Mining the Talk

Mining the Talk
Unlocking the Business Value in Unstructured Information

Scott Spangler
Jeffrey Kreulen

IBM Press
Pearson plc

Upper Saddle River, NJ • Boston • Indianapolis • San Francisco
New York • Toronto • Montreal • London • Munich • Paris • Madrid
Cape Town • Sydney • Tokyo • Singapore • Mexico City

ibmpressbooks.com

IBM Press Program Managers: Tara Woodman, Ellice Uffer
Cover design: IBM Corporation
Associate Publisher: Greg Wiegand
Marketing Manager: Kourtnaye Sturgeon
Publicist: Casey Radomsky
Acquisitions Editor: Bernard Goodwin
Managing Editor: Gina Kanouse
Designer: Alan Clements
Senior Project Editor: Kristy Hart
Project Editor: Jovana San Nicolas-Shirley
Copy Editor: Water Crest Publishing
Indexer: WordWise Publishing
Compositor: Bronkella Publishing
Proofreader: Williams Woods Publishing
Manufacturing Buyer: Dan Uhrig

Published by Pearson plc
Publishing as IBM Press

IBM Press offers excellent discounts on this book when ordered in quantity for bulk purchases or special sales, which may include electronic versions and/or custom covers and content particular to your business, training goals, marketing focus, and branding interests. For more information, please contact:

U.S. Corporate and Government Sales
1-800-382-3419
corpsales@pearsontechgroup.com

For sales outside the U.S., please contact:
International Sales
international@pearsoned.com

This Book Is Safari Enabled

The Safari® Enabled icon on the cover of your favorite technology book means the book is available through Safari Bookshelf. When you buy this book, you get free access to the online edition for 45 days. Safari Bookshelf is an electronic reference library that lets you easily search thousands of technical books, find code samples, download chapters, and access technical information whenever and wherever you need it.

To gain 45-day Safari Enabled access to this book:

- Go to http://www.awprofessional.com/safarienabled
- Complete the brief registration form
- Enter the coupon code GFHJ-XTYG-BYLN-Z4H3-F397

If you have difficulty registering on Safari Bookshelf or accessing the online edition, please e-mail customer-service@safaribooksonline.com.

Library of Congress Cataloging-in-Publication Data
Spangler, Scott.
  Mining the talk : unlocking the business value in unstructured information / Scott Spangler, Jeffrey T. Kreulen.
    p. cm.
  ISBN-13: 978-0-13-233953-7 (pbk. : alk. paper) 1. Data mining. 2. Soft computing. 3. Business intelligence. I. Kreulen, Jeffrey T. II. Title.
  QA76.9.D343S683 2007
  005.74—dc22
                              2007018683

        Pearson Education, Inc.
        Rights and Contracts Department
        501 Boylston Street, Suite 900
        Boston, MA 02116
        ISBN-13: 978-0-13-233953-7
        ISBN-10: 0-13-233953-6

Text printed in the United States on recycled paper at Courier Corporation in Stoughton, Massachusetts.
First printing, July, 2007

This book is dedicated to Norm Pass, for his unique ability to bring talented people together and motivate them to do great things. Without the benefit of his wisdom, encouragement, and enthusiasm, this book would not exist.

Contents

Contents

Preface

Let us begin by telling you what this book is not about. It is not about the spoken word, in any way, shape, or form. When we refer to *Mining the Talk*, "the talk" refers to words on the page, or to be more precise, words on the electronic page, not words out of the mouth. The reason we call it "talk" is not to be cute, but to emphasize the informal nature of the data being mined. Most data that is mined, or searched, or graphed is meant to be used in this way. That is usually why the data was put there in the first place. The collection and the analysis of the data go hand in hand. Not so with the type of data we refer to as "talk"—talk is put on the earth simply to be read. It is casual, unstructured, unpredictable, and diverse. You never know what to expect from talk, and that is what makes it so endlessly fascinating.

This book is not about text-mining research—at least not in a general sense, and certainly not in the sense that text mining is defined in the literature. We will not survey all the approaches or discuss the pros and cons of various algorithms. We will not describe any other methods beyond those we are intimately familiar with—those we use on a daily basis to peer into obscure data sets and make sense out of them.

This book is not about text search. If text search is akin to finding the needle in a haystack, this book is like plunging into the haystack (and not with the purpose of getting stabbed with the needle, though you might regard it as one possible benefit of such an action). If you enter a query into a search engine and receive a message that reads "results 1–10 of 1,837,220,135," you might pause to wonder about the results you don't see. This book has little to say about results 1–10. It's much more about the other 1,837,220,125—an area in which, to our minds, far too little effort is generally spent, when compared to the relative potential rewards of discovery.

This book is not about natural language processing (NLP). The techniques employed are statistical in nature, meaning that basic counting of regularly recurring text features is the basis for reasoning. No higher-level syntax or grammar is recognized or utilized in the processing of the unstructured information.

This book is not about a black box approach that magically transforms streams of characters into actionable ideas. It is about using whatever time and attention you are willing to invest in your unstructured mining endeavor in an effective manner to achieve a positive benefit in a reasonable time.

This book is, quite simply, a description of a method and its application—a method we have devised for getting useful information out of large amounts of unstructured data. It is a method we created in order to deal with the fact that standard approaches that were readily available were not getting the job done. When we achieved success in one area, we started applying this same approach to more and more kinds of data, with equal success. As the years passed and we were able to convince ourselves and others that this method was valuable, it started to become clear that the method needed to be published—to share the capabilities with a much wider audience and invite closer comments and scrutiny of what we have created. We are convinced that the potential of this method is just beginning to be tapped. But only with a much wider exposure and application will we ever find out the limits of just what it can do.

The purpose of this book is to both explain our approach to *Mining the Talk* and also to expand awareness of how and where our techniques can be applied to business data. We believe that the potential of this technology is only beginning to be tapped, and that a greater awareness in the business and technical community of what knowledge can be gleaned from unstructured information will likely lead to an explosion of application areas.

We assume that you, the reader, are investing time in this book because you are faced with the same kind of problems that we were: lots of data, not much structure, and a certainty that if you only had a reasonable approach (something better than searching or reading it line by line), you could utilize what's in the data to improve whatever endeavor your organization is currently engaged in. Although we cannot give you any magic formula that will effortlessly transform your unstructured data into useful information, we can promise you a systematic way to efficiently turn effort spent on your data into understanding—as much understanding as the data and your effort will allow. Is it a perfect solution? No way. Is it better than reading each text example that you want to understand? Almost certainly.

At the end of reading this book, we hope you feel, as we do, a sense of wonder and excitement about the vast ocean of unexplored unstructured content that lies waiting to be charted. We also wish you to come away with a healthy respect for the dangers and a realistic appraisal of the costs of such a voyage. This book contains a very realistic, practical approach to mining unstructured information. There's no trick to getting the knowledge you need out of the available data; it just takes intense focus, hard work, thoughtful planning, and finally, an open mind.

Who Should Read This Book?

We have made a conscious effort in writing this book to reach out beyond the data mining community. We have strived to write this book for a general audience, including business executives, engineers, and students having an interest in studying this field as a potential career. The audience for this book is primarily business professionals who have data management or analysis responsibility or needs. This would include business consultants, managers and executives, IT professionals, knowledge workers, market analysts, and those involved in the management of intellectual property. The reader benefits from the book by seeing how data and text-mining techniques and processes can be employed to solve real-world business problems. The book does not assume a high level of familiarity with data mining or analytic concepts. It is primarily a qualitative description of our technique, though some quantitative supporting details are supplied. There is no prerequisite background required of the reader, though a mathematical or analytic background will certainly help. This book is also very relevant to students in data mining or machine learning, because it demonstrates some proven, practical approaches to real-world text-mining problems that will complement the techniques typically taught in academia.

How This Book Is Organized

Chapter 1 of this book is an introduction to our methodology, describing the history of how and why we developed the *Mining the Talk* method, and including a high-level description of what the methodology actually consists of.

Each of the next five chapters describes a different application area of *Mining the Talk*. These are the following:

- Chapter 2, "Mining Customer Interactions": Interactions between your business and its customers

- Chapter 3, "Mining the Voice of the Customer": Customers (and others) discussing your business and its products online

- Chapter 4, "Mining the Voice of the Employee": Internal organizational communication
- Chapter 5, "Mining to Improve Innovation": Public information on technical innovation for collaboration and partnership
- Chapter 6, "Mining to See the Future": Technology and market trends

Chapter 7, "Future Applications," discusses some potential future applications of *Mining the Talk* techniques and then concludes the book.

The Appendix, "The IBM Unstructured Information Modeler Users Manual," contains a detailed description of software that implements the *Mining the Talk* methodology.

A Clarification on Personal Pronouns

When two people author a book, they seldom actually sit down together and write it. Typically, one writes, the other edits/corrects/appends, and then they switch roles. The actual writing itself is generally a solitary activity. Therefore, occasionally, it seems more natural to use the singular personal pronoun when one is required, even though technically "I" probably should say "we." We hope the reader will not find this inconsistency confusing. Please don't take this to mean that one of the two of us is taking ownership of or claiming credit for whatever section *we* are writing about. In general, all of this work has been a team effort between the two of us, as well as many others.

Software Applications

It is my fervent hope that you will emerge from reading this book with an immediate desire to try out these techniques on your own data. If you wish to do this on your own, you have our best wishes. Of course, if you would like some help, we at IBM have some wonderful tools that will get you started as quickly as possible; in fact, a demo version of one of these tools is available for download.

Everything we talk about in this book has been implemented as software, and the reader will notice many screenshots taken from these tools. It turns out that none of these software applications is actually currently for sale as a shrink-wrapped product. Instead, they are all "research assets" used internally at IBM and by IBM consultants on customer service engagements. However, it seemed unfair to tell you about our method, explain it in great detail, and then not give you the tools you need to try it out. Therefore, the folks at IBM Alphaworks have graciously agreed to provide a free demonstration copy of one of our early text-mining tools, IBM Unstructured Information Modeler, as an adjunct to this book. Here is the URL for those who are interested:

http://www.alphaworks.ibm.com/tech/uimodeler.

The user manual for this tool is contained in the Appendix. We hope you find this useful, and that it whets your appetite to try out our more advanced applications.

On the other hand, if you want to take our methods and create your own software solution to sell as a product, while we applaud your initiative and enthusiasm, you really should first discuss this with suitable representatives from IBM business development. IBM has sole ownership of all the intellectual property described in this book, all of which is protected by U.S. patents, both granted and pending. All rights reserved, etc., etc.

Acknowledgments

We would like to extend our gratitude to all the reviewers of this material, for supplying such critical feedback. This book is nothing like what it started out to be, and we think it is far better because of their input.

Much of the early work in eClassifier and other *Mining the Talk* tools came out of discussions with Dharmendra Modha and Ray Strong.

Other significant software contributions to *Mining the Talk* tools have come from Justin Lessler, Vikas Krishna, and James Rhodes. James has also been instrumental in developing the Explore, Understand, Analyze methodology and chemical annotation capability.

Case Studies were contributed by Larry Proctor and Ray Strong. Larry has also been a great contributor of ideas and the primary provider of external customers for our work.

We would like to thank all the great folks at Masterfoods/Mars for being such great partners in our recent *Mining the Talk* endeavors and for allowing us to reference them in this book.

We would also like to express appreciation to some of the early and longstanding users of our technology, especially Kristine Lawas and James Newswanger for supporting the use of eClassifier for Jams; Jeff Biegel, Martha Carr, and Karen Butler for use of our tools to support helpdesk analysis; and Steve Boyer for using our techniques for analyzing patents and the life sciences research area.

A special thanks to the IBM Managers and Executives throughout these many years who have patiently supported our research as it has grown to maturity: David C. Martin, Norm Pass, Bill Cody, Mike Wing, Jim Spohrer, Anant Jinghran, Robert Morris, Jim Carrubba, and Mark Dean.

And finally, a deep debt of gratitude is owed to our wives and families for supporting us through the extra hours this book required of us that might have otherwise been spent with them. The fault is your own, for it is your confidence in us and unflagging support of our careers that has made this book possible.

About the Authors

W. Scott Spangler

IBM Research Division, Almaden Research Center, 650 Harry Road, San Jose, CA 95120 (email: spangles@almaden.ibm.com; ph. 408-927-2887)

Scott Spangler is a Senior Technical Staff Member who has been doing knowledge base and data mining research for the past 20 years—since 1996 at the IBM Research Lab and previously at the General Motors Technical Center, where he won the prestigious "Boss" Kettering award (1992) for technical achievement. He currently works in IBM Almaden Services Research, where he designs and implements new methodologies for data visualization and text mining. Mr. Spangler holds a B.S. degree in math from the Massachusetts Institute of Technology and an M.A. in computer science from the University of Texas.

Jeffrey T. Kreulen

IBM Research Division, Almaden Research Center, 650 Harry Road, San Jose, CA 95120 (email: kreulen@almaden.ibm.com)

Dr. Kreulen is Senior Manager of Services Oriented Technologies and Senior Technical Staff Member at the IBM Almaden Research Center. He holds a B.S. degree in applied mathematics (computer science) from Carnegie-Mellon University, and an M.S. degree in electrical engineering and a Ph.D. in computer engineering from Pennsylvania State University. Since joining IBM in 1992, he has worked on multiprocessor systems design and verification, operating systems, systems management, web-based service delivery, integrated text and data analysis, and the science of services.

I

Introduction

People are talking about your business every day. Are you listening?

Your customers are talking. They're talking about you to your face and behind your back. They're saying how much they like you, and how much they hate you. They're describing what they wish you would do for them, and what the competition is already doing for them. They are writing emails to you, posting blogs about you, and discussing you endlessly in public forums. Are you listening?

Other businesses and organizations are talking too. Researchers talk about new technologies and approaches you might be interested in. Other businesses describe innovations you could leverage in your products. Your competitors are revealing technical approaches and broadcasting their strategies in various publications. They talk about what they are working on and what they think is important. Are you listening?

Your employees are also talking. They are producing great ideas that are languishing for lack of the right context to apply them. They are looking for the right partners to help them innovate and create the next big thing for your company. They reveal new ways to improve your internal processes and even change the entire vision for your company. Are you listening?

All of this talk is going on out there now, even as you read these pages. And you can listen—if you know how. This book is about how we learned to listen to the talk and to turn it into valuable business insights for our company and for our customers. Now we would like to share that knowledge with you.

A Short Story…"The Contest"

Writing this book has been a project that beckoned for many years. We had started and stopped multiple times. We knew we wanted to write the book, but we had trouble convincing ourselves that anyone would want to read it. At a gut level, we knew that what we were doing was important and unique. However, there were a lot of competing methods and products, with more added every day, and we could not spend all of our time evaluating each of them to determine if our approach was measurably superior. Then, in May 2006, an event happened that in one day demonstrated convincingly that our approach was significantly better than all the other alternatives in our field. The results of this day would energize us to go ahead and complete this book.

It began when a potential client was considering a large unstructured data mining project. Like most companies, they had a huge collection of documents describing customer interactions. They wanted to automatically classify these documents to route them to the correct business process. They questioned whether or not this was even feasible, and if so, how expensive would it be. Rather than invite all the vendors in this space to present proposals, they wanted to understand how effective each technical approach was on their data. To this end, they set up the following "contest."

They took a sample of 5,000 documents that had been scanned and converted to text and divided them manually into 50 categories of around 100 documents each. They then invited seven of the leading vendors with products in this space to spend one week with the data using whatever tools and techniques they wished to model these 50 categories. When they were done, they would be asked to classify another unseen set of 25,000 documents. The different vendors' products would be compared based on speed, accuracy of classification, and ease of use during training. The results would be shared with all concerned.

That was it. The "contest" had no prize. There was no promise of anything more on the client's part after it was over. No money would change hands. Nothing would be published about the incident. There was no guarantee that anything would come of it. I was dead set against participating in this activity for three very good reasons: 1) I thought that the chances it would lead to eventual business were small; 2) I didn't think the problem they were proposing was well formed since we would have no chance to talk to them up front to identify business objectives, and from these to design a set of categories that truly reflected the needs of the business as well as the actual state of the data; and 3) I was already scheduled to be in London that week working with a *paying* customer.

I explained all of these reasons to Jeff, and he listened patiently and said, "You could get back a day early from London and be there on Friday."

"So I would have one day while the other vendors had five! No way!"

"You won't need more than one day. You'll do it in half a day." I didn't respond to that—I recognize rank flattery when I hear it. Then Jeff said, "I guess you really don't want to do this."

That stopped me a moment. The truth was I did want to do it. I had always been curious to know how our methods stacked up against the competition in an unbiased comparison, and here was an opportunity to find out. "OK. I'll go," I found myself saying.

As planned, I arrived at the designated testing location on Friday morning at 9AM. A representative of the client showed me to an empty cubicle where sat a PC that contained the training data sample. On the way, he questioned me about whether or not I would want to work until late in the day (this was the Friday before Memorial Day weekend). I assured him that this would not be the case. He showed me where on the hard drive the data was located and then left. I installed our software[1] on the PC and got to work.

About an hour later, he stopped by to see how I was coming along. "Well, I'm essentially done modeling your data," I said. He laughed, assuming I was making a joke. "No, seriously, take a look." We spent about an hour perusing his data in the tool. I spent some time showing him the strengths and weaknesses of the classification scheme they had set up, showing him exactly which categories were well defined and which were not, and identifying outliers in the training set that might have a negative influence on classifier performance. He was quite impressed.

"So, can you classify the test set now?" he asked.

"Sure, I'll go ahead and start that up." I kicked off the process that classified the 25,000 test documents based on the model generated from the training set categories.

We watched it run together for a few seconds. Then he asked me how long it would take. I tried to calculate in my head how long it should take based on the type of model I was using and the size of the document collection. I prevaricated just long enough before answering. Before I could give my best guess, the classification had completed. It took about one minute.

"So that's it? You're done?" he asked, clearly bemused.

"Yes. We can try some other classification models to see if they do any better, but I think this will probably be the best we can come up with. You seem surprised."

He lowered his voice to barely a whisper. "I shouldn't be telling you this, but most of the other vendors are still here, and some of them still haven't come up with a result. None of them finished in less than three days. You did it all in less than two hours? Is your software really that much better than theirs? How does your accuracy stack up?"

"I don't know for sure," I answered truthfully, "but based on the noise I see in your training set, and the accuracy levels our models predict, I doubt they will do any better than we just did." (Two weeks later, when the results were tabulated for all vendors, our accuracy rate was almost exactly as predicted, and it turned out to be better than any of the other participating vendors.)

"So why is your stuff so much better than theirs?" he asked.

"That's not an easy question to answer. Let's go to lunch, and I'll tell you about it."

What I told the client over lunch is the story of how and why our methodology evolved and what made it unique. I explained to him how every other unstructured mining approach on the market was based on the idea that "the best algorithm wins." In other words, researchers had picked a few sets of "representative" text data, often items culled from news articles or research abstracts, and then each created their own approaches to classifying these sets of articles in the most accurate fashion. They honed the approaches against each other and tuned them to perform with optimum speed and accuracy on one type of unstructured data. Then these algorithms eventually became products, turned loose on a world that looked nothing like the lab environment in which they were optimally designed to succeed.

Our approach was very different. It assumed very little about the kind of unstructured data that would be given as input. It also didn't assume any one "correct" classification scheme, but observed that the classification of these documents might vary depending on the business context. These assumptions about the vast variability inherent in both business data and classification schemes for that data, led us to an approach that was orders of magnitude more flexible and generic than anything else available on the market. It was this flexibility and adaptability that allowed me to go into a new situation and, without ever having seen the data or the classification scheme ahead of time, quickly model the key aspects of the domain and produce an automated classifier of high accuracy and performance.

In the Beginning...

In 1998, a group from IBM's Services organization came to our Research group with a problem. IBM Global Services manages the computer helpdesk operations of hundreds of companies. In doing so, they document millions of *problem tickets*—records of each call that are typed in by the helpdesk operator each time an operator has an interaction with a customer. Here is what a typical problem ticket looks like:

```
1836853 User calling in with WORD BASIC error when opening files in word. Had
user delete NORMAL.DOT and had her reenter Word, she was fine at that point.
00:04:17 ducar May 2:07:05:656PM
```

Imagine millions of these sitting in databases. There they could be indexed, searched, sorted, and counted. But this vast data collection could not be used to answer the following simple question: What kinds of problems are we seeing at the helpdesk this month? If the data could be leveraged to do this analysis, then some of the more frequent tasks could potentially be automated, thus significantly reducing costs.

So why was it so hard to answer this question with the data they had? The reason is that the data is *unstructured*. There is no set vocabulary or language of fixed terms used to describe each problem. Instead, the operator describes the customer issue in ordinary everyday language...as they would describe it to a peer at the helpdesk operations center. As in normal conversation, there is no consistency of word choice or sentence structure or grammar or punctuation or spelling in describing problems. So the same problem called in on different days to different operators might result in a very different problem ticket description. This kind of unstructured information in free-form text is what we refer to as "talk." It is simply the way humans have been communicating with each other for thousands of years, and it's the most prevalent kind of data to be found in the world. Potentially, it's also the most valuable, because hidden inside the talk is little bits and pieces of important information that, if aggregated and summarized, could communicate actionable intelligence about how any business is running, how its customers and employees perceive it, what is going right and what is going wrong, and possibly solutions to the most pressing problems the business faces. These are examples of the gold that is waiting to be discovered if we can only "Mine the Talk."

And so with this challenge began the journey that culminated in this book.

The Thesis

The purpose of this book is to share with you the insights and knowledge that we have gained from the journey we have been on for nearly a decade. We are applied researchers and software engineers that have been developing technologies to address real-world business problems. We have implemented and experimented with variations of most approaches and algorithms that are espoused in the literature, as well as quite a few new techniques of our own. Through trial and error, insight, and sometimes good luck, we have come up with an approach, supported by technology, that we think will revolutionize the definition of business intelligence and how businesses leverage information analytics into the future.

Our work can be summarized in one simple thesis:

> A methodology centered around developing taxonomies that capture both domain knowledge and business objectives is necessary to successfully unlock the business value in all kinds of unstructured information.

In this introduction, we will take you through the thinking that has led us to this conclusion, and outline the methodology we use to *Mine the Talk* to create lasting business value.

The Business Context for Unstructured Information Mining

In parallel to, and in collaboration with, technological progress, businesses have adapted and evolved to better leverage structured and unstructured information analytical capabilities. This is part of a larger phenomenon sometimes referred to as the co-evolution of business and technology.

The Enterprise Ecosystem

Gone is the day of the monolithic enterprise. To create efficiencies, most industries have disaggregated into their component parts. For example, in the automotive industry, the manufacturers do not mine the ore to make the steel to fabricate the parts that make up their products. All of these tasks are performed by specialized companies for the automotive industry, and as many other potential industries and customers as possible, in order to maximize their return on investment. Similarly, as a consumer, you do not actually buy or service your vehicle from the manufacturer, but there is a selection of dealers and service providers to choose from. Today's enterprise exists in a complex network of suppliers, vendors, business partners, competitors, and industries, which we call the enterprise ecosystem (see Figure 1-1).

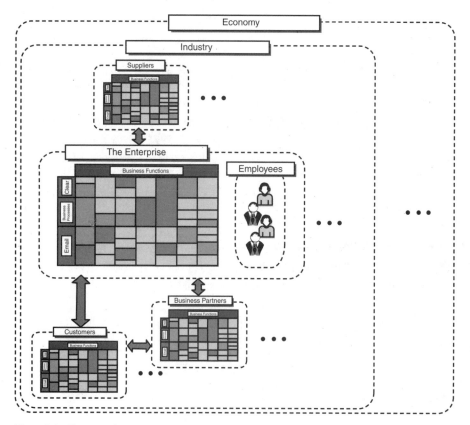

Figure 1-1   The enterprise ecosystem

An increasingly important aspect of the enterprise ecosystem that creates an integrating backdrop is the information space. This consists of all human knowledge accumulated in its various forms: written, spoken, and otherwise. This is manifested in communication mediums such as newspaper, magazines, books, television, and the Web. With the growth of the internet and electronic media, the rate of growth in the information space is increasing exponentially. But more information is not always better. Figuring out what is important is becoming an increasingly difficult problem.

Services Industry Growth

A second trend in the evolution of business is the significant growth of the services sector. Over the last century, the world's labor force has migrated from agriculture to goods manufacturing to services (see Figure 1-2). This largely has to do with efficiency gains in agricultural and manufacturing processes through technological innovation and labor optimization. There is no reason to believe that this won't occur in the services sector as well, so the advantage will go to those who lead in this process, not those who ignore it or resist it.

Top Ten Nations by Labor Force Size
(about 50% of world labor in just 10 nations)
A = Agriculture, G = Goods, S = Services

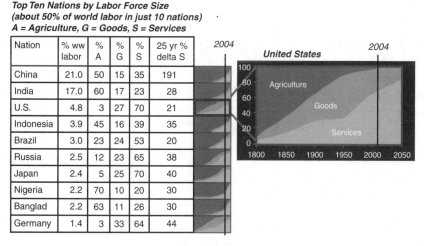

Nation	% ww labor	% A	% G	% S	25 yr % delta S
China	21.0	50	15	35	191
India	17.0	60	17	23	28
U.S.	4.8	3	27	70	21
Indonesia	3.9	45	16	39	35
Brazil	3.0	23	24	53	20
Russia	2.5	12	23	65	38
Japan	2.4	5	25	70	40
Nigeria	2.2	70	10	20	30
Banglad	2.2	63	11	26	30
Germany	1.4	3	33	64	44

Figure 1-2 Services industry growth

So why is this important in the context of *Mining the Talk*? Services, by their nature, are more unstructured. Services involve an interaction between the service provider and the customer. Customers are integral to the process, because they are involved with the co-production of value between a provider and a consumer. This makes each transaction inherently unique. When modeling or capturing this process, this uniqueness or variability lends itself to a more unstructured representation. With the explosion of the services sector and its affinity to unstructured information, the ability to extract value from this information will only grow in importance.

One of the techniques to create efficiencies in agriculture and manufacturing was process standardization. This is made somewhat more difficult in services with customers in the loop, because in many cases, they may not care about your process efficiencies. We can all relate to being annoyed by complex phone navigation trees to try to get to the right person or service to handle our concern. It is clear that business process standardization will continue and is necessary, but those who do it most effectively without alienating customers will have a distinct advantage.

From Transaction to Interactions and Relationships

It is no longer sufficient to only look at the attributes of a transaction with customers at the boundary of the enterprise to understand your business. Businesses need to look at the lifecycle of their interactions within the business ecosystem (see Figure 1-3). This means all of the interactions that you have with your customers, suppliers, business partners, employees, and competitors, as well as the industries and economies in which you compete. On its face, this can seem either obvious, insurmountable, or both. However, there is hope, and *Mining the Talk* will help get you there.

How many times have you heard the sage business advice, "listen to your customers"? Although this is good advice, it is necessary but not sufficient. You will also need to listen to your employees, because they are closest to the action. Your vendors, suppliers, and business partners are also a source of incredible information. In addition, the information space, what is being said in the press, on the Web, and in the technical literature, are other sources that can be utilized. All of this requires constant attention and monitoring. These are not transactions to be counted and sorted, but they are ongoing interactions and relationships that need to be understood and leveraged.

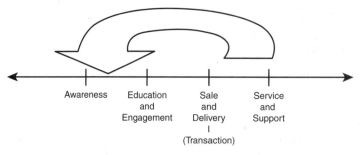

Figure 1-3 Interaction lifecycle

Capturing Business Objectives and Domain Expertise

In our journey of discovery, we have seen one mistake made repeatedly. We have seen static business models and static data models try to be used to model inherently dynamic business processes, particularly at the point of interaction. For example, virtually every customer relationship management system we have come across has a manual classification scheme (or taxonomy) that is meant to be used by the service agent to classify the nature of the customer interaction. This approach has two major flaws. First, as soon as the classification scheme is published, it is out of date, because interactions with your customers are unpredictable and continually changing. Second, even if the classification scheme was representative of your customer interactions, it is unreasonable to expect any number of service agents to classify their interactions with their customers in a consistent way and with high quality. This very often makes such classification data completely useless, or, more dangerously, misleading. This issue is true throughout the business ecosystem where unstructured information exists.

An adaptable data model is critical when incorporating unstructured information mining. One problem commonly encountered is that the analysis typically leads to more questions. In business intelligence or data mining, if the data model is not designed to handle the new question, the data model must be modified and the data manipulated and reloaded, which is often a difficult and cumbersome process, many times taking months. This problem is compounded even more with unstructured information because of its very nature. It is important to be able to add or enhance existing taxonomies, classifications, or extracted data as the information leads you through the discovery process.

Additionally, it is important to combine the right mix of algorithmic assistance with domain expertise. We have found that most people naively want to push a button and magically receive the answer. However, we have come to the conclusion that, particularly with unstructured information, the analytical process cannot be fully automated. Even for structured information, it typically needs an analyst in the loop to interpret the results. For unstructured information, an analyst is required in the loop to help guide the process with a combination of algorithmic assistance, a useful set of metrics to assist in the interpretation, and the analyst's domain expertise. The key is to make efficient use of this expensive and scarce resource, not to eliminate it entirely.

A Common Analytical Methodology

We struggled for some time and went through multiple iterations before we settled on a common analytical methodology that spans domains, business objectives, and information sources. Our method has three major phases: *Explore*, *Understand*, and *Analyze*.

Each of these phases leverages different capabilities that build on each other. However, it is not always necessary to use every phase or capability. For very large information collections, we have developed the capabilities in *Explore*, and we will discuss this in Chapter 5, "Mining to Improve Innovation." Most of this book will concentrate on the *Understand* and *Analyze* phases, which are the unique differentiators and the key to unlocking the business value of unstructured information in *Mining the Talk*. In this section, we introduce each of these concepts and describe what they entail.

Explore

Many times we are dealing with very large repositories of information. Depending on our information source and our business objective, not all of the information will be relevant. For example, if you are interested in analyzing the Web to understand issues around a specific brand, you only need the portion of the Web that pertains to that brand. If you are analyzing patents related to a technology area, you only need the patents that are relevant to that area. We use a combination of techniques to locate the relevant set of information from a larger set. With structured information, we can use various queries; for unstructured information, we can use search, and we can combine them in different ways using various set operations. We call this process *Explore*.

Queries

We use *query* as the term to describe how we use structured fields in a database to select the subset of information that is of interest. For example, we can select customers based upon their location, the product they have purchased, or the time frame that we wish to investigate. We can select patents based upon the assignee, the inventor, or the classification code. These are all typically structured fields that are stored in a database. These types of queries are quite simple to perform using the standard SQL query language to find the sub-collections of interest. This technique is very powerful and effective, given you have the appropriate attributes in the database and know which of their values will select the subset that is relevant to address the issue being analyzed.

Search

Search is the process of finding those documents that contain specific words or phrases in their unstructured text. We use search as the means to find collections of documents that have concepts of interest within them, rather than to find individual documents. Although it is a valuable tool, search is not the solution to all problems. The use of language does not always lend itself to easily disambiguate concepts. Some words have more than one meaning, known as homonyms. For example, using "shell" as a query will likely return information on sea shells, Shell Oil, Unix shell, egg shells, and many others. Disambiguation is one problem, but coverage is another. Some meanings can be described with more than one word, known as synonyms. For example, we have found that valium has more than 150 unique names—have fun typing that query.

Set Operations

Because in many cases no single query or search is sufficient to get to the optimally desired collection for deeper analysis, we have found it necessary to be able to perform set operation on collections. The most commonly used operations are join and intersect. Joins are useful in combining multiple searches for synonyms. Intersection is useful when you are looking for the subset that has two attributes that could be from either the structured or unstructured fields. In some cases, when the result of a combination of queries and searches is still too large to effectively analyze in a reasonable time, sampling techniques may be used to select a statistically valid subset.

Recursion and Expansion

Results of queries and searches can be used as input to subsequent Explore operations. This allows us to refine the subject of our mining study incrementally as we learn more about the data. Also, we can use query expansion to take the results of a query done on a subset of the data and apply it to the entire data collection.

Understand

The result of the *Explore* phase is a collection of information that covers the topic of interest. The *Understand* phase is about discovering what the information contains. We have developed a unique method of creating structure from unstructured information through the process of taxonomy generation and refinement. We use a combination of practical steps, statistical techniques, algorithms, and a methodology for editing taxonomies that allows for the flexible capture of domain expertise and business objectives. We call this process *Understand*. The Understand process works in two directions: the analyst understands the underlying structure inherent in the unstructured information, and the models captured as a result of the analyst's edits represent an understanding of domain knowledge and business objectives.

Statistics are fundamental to our *Understand* process. We are all familiar with the idea of summarizing numerical data with statistical techniques. For example, a grade point average is a way to summarize your overall academic performance. It doesn't tell you everything, but most people have agreed that it is a pretty good indicator. What about something more complex, like a sporting event? Pick your favorite sport—whether it is baseball, basketball, tennis, or football—and there are usually various ways to summarize the game or match that allow you to understand the essence of what transpired. Such summaries are no substitute for watching the game, but they can convey a lot of information about the game in a very small space.

Partitioning

If you have a large body of text, there is probably one or more natural ways to partition it into smaller sections. A book naturally falls into chapters, and each chapter into paragraphs, and each paragraph into sentences, just as a baseball game has innings and innings have outs. Breaking a large document into smaller entities makes it much easier to summarize the message of the text as a whole, because it makes statistics possible. If we try to summarize a baseball game without breaking it down by innings and outs, we are left with only the final score. But if we can break down the game into innings or at-bats and measure what happened during each of these smaller units (e.g., hits, walks, outs), then we can create meaningful statistics such as *Earned Run Average* or *On Base Percentage*.

There may be many suitable ways to do partitioning, each with its own advantage. However, the best methods for partitioning are those that produce a section that talks about only one concept with respect to the questions we want answered. The level of granularity should roughly match that of the desired business result. The analogy in baseball is that we measure innings for pitchers and at-bats for batters. The different levels of granularity make sense for different kinds of outcomes that need to be measured.

Similarly, if we want to understand the issues for which customers are calling into a call center, then individual problem records, which may span multiple calls, are the right partitioning. On the other hand, if we wish to understand better what affects customer satisfaction, we may decide to analyze each individual call record. A customer might be both satisfied and dissatisfied during the course of resolving an issue, and we want to isolate the interactions in order to analyze the underlying causes.

Feature Selection

Once the partitioning granularity is properly adjusted, we need to decide what events we are going to measure and what statistics we will keep. In a baseball box score, we don't measure everything about the game. For example, we don't know the average number of swings each batter took, or the number of pitches each pitcher threw. We could measure these things if they were important to us, but that level of detail is not interesting to the average baseball fan. Similarly in statistical analysis of text, we could measure the average number of times each letter of the alphabet occurs. We could measure the average word length, or the number of words in sentences. In fact, such statistics are used as a means for roughly measuring how "readable" a section of text will be for readers of various grade levels.[2] However, these kinds of statistics are not helpful to answer typical business questions, such as "What are my customers most unhappy about?"

So what are the right things to measure about each text example? The answer is, it all depends. It depends on what we want to learn and what kind of text data we are dealing with. Word occurrence is a good place to start for most types of problems, especially those where you don't have much specific domain knowledge to draw upon and where the language of the documents is fairly general. When the text is more technically dense or focused on a very specialized area, then it may make sense to also measure sequences of words, also known as phrases, to get a more precise kind of statistic.

We use word and phrase occurrence as the features of a document. However, we don't use every word and phrase, because there can be a very large number of them and they are not all meaningful or useful. We use a combination of techniques to reduce the feature space to a more manageable size. We eliminate non-content–bearing words, called stopwords, such as "and" and "the." We also remove repetitive or structural phrases (we call them stock phrases). If every document contains "Copyright IBM" or "IBM Confidential," then it can safely be removed. We also combine features using a synonym list. This can be done manually where deemed appropriate or automatically through a technique called stemming. Stemming allows "jump," "jumping," and "jumped" to be treated as one. There are also various domain-specific synonym lists that can be used where stemming will fall short. Finally, we remove features that occur infrequently in the document collection because these tend to have little value in creating meaningful categories. Once we have reduced the features to a manageable size, we can use this to create summary statistics for each document. We call the collection of all such statistics for every document in a collection the *vector space model*.

Clustering

We use clustering to quickly and easily seed the process of taxonomy generation. *Clustering* is an algorithmic attempt to automatically group documents into thematic categories. These thematic categories, which together constitute a taxonomy, give an overview of what information the document collection contains. There are many different clustering algorithms that could be used, and our approach could support them all. However, we have relied heavily on variations of the k-means algorithm, because it is fast and does a reasonable job. We have also developed our own algorithm, which we call *intuitive clustering*, that we also employ.

Taxonomy Editing

Clustering is a wonderful tool, but we rarely find it to be sufficient. No matter how good the algorithmic approach to clustering becomes, it cannot embed the nuance of business objectives and the variations of language from different information sources within an algorithm. This is the critical missing element that our method incorporates. We have developed a unique set of capabilities that allow for an analyst or domain expert to quickly assess the strengths and weaknesses of a taxonomy and easily make the changes necessary to align the taxonomy with business objectives.

Analyst knowledge about the purpose of the taxonomy trumps every other consideration. Thus, a category may be created by an analyst for reasons that have nothing to do with text features. An example would be a category of "recent" documents—those created most recently out of all the documents in the corpus. Depending on the business analysis goals, such a category may be very important in helping to understand emerging trends and issues.

Ideally, the name of a category should describe exactly what makes the category unique. An analyst may decide to change a system-generated name to one that is better aligned with the analyst's view of what the category contains. This category renaming process thus becomes an important way that domain expertise is captured.

In addition to the name, a category can also be described by choosing examples that best summarize the overall content. We describe these as "Typical Examples" because they are selected by virtue of having all or most of the features that typify the documents in the category as a whole. Using the vector space model, it is possible to automatically compare examples and select those that have the most typical content. By reading and understanding typical examples, it is possible for the analyst to make sense of a large collection of documents in a relatively short period of time.

It is also important to measure the variation within a category of documents. If there is a statistically large variation among the documents within a category, this may indicate that the category needs to be split up, or subcategorized. We call the metric that measures within category variation *cohesion*. Additionally, it is important to measure the similarity between categories. We call this *distinctness*. Categories with low distinctness scores indicate a potential overlap with another category. This overlap may indicate the need to merge two or more categories together.

The categories created using clustering and summarized with various statistics can also be edited based on this understanding. This is where analysts adds their domain knowledge and awareness of the business problem to be solved to the results—creating categories that are more meaningful.

There are many kinds of editing that are typically employed, at all levels of the text categorization. Categories can be merged or deleted. They can be created wholesale from documents matching individual words, phrases, or features. Categories can be edited— splitting off subsets of a category to create new categories. Documents can be selectively removed from one category and placed in another.

The taxonomy editing process can be thought of as the human expert training the computer to understand concepts that are important to the business. There may be many different types of categorizations that can be created on the same set of data, each representing a different important aspect of the information to the enterprise.

Visualizations

The visual cortex occupies about one third of the surface of the cerebral cortex in humans. It would be a shame to waste all of that immense processing power during the *Understand* process. We employ visualizations of taxonomies to create pictures of the information that the human brain can process in order to locate areas of special interest that contain patterns or relationships. There are many types of visualizations that can be used to show relationships in structured and unstructured information. Scatter plots, trees, bar graphs, and pie charts can all help in the process of understanding the information, and in modifying taxonomies to reflect business objectives.

The vector space model of feature occurrence in documents is the primary data source for automatically calculating visual representations of text. Using this representation, a document becomes not just words, but a position or point in high-dimensional space. Given this representation, a computer can "draw" a set of documents and allow a human analyst to explore the text space in much the same way an astronomer explores the galaxy of stars and planets.

Analyze

At the end of the *Understand* phase, we have one or more taxonomies that represent characteristics of the unstructured information, along with a feature set that describes the individual documents that make up each taxonomy. But a taxonomy by itself rarely achieves the business objectives of mining unstructured information. The final step is to take combinations of structured and unstructured information and look for trends, patterns, and relationships inherent in the data and use that to make better business decisions. We call this process *Analyze*.

Trending

Timing is everything in comedy, in life, and in business. Knowing how categories occurred in the data stream over time will often reveal something interesting about why that category occurs in the first place. Trend analysis is also useful for detecting spikes in categories as well as in predicting how categories will evolve in the future. Trending can be interesting from a historical perspective, but it is usually most valuable when used to detect emerging events. If you can detect a problem in your business before it costs you a lot of money, that goes straight to the bottom line. If you can spot a trend before your competition, you have a leg up.

Correlations

Taxonomies capture the concepts embedded in unstructured information. Co-occurrence analysis reveals hidden relationships between these concepts and other attributes or between categories of different taxonomies. For example, we can look for a relationship between technology areas and companies to see where our competition is investing. Or we can find a correlation between a specific factory and a certain kind of product defect.

A correlation is based on the simple idea that two different phenomenon have occurred together more than expected. For example, if 100 customers who talked to a specific call center representative ended up dissatisfied with their overall customer experience, then depending on the total percentage of unsatisfied callers and the total percentage of calls that particular representative took, we could calculate whether there was a correlation between dissatisfaction and talking to this representative. Keep in mind that, even if there is such a correlation, it doesn't mean that this representative is actually responsible for the poor customer satisfaction. It could be that this person only works during weekends and that people who call on the weekends are generally more dissatisfied. This example serves to show that correlations are not causes. They are simply indicators of potential explanations that should be explored further. Think of them as "leading indicators" of business insights.

Classification

One you have a taxonomy that models an important aspect of the information, it is important to be able to apply this classification scheme to new unstructured data. Many classification algorithms exist, and we have incorporated a large variety of them into our approach, allowing us to select the best algorithm for a given taxonomy and information collection. The specifics of how we do text classification is a more technical subject that is beyond the scope of this book. However, the general approach is to pick the algorithm that most accurately represents each category, based on a random sampling of the documents in that category being used to test the accuracy of each modeling approach.

Applications for *Mining the Talk*

Although the number of possible different applications for unstructured mining is virtually limitless, we will explore in-depth applications that fall into five major categories.

Customer Interaction

This is the mining of information coming from unstructured interactions between representatives of the business and customers. It is one of the most common forms of information that nearly every business possesses. This kind of information is good for providing insights into your current processes, what's working and what's not, and identifying areas of potential cost reduction or quality improvement.

Voice of the Customer

This type of mining also involves the customer, or potential customer, but the difference is there is no direct dialog with the business. This includes mining of customer monologues available from surveys, discussion forums, or web logs. This kind of information is useful for discovering what your customers think about you and about your industry. It can provide ideas for improving your products, burnishing your image, or inventing innovative new service offerings.

Voice of the Employee

In this area, the information comes from internal surveys, suggestion boxes, employee discussion events, or open employee forums. This data can provide the business with valuable insight into the collective consciousness of the organization. Such insight can help set a company's vision or generate new ideas for innovation. The results of this kind of mining may help bring disparate groups of the company together to collaborate on new projects and opportunities.

Improving Innovation

Mining the Talk to improve innovation involves looking at both internal and publicly available information sources to find potential ways to innovate through partnering with other businesses. The patent literature is one good source to look for potential opportunities for cross licensing or joint development programs. This data can also be mined to gauge the potential viability of new technologies or product offerings.

Seeing the Future

The ability to see a little bit further ahead than your competition is a crucial competitive advantage. Mining a wide spectrum of publicly available unstructured information sources over time can help the business spot important product and technology trends as they emerge. It can also help in gaining time to react to emerging external events before they become major business catastrophes.

Figure 1-4 shows how the application areas described in the remaining chapters of this book cover the business ecosystem.

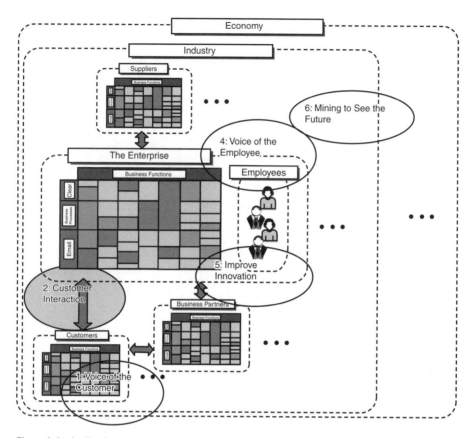

Figure 1-4 Application areas by chapter

The Transformation Process

As we wrote this book, we noticed that the documented examples and case studies followed a general pattern. Based on our experience of working within our own company and working with clients in many different industries, we have found that it is very difficult to get to the full scope of mining unstructured information's potential in one big step. We have found the process to be iterative. As the users and consumers of *Mining the Talk* become more familiar with the approach and build trust that it will achieve the results intended, they will embrace and expand the scope.

Each new potential customer of our approach believes that their situation is unique and their data is different. So typically, we go through a process of showing them the efficacy of our approach on a limited set of their data. This allows us to collaborate with the customer in exploring the data and enables them to envision the potential of the endeavor. This is usually followed by an enhanced proof point in a major application area, but one still focused on a limited portion of the business. Once the business value is achieved on this proof point, we are on our way to a full-scale deployment and exploring additional potential opportunities in other parts of the business.

This breaks down roughly into five key steps for business transformation process enabled by *Mining the Talk*: 1) Identify the business drivers; 2) Identify the key information sources; 3) Identify what we can learn; 4) Set up an initial unstructured mining process; and 5) Establish a sustainable process that can continue to create value. Subsequent chapters will cover each of these steps in more detail, for each of the application areas.

Summary

We hope this introduction has motivated you to learn more about what this amazing method we call *Mining the Talk* can do. By this point, you should be convinced that there is a growing problem faced by businesses due to ever-increasing complexity of relationships and interactions, and that mining of unstructured information is a potential solution to this problem. We have also introduced the basic premise behind our method, which is that mining of unstructured information requires the capture of domain knowledge and business objectives if it is to consistently succeed. We trust the rest of this book will convince you that this premise is correct.

In subsequent chapters, we will take you on our journey through five application areas of our approach, giving you specific insights into how our approach can be used to address needs within the business. As we go through these application areas, the steps of the *Mining the Talk* methodology will be fleshed out. The next three chapters will address the informal talk that occurs with customers and employees. Subsequently, Chapters 5 and 6, "Mining to See the Future," will address more formal talk that is found in technical literature, patents, and the Web. Finally, in Chapter 7, "Future Applications," we discuss some potential future applications of *Mining the Talk*.

Endnotes

1. This software is called IBM Unstructured Information Modeler, and the appendix of this book describes it in detail.
2. There are many well-established formulas for calculating the readability and grade level of a text sample based on word length, syllables, sentence length, and so on. Here is a reference for more information on these approaches: http://www.readability. info/info.shtml.

2

Mining Customer
Interactions

This chapter will show how we use *Mining the Talk* techniques to solve real-world business problems using actual examples. By the end of this chapter, the reader should have a basic grasp of our methods and how they work. This chapter goes into some detail concerning how we represent information and the algorithms we employ. We hope you will find our approach surprisingly simple. The simplicity of the approach is what makes it so generally applicable to such a wide range of information sources and business problems.

In the beginning of this chapter, we set the stage by motivating *Mining the Talk*, comparing it to search—the most common method of accessing unstructured information. We then focus on customer interactions as an application domain for our method. Next, we describe the high-level process used to apply *Mining the Talk* principles in business environments. The rest of the chapter consists of two detailed real-world examples illustrating our methods applied to customer interaction scenarios.

A Brief Analogy to the Physical World

How do you ask for directions if you don't know where you are going? That's a problem I often face when traveling on business and staying in a hotel in a strange city. Suppose you're visiting on business, but the meetings don't start until tomorrow and there's plenty of daylight left today. You would like to walk around a little, see something of the countryside, maybe find a nice local restaurant to eat a meal, and then stroll back. Ideally, you would like to see something during your walk that helps you experience the place, so you remember it after you've come home—sort of like an adventure, without the danger or risk.

So you go to the hotel desk and ask for…what? Directions to where? Advice on how to discover something interesting? For lack of a better question, you ask if they have a map of the local area. Fortunately they do, and one that is thoughtful enough to have already marked your current location on it. With this in hand, you set off on your excursion.

This experience is a lot like *Mining the Talk*. In *Mining the Talk*, you are not looking for a single document that will answer your question—you may not even be looking for a single answer. Instead, you want to find out what you don't already know. You want enlightenment. You want an experience, something that will widen your view of the world and expand your vision of your company and its place in the universe. This is the principle difference between *Mining the Talk* and search. Search is like what you do when you ask the hotel clerk for directions to the "best restaurant" in the area. Search assumes you have a clear idea of what you want to find, and a clear way to describe it. Of course, if your idea of "best restaurant" is very different from the hotel clerk's idea, then search may still fail to get you what you want. This illustrates the point that even problems that seem like search may really be mining problems in disguise. The key criteria for search are as follows:

1. A specific question to be answered.
2. An unambiguous way to communicate the question.

If both criteria are met, then a search may succeed. If not, it will almost certainly fail. In that case, it's time to take a journey of discovery.

In order to explore effectively, you need more than your own two feet. You really need a map. To see why, let's return to our city excursion. As you walk out of the hotel lobby, you are faced with several possible directions in which to walk, and no real information upon which to base your decision. If possible, you would prefer to walk in a direction that will be less populated and more scenic than the others. You look around to see if you can tell this from the immediate area, but the buildings that surround you prevent you from seeing very far in any direction. Here is where the map comes in handy.

In one direction, you can see dense intersecting streets and in another direction a major highway. These don't look too promising. You decide to set off in a third direction where there is a local university and a less-dense street pattern. This leads you on the sort of walk you were looking for—scenic, not too much traffic, and eventually a small, out of the way, cozy restaurant, off the beaten path, where you get a pleasant meal before heading back to the hotel. Using the map, you go a different way than you came, saving time and also seeing some different scenery.

A successful excursion. You might have been able to do something similar without the map, if you had been lucky or patient, but even if you had, the result would have been less satisfactory. The map actually helped in two important ways. It helped you find something valuable, and it showed you that what was found was the best available. The map gives you a sense of the possible. Without it, you might always have wondered what lay along the road not taken.

This "sense of the possible" is very much what *Mining the Talk* provides. Very often it's not only what you find that's important, but what is not found. What is needed is the equivalent to a map for unstructured information. We need something that describes the lay of the land, giving some direction and an organized way to go about the process of creating insight from information. Our map for unstructured information is a taxonomy. A taxonomy is the core concept in *Mining the Talk*, and in this chapter, we will spend significant time discussing how to create one and what they are good for once you have one.

Rather than begin by describing taxonomies in the abstract, we thought it would be more instructive to set the stage by describing a typical problem domain in which taxonomies can be used to make sense of unstructured information. This is the domain of "customer interactions."

Transactions Versus Interactions

Every business deals with customers. Most businesses (at least the legal ones) keep a record of every customer exchange. This data can take on many forms, but for the sake of simplicity, we reduce these forms to two overall categories that we refer to as *transactional* and *interactional*.

Transactions are the exchange of a customer's money for a product or service. The data we record about transactions is typically *structured*. What is recorded about each transaction is identical. Typical examples of transactional data are the amount of the purchase, the items purchased, the location of the purchase, and the date and time of the purchase. One transaction looks much like another; only the actual values change with each transaction. The possible values of the transactional data are known ahead of time. Existing business intelligence tools are the industry standard for analyzing this type of information.

Interactions are another matter. Typically, a customer interaction involves an unstructured exchange of some kind. Usually, the customer talks first, in speech or text, by asking some kind of question, requesting some specific service, presenting a problem, or providing other input to the business. The business then replies to the customer, attempting to satisfy the customer's needs. The dialog may continue as each side gathers more information and tries to achieve a mutually agreeable conclusion.

Interactions may or may not generate interactional data. There is no absolute requirement that customer interactions be recorded for them to be effective. However, most businesses at some point begin to keep records of their customer interactions. These are usually recorded as transcripts or summaries of the dialog that took place between a business representative and the customer. Unlike transactional data, interactional data does not have a fixed format. There is no way to accurately predict ahead of time what the customer will request in every situation, how the business will respond, or how the customer will receive this response. The interaction is *unstructured*. This means interactional data must also be unstructured. A fixed database schema with pre-defined values cannot capture every possible form a customer and business dialog might require, without resorting to free-form text fields. Some customer service applications attempt to apply structure to the unstructured interaction by having the person who takes the call manually classify each customer interaction into one of a predefined set of categories. This approach seldom works in practice because it is impossible to predict all important interaction issues that may arise ahead of time.

The line between transactions and interactions is not a fixed one. Over time, interactional data may evolve into transactional data as the interaction process matures. One example would be automated customer help systems that become routinized and can be reduced to a transactional form. This does not mean that analysis of interactional data is an intermediate step on the way to transactional maturity. No matter how mature the customer interaction process becomes, there will always be unforeseen and unstructured customer interactions that take place, and the need to document and analyze these should be a permanent part of any dynamic enterprise. Collecting and analyzing unstructured data for customer interactions is essential to providing necessary insight into what you don't already know about your business processes.

Business Drivers for Interactional Analysis

Just because interactions between businesses and customers exist, and are sometimes captured, does not imply that analysis is warranted. There needs to be a specific business purpose that drives the analysis. Information analysis absent business objectives is seldom fruitful. One important motivation is driven by the fact that customer interactions are not free. Customer interactions require the time and effort of a trained staff along with the infrastructure to support them. Therefore, reducing expenses through improved efficiency in customer interactions is frequently a primary driver of analysis. Cost reduction may be achieved via automated call handling as the interactions between business and customer become routinized. Another possibility is to reduce the average length of time each customer interaction requires, thus reducing the total labor required. Finally, the average level of expertise needed by the call taker may be reduced by leveraging knowledge support systems, thus again reducing the total labor expense.

Having high customer satisfaction is important to every business, because a happy customer buys more products and services. A happy customer also tells his friends. Customer satisfaction improvements can be realized through better and more consistent interactions on the part of call center employees. Speed and quality of service are important to improving the overall customer experience.

Additionally, detecting new customer requirements expressed in these interactions may lead to new product ideas. Detecting trends or patterns in areas of dissatisfaction may point to product or manufacturing defects that could be addressed. Finally, the business may discover hidden patterns in customer interactions that may lead to insights resulting in process improvements.

Every customer interaction analysis situation can be unique. Capturing the business objectives early and incorporating them into the analysis process is critical to achieving success. This may seem straightforward, but it is seldom practiced.

Characteristics of Interactional Information

There are common characteristics that are frequently recorded for all customer interactions. The information typically contains both structured and unstructured components.

Structured Information

Structured information associated with customer interactions consists of the known attributes of the interaction, the customer, and products. Examples include the following:

- **ID**—A unique identifier given to the customer interaction record.
- **Date and Time**—The date and time the customer interaction took place. There may be several *timestamps* to cover important milestones for a multi-interaction dialog, such as when the issue was opened, diagnosed, or closed.
- **Customer Information**—Who is the customer, what is their email address and phone number, and other demographic information.
- **Business Information**—Information about the business representative and their important attributes.

- **Location Information**—Where the customer and business representative are physically located.

- **Product Information**—Which make, model, brand, product, or service is related to the interaction.

- **Categorization**—A categorization of the customer concern into one or more predefined categories. Usually this categorization is done by the business representative, but sometimes it is by the customer.

Structured information plays a role in selecting the unstructured information to analyze. For example, we can use it to select customer interaction data for a particular product, date range, or call center. Later on, we also use structured information during the analysis phase. Correlations between the unstructured and structured data often form the backbone of our analysis conclusions.

Unstructured Information

Unstructured information captures everything else that happened during the interaction between the customer and the business that got recorded. Typically, this includes the following information:

- **Customer Issue Description**—What issue or question does the customer have with the business or its products?

- **Resolution Description**—How did the business respond to the customer?

- **Other Process Information**—What were the intermediate steps that were taken to find a resolution to the customer request?

Unstructured information is the meat on the bones of structured data. It's where the insight lies that will help us achieve the business objectives we set out with originally. *Mining the Talk* is how we get at that insight in a cost-effective way.

What Can We Learn from Customer Interactions?

Unstructured information related to customer interactions can teach us many things about our customers and how they relate to the business. For example:

1. What are the most common issues that customers have? This can be important because it may reveal "low hanging fruit" or areas where automation or other process changes will have the greatest business impact.

2. Where are the areas of dissatisfaction? These are the areas where you have a chance to have the biggest impact on improving overall customer satisfaction. Sometimes even customers who were dissatisfied in the past may be won back if you can identify them and offer appropriate incentives to make up for any perceived lack of performance on your part.

3. If the customer interaction process is breaking down, at what point does that usually occur? Knowing the weak points in your customer interaction process is the first step toward improving it. Unstructured customer interaction information is often the only place where such details are kept.

4. Who is doing a good job and who is doing a poor job of customer interaction? Once you know the weak points in the process, the next step is to take appropriate measures to ensure change.

5. What are the major drivers of cost in typical customer interaction? Combining unstructured analysis with structured information concerning call duration or time required to close a customer issue can lead to identification of key cost drivers in the customer interaction process.

6. What are the emerging trends in customer issues? Trends are helpful in pointing you toward emerging issues that can be headed off before they become major headaches.

The *Mining the Talk* Process for Customer Interactions

After many implementations, we realized the process of *Mining the Talk* for customer interactions has distinct phases. This section discusses each of these phases at a high level, to help set the context for the detailed examples that come later.

Understanding Business Objectives

The first step is to understand what the primary unmet needs of the business are in relation to customer interaction. Is there a known customer satisfaction issue? Is there a cost competitiveness problem? Are there any clues or theories as to why the customer is dissatisfied or as to what the primary drivers of unnecessary cost are? Who are the owners of the existing process, and what are the parameters of the process that can be changed? If these questions are not answered early, it will be difficult for *Mining the Talk* to achieve its true potential value.

Demonstration of Capabilities

When discussing opportunities for *Mining the Talk* solutions, it is seldom adequate merely to describe how mining of unstructured information can lead to business value. The value of the solution must be demonstrated. The stakeholders must be convinced of the need to invest time and resources, and they need to be educated on the type of data and kinds of problems that can be tackled with a mining approach. In most cases, the stakeholders will have only the most rudimentary understanding of the potential insights unstructured mining can produce. These misconceptions can quickly lead mining efforts down the wrong path—by selecting the wrong problem to tackle or the wrong information to tackle the problem with. Imparting an understanding of what is possible by mining customer interaction data will help facilitate the discussion of specific areas of the business that might benefit from the application of this technology. Demonstrating capabilities using past scenarios that have similar characteristics to the situation at hand is the most effective technique to ensure that the initial efforts will be properly focused.

Survey of Available Information

In order to achieve value by *Mining the Talk*, there must be a reasonably complete collection of information describing a significant sample of customer interactions. A survey of the available information sources should include the following:

- Call center logs
- Customer emails
- Chat or instant messaging transcripts
- Voice transcripts from customer calls
- Customer suggestion line databases

The first characteristic of good information is that it directly addresses the defined business objectives. It should have at least one free-form text field (unstructured information) whose content is relevant. The data should cover some significant time period, a few months at least, to ensure that any significant trends can be detected. Ideally, it should be a mixture of both structured and unstructured values. Additionally, there should be a significant amount of data available, more than could be easily read and understood by a single person in a reasonable amount of time.

Information Acquisition and Preparation

Before analysis can be performed, the data must first be properly prepared. This is the process of *Extracting* the data from where it resides, *Transforming* it into a format that the analysis tool can read, and *Loading* the data into the analysis tool data repository. This process is commonly referred to as *ETL*. The *ETL* process can consume the most time and resource in an analysis project. This is due to several factors, among these being: 1) getting efficient access to data is often non-trivial, due to local storage or security issues; 2) understanding the meaning of the data and the data schema is frequently difficult; 3) identifying and handling inconsistencies in the content can take time (e.g., missing values, incorrect types); 4) normalization (i.e., correcting values that seem different in the data, that actually mean the same thing) of structured fields is often a problem as well. After these issues are dealt with, the data can be extracted from where it resides, transformed into a format that is more desirable for mining, and then loaded into whatever repository the mining tool can access.

Divide and Conquer—Create an Initial Taxonomy

Creation of the taxonomy is the first step in breaking the analysis into manageable chunks. We employ a divide and conquer approach. Although it can be hard to understand a large collection of documents, it is possible to look at and comprehend a smaller set of documents when each set has a common theme. Our method derives the initial taxonomy directly from the information so that we can discover the known and unknown aspects of the customer interaction process. We use clustering to automatically generate disjoint categories made up of documents that share common elements. The structure of these categories and the method of generation helps ensure that no major areas of potential customer interaction insight present in the data are missed.

Capturing Domain Expertise Through Taxonomy Refinement

The initial taxonomy created by clustering is just the starting point. To be truly effective, the categories in a taxonomy must align with the business purpose of the analysis. The only way to ensure that this happens is through editing of the taxonomy categories. An analyst refines the taxonomy to ensure that each category is valid and makes sense in the context of the objectives. The refinement process includes ensuring that the membership of each category is accurate, the category is named with an appropriate label, and there are no "indistinct" and conceptually unclear categories. Doing this correctly ensures that the analysis will produce meaningful results.

Frequently, the most fruitful insights come during this stage of the process. Evaluation of large categories of customer interactions leads to the identification of significant issues that should be addressed. Addressing these issues may lead to process changes that reduce the number of interactions, improve performance of the business representative, or lower the cost of the customer interactions. Using this analysis, the consequence of a change to the customer interaction process (through automation or training) can be accurately gauged, based on frequency of customer interactions in that category. This leads directly to a business case for making the hypothetical process change.

More than one taxonomy may be necessary to capture all of the business objectives. Every taxonomy is in some sense a simplification of the underlying information from which it was derived. Multiple taxonomies help ensure that all important concepts are accurately captured, which means no important information will be lost in the translation from unstructured information to structured taxonomic categories. Multiple taxonomies provide the ability to view the data from different perspectives. For example, taxonomies may be based on the type of customer issue, the process used to solve the customer issue, or how satisfied the customer was with the result. This is a powerful technique, because different taxonomies can be analyzed together to discover heretofore unappreciated relationships and patterns. An example would be correlations found between unsatisfied customers and certain processes they were subjected to.

Look for Trends and Correlations

Once an accurate set of categories are created that reflect both the contents of the data and the objectives of the business, the next step is to look for any correlations between these categories and other structured attributes. This would include the following:

- The evolution of categories over time to spot emerging trends.
- A high co-occurrence between a category and a structured attribute, such as product or location to detect any underlying systemic causes.
- Measuring average call duration (time between initial customer call and close out) across categories to see if any unusual patterns emerge that might indicate problems with the customer interaction process.

Each of these correlations, when they occur, indicate a place for investigation of possible process problems. Looking at specific examples for each correlation is required to verify that the correlation actually corresponds to an interesting phenomenon, and is not simply a coincidence.

Stakeholder Review

All of the insights from analysis should be summarized in a report for the business stakeholders. This report should include the relevant categories and interesting correlations, along with their statistical significance and supporting examples. Where possible, the report should highlight those areas where some action or process improvement will likely lead to the greatest benefit.

Frequently a demonstration of the actual data loaded into an interactive mining and visualization tool[1] will be useful to allow the stakeholders to explore the customer interaction taxonomy themselves and brainstorm about potential process improvements that the analyst may have missed.

Establishing a Continuous Process

Once a proof point has established the value of mining customer interactions, it is time to take *Mining the Talk* to the next level. Systems and processes must be put in place and used regularly to gain insights from a continuing stream of customer interaction information. Every implementation will be different, but this section describes what the major issues are for making mining of customer interactions an ongoing concern.

The ETL, Classification, and Reporting Process

Automatic data feeds are created that send all relevant information to a mining engine on a regular basis. The ETL process designed previously is automated and applied to create an input data stream for classification. The taxonomies developed with domain expertise are used to classify the information stream into meaningful categories. Significantly high occurrence levels in any category, or in any combination of attributes, can be flagged to generate system alerts. These alerts may lead directly to actions taken by the business to improve customer interaction.

Coming Full Circle: Interactional Data Becomes Transactional

By leveraging the developed taxonomies to enable automatic classification on the unstructured information, we can now save the results as additional structured fields. In a sense, we are taking the knowledge we have gained from the unstructured information mining exercise and applying it to the data collection process to make it more intelligent, turning what was purely interactional data into transactional data. Now we can use our familiar suite of Business Intelligence tools to analyze this information to monitor our customer interaction processes going forward.

The trade-off here is going from the details about the customer interaction captured in the unstructured information to a more general description captured in the resulting structured information. Although some information may be lost, we are also eliminating some noise, obscuring the signal we want to detect. Using the captured knowledge from mining interactions to boost the signal and decrease the noise will improve data consistency, increase the scalability, and widen the applicability of each analysis. Continued analysis of the unstructured information will always be needed to adapt to changing business conditions and emergent customer interaction behaviors.

Measuring Effectiveness

Taxonomies need to be maintained over time. Their effectiveness needs to be continually monitored and the taxonomies and alert thresholds adjusted as the environment in which the business operates changes. The sensitivity and frequency for monitoring and adjustment is business dependent; some businesses, processes, and industries are more stable than others. To help with this, automated tools may be put in place to detect degradations in classifier quality.

Expand the Application of *Mining the Talk*

Success in one area of the business leads to opportunities in additional application areas. Leveraging the success in one area will encourage analysis of other unstructured information sources relevant to customer interaction.

Applications that combine input from multiple sources into a single mining workbench are often the most effective. Having multiple sources that verify or qualify conclusions from a single source makes the conclusions even more meaningful and reliable.

Customer Interactions Examples

Next we will work through two detailed examples. This first will be a call center for a Fast Consumer Goods Company, where we will describe how to build an initial feature space, create a taxonomy, and analyze that taxonomy versus structured information. In our second example, we will delve into the operations of a computer helpdesk, where we will address feature space and taxonomy editing in detail.

Example 1: Fast Consumer Goods Company: Customer Call Line

A Fast Consumer Goods Company has a toll-free number for customers to call for complaints, questions, and comments on products. Most of the information collected related to each call is structured, including attributes like product name, geographic location, manufacture source, and the date. One of the fields is unstructured and contains a short (usually 10–20 word) description of the customer issue. The simplicity of this data serves to clearly illustrate the most basic process for creating a taxonomy to derive business insights for the company.

Building the Feature Space

Given a large number of unstructured call descriptions—in this case, over 15,000—how do you begin to make sense of it? Where do you even start? As we said earlier, you need a map to begin. This section will describe how to create such a map. Keep in mind as we go through the details of text feature generation that this is not something you do with pencil and paper. Software will be required to perform many of the tasks described. Given such software, the actual mining process goes very rapidly. On this data set, it takes less than a minute to generate a features space and an initial taxonomy from it.

The foundation of any map is a well-defined coordinate system. For a two-dimensional road map, that is longitude and latitude. For a topographical map, there is a third dimension added using elevation lines. For our unstructured information map, we will use a multi-dimensional feature space, but one having many more than three dimensions. The dimensions in our features space are the words and phrases that occur in the information collection. The values for each dimension are the number of times each word or phrase occurs in each document. The documents are like locations on a map whose coordinates correspond to their word and phrase counts.

This scheme for representing documents is commonly known as a "bag of words" or the vector-space model. This scheme eliminates the order and punctuation that make a document readable. This is like what would happen if you took all the words and phrases in a typed version of the document and cut them out (like a kidnapper creating a ransom note) and put them in a bag and shook them up. Someone else who came along and opened the bag would find it impossible to read the original document, because the ordering would be lost. But they still might be able to determine the subject matter of the document. Perhaps they could infer from this bag of words what "kind" of document it was originally. That's exactly how we are going to use our bag-of-words representation, not to "read" the text, but to glean the essence from each document.

Referring to a document as a particular "kind," is a form of classification. Classification requires a taxonomy of categories from which to choose. In the next section, we discuss what taxonomies are and how we create them from unstructured information. Our bag-of-words feature space is used to generate a taxonomy automatically using a technique called clustering.

Taxonomies and Text Clustering

It is worth spending a little time on what taxonomies are before we talk about how to generate them. A *taxonomy* is a classification of objects into disjoint sets, meaning each object belongs to a single category. The objects that are contained in the same category share some characteristics.

In science, classification schemes, such as those describing the physical elements in chemistry and the animal species in biology, are examples of taxonomies based on common physical characteristics.[2]

It is a well-known maxim in science that the most difficult part of doing research is in not finding the answers to questions, but in asking the right questions in the first place. Classification and taxonomy generation are powerful tools in the search for the right question. Scientists in all disciplines classify things in order to discover similarities, and in finding these similarities ask the questions about underlying structure that ultimately leads to a greater understanding of the universe. Text taxonomy creation is the search for a different kind of knowledge using the same strategy.

Now that we motivated why we want to create taxonomies, how do we create them? We begin by using the words and phrases in the documents as features, and then group documents with words and phrases in common. This approach assumes that these features are a good substitute for an underlying semantic commonality. The analyst determines the underlying structural explanation for the common features. This last step is critical, because it ensures the category is not a chance collection of documents with similar word content and no inherent meaning.

How does clustering actually work? It all begins with the feature space. We will discuss the feature space in more detail later in the chapter, but for now just remember that they are the words and phrases that occur in documents. For the purposes of clustering, each example in a collection is converted into a numeric representation. To accomplish this, each unique word is assigned a unique integer, and for each example, we count how many times each word occurs. Here's what that word occurrence matrix might look like for three simple examples (see Figure 2-1).

Example	product	rice	object	plastic	found	sauce	jar	piece	polythene	returning
found plastic object in rice product	1	1	1	1	1	0	0	0	0	0
plastic piece found in sauce jar	0	0	0	1	1	1	1	1	0	0
polythene in the product-returning	1	0	0	1	0	0	0	0	1	1

Figure 2-1   Text converted to feature space

This is how text turns into numbers—numbers that can be reasoned about by a machine allowing a computer to compare two different text examples and determine how similar they are. If two documents are considered "similar" to the degree that they have similar word content, all we need is a metric with which to compare documents based on these numbers. For this, we turn to the standard Cartesian coordinate system that most of us are familiar with from our high school math classes. In this system, points that are described by a vector of numeric values can be plotted, with rows representing points and columns representing dimensions.[3] There are a couple of ways we could mathematically measure the similarity between two such numeric vectors. One approach would be Euclidean distance. This is calculated with the well-known formula:

$$d(a,b) = \sqrt{\sum_i (a_i - b_i)^2}$$

However, Euclidean distance can be problematic in this context because a long document may be "far" from a short document by virtue of having more words, even if both documents talk about the same subject.[4] If you think about it, what we really want to measure for the purposes of document similarity is not absolute distance, but orientation. If we draw a line between the origin and each of the points we wish to compare, it is the angle of that line that indicates the relative orientation and therefore the nearness of the two points—or to be more specific, the cosine of that angle.[5]

Cosine distance is the basic evaluation metric we use in our approach when it comes to comparing two documents, a document and a document category, or two different document categories. The beauty of this approach is it reduces the complexity of comparing two dissimilar documents down to a single equation that produces one numeric output, whose value lies within a fixed range. That's really a very powerful simplification.

But always remember that it's just a number. No matter how many decimal places you accurately calculate, it won't tell you why the documents differ or give you any context concerning if the difference is truly important. It's only as good as the underlying set of features that describe each document. If the features are irrelevant for the task you are trying to accomplish, then there is not much chance that anything useful will be gained from any distance metric. We will address this issue more later in the chapter where we describe how to generate a good feature space.

Now that we have a powerful way to numerically compare documents, we need a way to describe a document collection. This is necessary in order to compare a single document to a collection to determine whether that document belongs to that collection, and if so, how well it fits. To model a document collection, we introduce the concept of a "centroid." A *centroid* is the average of all the document vectors in a collection.[6]

Using feature spaces, centroids, and cosine distance, we have a way to numerically compare document collections to documents. We are ready to begin to understand how document clustering works. A cluster is nothing more than a document collection that has a centroid associated with it. A set of clusters that completely categorizes a set of documents is called a taxonomy. The process of generating a taxonomy from a collection of documents is called *clustering*.

There are several methods of clustering; some of them have been around for decades, and others were developed more recently. In this example, we will cover two methods that we have found to be most effective in creating meaningful taxonomies from document collections—in particular, those collections consisting primarily of short documents containing one concept. We assume in *Mining the Talk* that the clustering is performed by software, but it is valuable to understand the process in order to properly interpret the results.

K-means Clustering

K-means clustering derives its name from the variable k, which represents the number of clusters to be generated, and "means," which refers to the centroid that models each cluster.[7] K-means begins by choosing k cluster centroids. Each document is assigned to the cluster with the closest centroid. The centroid is recalculated based upon the mean of the actual documents that were closest to the centroid. The documents are reassigned based upon the new centroid. This process repeats until the process produces minimal changes to the centroids.

An interesting characteristic of k-means is it doesn't have only one solution for a given document collection and choice of k. The initial centroids actually determine the final answer we will get, so it's a pretty important step. However, no one really knows the best approach to selecting the initial set of centroids. In fact, there's probably no one approach that works for all data.

Why is that? Because, what makes a clustering, or any taxonomy, good or bad is not simply the data that makes up the categories, but the purpose for which you want to use the taxonomy in the first place. So on the same set of data, a clustering that is ideal for one business purpose, may fall completely short in its usefulness for some other business purpose.

As an example, take our Fast Consumer Goods Company collection of customer comments. There are at least two business purposes one could have for this kind of data: 1) To understand what about the products makes customers happy or unhappy and to identify potential actions that might improve customer satisfaction; and 2) To identify specific, recurring problems in the production and distribution chain, and thereby identify the underlying causes in order to address them.

It is very unlikely that both of these questions can be addressed well with the same taxonomy. Although a "recurring problems" taxonomy might have many categories, one for each kind of problem, a "satisfaction" taxonomy might consist of just three simple categories:

- Satisfied customers
- Unsatisfied customers
- Other

If there's no one right taxonomy, then it makes sense that there's no right way to start *k*-means in order to generate the perfect clustering. An approach often taken is to begin with a set of *k* random centroids. This means that each time you run *k*-means on the same set of information, you may get a different result. That's a little unsettling, but it is indicative of the nature of the problem we are trying to solve—one in which clustering alone can only get you so far toward the desired result. To get the rest of the way requires human expertise. More on this subject later when we go over the second customer interaction example.

Naming Clusters

Clustering using *k*-means gives us a partitioning of the documents into distinct categories. What next? A partitioning by itself is not very helpful. For example, we could randomly assign each document to one of *k* categories. This would produce a taxonomy, but not one that would have any useful application. What makes a taxonomy helpful is the documents in each category have something in common. By definition, the members of a *k*-means–generated category have in common a greater affinity for that category's centroid than any of the other categories' centroids. Unfortunately, that's not a natural concept for a human analyst to understand. We need something more intuitive than a centroid to communicate the concept that a category represents. This is where cluster naming plays a role.

The name of a cluster should communicate as succinctly as possible what makes that cluster unique in the taxonomy. The name should identify a distinct concept that the members of the cluster all share, but that is not generally true of most other documents. We call this approach *cover naming*, because it tries to cover as many examples in the category as possible with the name. Ideally, if we could find exactly one dictionary term all the documents in a cluster shared, and that term would not be more frequent in the cluster documents than in other documents in our collection, then that would be a good name for our cluster. Failing that preferred scenario, if we have multiple words that occur in all documents in a cluster, then all such words connected by "and" would make a good name.

What if a category contains a set of examples that have no dictionary word in common? The best you can do is to construct a multiple word name. The first word is the most common. The second word is the most common word shared by those examples not containing the first word. These two words connected by an "or" create a cluster name. More words can be added to sufficiently cover the documents in the category.[8] Eventually, the name of the category might get too long to be helpful in terms of gaining a quick understanding of the category. In that case, we give the category a special name, like "Miscellaneous," to indicate that there is no straightforward way to describe the contents.

Figure 2-2 shows the Fast Consumer Goods Company call center information after a *k*-means clustering and cluster naming. We will explain cohesion and distinctness in the next example. This figure serves to illustrate one way in which this large collection of information can be broken down into its components using clustering.

	Class Name	Size	Cohesion	Distinctness
1	mail_card	79 (0.52%)	88.62%	97.95%
2	hbc	147 (0.96%)	76.33%	86.31%
3	damage	102 (0.67%)	73.23%	85.65%
4	buy	32 (0.21%)	70.94%	93.72%
5	heat_bloom	571 (3.74%)	70.68%	91.18%
6	stockist	81 (0.53%)	65.14%	93.11%
7	free	403 (2.64%)	64.26%	90.32%
8	white	32 (0.21%)	62.98%	77.61%
9	enquiry	39 (0.26%)	62.72%	92.90%
10	calendar	298 (1.95%)	62.06%	72.88%
11	recipe	216 (1.42%)	61.50%	64.85%
12	taste	86 (0.56%)	58.49%	92.23%
13	availability	741 (4.86%)	57.81%	92.97%
14	revels	89 (0.58%)	57.65%	89.53%
15	pet	42 (0.28%)	56.31%	95.87%
16	pack	665 (4.36%)	56.05%	69.56%
17	promises	35 (0.23%)	55.36%	94.12%
18	chicken	91 (0.60%)	53.87%	74.15%
19	advert,music	85 (0.56%)	52.68%	82.99%
20	chocolate	64 (0.42%)	51.60%	77.61%
21	query	216 (1.42%)	51.28%	90.32%
22	box	203 (1.33%)	50.71%	81.96%
23	pouch	251 (1.65%)	49.22%	85.79%
24	wrong,breed,vet	215 (1.41%)	49.00%	95.35%
25	date	209 (1.37%)	48.76%	92.26%
26	product	496 (3.25%)	48.26%	88.71%
27	code	591 (3.87%)	47.84%	78.01%
28	open	281 (1.84%)	46.72%	84.70%
29	cat	576 (3.78%)	46.19%	89.99%
30	return	489 (3.21%)	46.17%	75.62%
31	bag	298 (1.95%)	45.28%	81.49%
32	pouches,tuna	128 (0.84%)	44.43%	86.29%
33	suitable,wants,vegetarian	188 (1.23%)	44.12%	92.76%
34	kitten,reffered	257 (1.68%)	42.82%	69.56%
35	feed,puppy	574 (3.76%)	42.44%	84.76%
36	request,information	384 (2.52%)	41.46%	64.85%
37	missing,sweet	350 (2.29%)	39.98%	72.88%
38	bar,peanut,snicker	431 (2.83%)	39.55%	85.65%
39	email,reply,response,u...	84 (0.55%)	38.75%	76.62%
40	hard,light,find	149 (0.98%)	37.86%	89.69%
41	content,fat,pasta,med	117 (0.77%)	37.63%	85.47%
42	rice,mouldy	476 (3.12%)	37.46%	85.79%
43	empty,seal,wrapped,pa...	270 (1.77%)	34.82%	80.57%
44	dog,tin	617 (4.05%)	34.41%	84.76%
45	jelly,gravy,beef	199 (1.30%)	34.23%	74.15%
46	plastic,piece,clip,blue	233 (1.53%)	31.27%	75.62%
47	ask,back,send,email	105 (0.69%)	29.61%	76.62%
48	Miscellaneous	1148 (7.53%)	14.98%	80.74%
49	NONE	1820 (11.93%)	0.00%	100.00%
	TOTAL / AVERAGE	15253	39.32%	84.82%

Figure 2-2 K-means clustering result on FCG data set

Intuitive Clustering

The process involved in finding good names for clusters generated by *k*-means led us to create a new clustering approach that has proven to be effective for generating good initial categorizations. This approach helps the analyst quickly understand the theme of each category in the taxonomy, simply by reading each category name. We call the approach *Intuitive*, because the goal of the method is to generate intuitively obvious clusters, rather than mathematically well defined.

The method builds on the observation that the best clusters generated using *k*-means are those named with a single dictionary term. It starts by finding such terms and building clusters around them, instead of vice-versa. The problem is reduced to one of finding a way to identify the best terms for the purpose of generating clusters. For this, we use the cohesion metric. We define the *cohesion* of a term to be the average distance of every document that contains that term from a centroid formed by the average of all documents that contain the term.

Simply put, cohesive terms are those which have the property that the documents that contain them are similar to each other. It turns out that, in general, this makes a good concept to build a category around, especially when the documents being clustered are relatively short, as is the case with the Fast Consumer Goods Company customer calls.[9]

Figure 2-3 shows the results of Intuitive clustering on this set of data.

Looking at a list of cluster names is only a first step in our journey. The taxonomy provides us with a map. Using the map, we are ready to explore. When the client looked at the intuitive taxonomy, three categories stood out as being especially interesting:

1. heat_bloom confirm
2. damage
3. gluten_free

These categories were interesting because they were not about specific products or seasonal items, but they identified a specific issue that could apply across many products. Here are some typical examples for each of these three categories:

heat_bloom

Number	Text Description
1	Heat bloom confirmed
2	Heat bloom confirmed 8 x 54g
3	"Heat bloom confirmed"

eClassifier: C:\data\mars\../text.dat

File   Edit   Execute   View   Subclass   Help

| Dictionary Tool | View Selected Class | Subclass | Merge Classes |

Taxonomy Level: Root

	Class Name	Size	Cohesion	Distinctness
1	heat bloom_confirm	320 (2.10%)	88.00%	22.86%
2	mail	85 (0.56%)	84.68%	96.09%
3	heat_bloom	153 (1.00%)	80.40%	22.86%
4	care_pack	301 (1.97%)	78.59%	43.72%
5	gluten_free	287 (1.88%)	77.22%	45.14%
6	advent_calendar	210 (1.38%)	74.00%	67.63%
7	vet	57 (0.37%)	73.36%	92.67%
8	breed	111 (0.73%)	72.92%	92.05%
9	hbc	204 (1.34%)	71.37%	86.48%
10	vegetarian	109 (0.71%)	71.28%	92.34%
11	advice	147 (0.96%)	69.08%	49.46%
12	stockist	123 (0.81%)	64.30%	93.91%
13	advert	101 (0.66%)	62.71%	90.18%
14	damage	193 (1.27%)	62.52%	78.75%
15	peanut	70 (0.46%)	61.71%	88.68%
16	date	131 (0.86%)	61.47%	92.99%
17	recipe	106 (0.69%)	60.97%	68.84%
18	availability	689 (4.52%)	60.67%	93.24%
19	reffered	65 (0.43%)	59.90%	92.25%
20	voucher	110 (0.72%)	59.81%	81.56%
21	enquiry	91 (0.60%)	59.37%	87.37%
22	hard	93 (0.61%)	59.31%	89.27%
23	tin	197 (1.29%)	58.57%	81.55%
24	kitten	91 (0.60%)	58.28%	76.39%
25	query	144 (0.94%)	58.26%	89.56%
26	pet	67 (0.44%)	58.19%	94.02%
27	mould	78 (0.51%)	57.51%	83.73%
28	taste	117 (0.77%)	57.44%	92.90%
29	pouches	138 (0.90%)	57.36%	87.01%
30	chocolate	77 (0.50%)	56.95%	95.48%
31	feed	226 (1.48%)	56.88%	49.48%
32	mouldy	87 (0.57%)	56.55%	76.34%
33	sweet	124 (0.81%)	56.26%	87.46%
34	buy	81 (0.53%)	56.05%	91.83%
35	revels	148 (0.97%)	55.89%	87.02%
36	content	107 (0.70%)	55.78%	91.53%
37	request	312 (2.05%)	55.76%	68.84%
38	box	113 (0.74%)	55.56%	86.54%
39	free	105 (0.69%)	54.65%	45.14%
40	puppy	184 (1.21%)	53.76%	66.05%
41	confirm	125 (0.82%)	53.65%	57.83%
42	complete	81 (0.53%)	53.42%	85.35%
43	missing	182 (1.19%)	53.37%	67.63%
44	jelly	85 (0.56%)	53.02%	82.13%
45	pouch	272 (1.78%)	52.96%	86.56%
46	bag	184 (1.21%)	52.89%	85.64%
47	chicken	143 (0.94%)	52.86%	82.13%
48	receive	82 (0.54%)	52.82%	81.56%
49	open	134 (0.88%)	52.72%	76.34%
50	food	95 (0.62%)	52.69%	76.39%
51	bar	280 (1.84%)	52.45%	84.89%
52	pack	497 (3.26%)	52.40%	43.72%
53	cat	473 (3.10%)	50.79%	86.81%
54	sauce	213 (1.40%)	50.84%	90.05%
55	product	406 (2.66%)	50.16%	87.55%

Visualization   Class View   **Class Table**   Class Tree

Figure 2-3   Intuitive clustering result

Heat bloom is a kind of spoilage. It would make sense to see if this category has a correlation with certain products, factories, or stores to determine the root cause.

gluten_free

Number	Text Description
1	Gluten free
2	Product X—Gluten free
3	Product Y—Gluten free

Gluten is a substance found in wheat flour that is indigestible in some individuals. A significant numbers of calls might indicate that better package labeling is needed on some products.

damage

Number	Text Description
1	ProductX 26gx6 machine damaged
2	ProductY machine damaged
3	ProductZ machine damaged

Damaged products lead one to wonder if there might be some underlying process issue that is systematically causing the damage. The next section explores this particular issue in depth.

In each case, we have found something interesting and understood what each category means. Now, we can use the structured information in the customer interaction data to discover patterns that might lead to insights about underlying causes or corrective actions.

Correlations Between Structured Data and Unstructured Categories

Products can be damaged at any phase of the manufacturing and distribution process. If the damage levels are significant, we can look for correlations with structured features that might help indicate a root cause. For example, for the calls in the damage category, we can test for a correlation with the factory of origination.

Our preferred method for visualizing the relationships of two independent variables is via a co-occurrence table (cotable). In this case, the taxonomy membership is one variable and the factory of origination is the other. This lets us see how the data breaks down across all the combinations of categories and factories. Figure 2-4 shows this breakdown for the Fast Consumer Goods Company data.

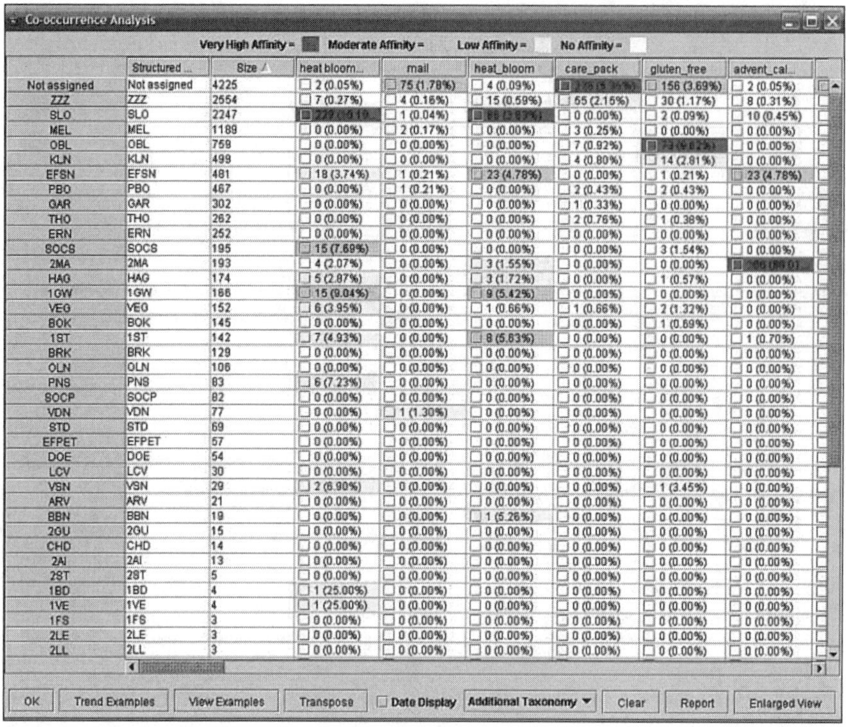

	Structured ...	Size	heat bloom...	mail	heat_bloom	care_pack	gluten_free	advent_cal...
Not assigned	Not assigned	4225	2 (0.05%)	75 (1.78%)	4 (0.09%)	[illegible]	156 (3.69%)	2 (0.05%)
ZZZ	ZZZ	2554	7 (0.27%)	4 (0.16%)	15 (0.59%)	55 (2.15%)	30 (1.17%)	8 (0.31%)
SLO	SLO	2247	[illegible]	1 (0.04%)	[illegible]	0 (0.00%)	2 (0.09%)	10 (0.45%)
MEL	MEL	1189	0 (0.00%)	2 (0.17%)	0 (0.00%)	3 (0.25%)	0 (0.00%)	0 (0.00%)
OBL	OBL	759	0 (0.00%)	0 (0.00%)	0 (0.00%)	7 (0.92%)	[illegible]	0 (0.00%)
KLN	KLN	499	0 (0.00%)	0 (0.00%)	0 (0.00%)	4 (0.80%)	14 (2.81%)	0 (0.00%)
EFSN	EFSN	481	18 (3.74%)	1 (0.21%)	23 (4.78%)	0 (0.00%)	1 (0.21%)	23 (4.78%)
PBO	PBO	467	0 (0.00%)	1 (0.21%)	0 (0.00%)	2 (0.43%)	2 (0.43%)	0 (0.00%)
GAR	GAR	302	0 (0.00%)	0 (0.00%)	0 (0.00%)	1 (0.33%)	0 (0.00%)	0 (0.00%)
THO	THO	262	0 (0.00%)	0 (0.00%)	0 (0.00%)	2 (0.76%)	1 (0.38%)	0 (0.00%)
ERN	ERN	252	0 (0.00%)	0 (0.00%)	0 (0.00%)	0 (0.00%)	0 (0.00%)	0 (0.00%)
SOCS	SOCS	195	15 (7.69%)	0 (0.00%)	0 (0.00%)	0 (0.00%)	3 (1.54%)	0 (0.00%)
2MA	2MA	193	4 (2.07%)	0 (0.00%)	3 (1.55%)	0 (0.00%)	0 (0.00%)	[illegible]
HAG	HAG	174	5 (2.87%)	0 (0.00%)	3 (1.72%)	0 (0.00%)	1 (0.57%)	0 (0.00%)
1GW	1GW	166	15 (9.04%)	0 (0.00%)	9 (5.42%)	0 (0.00%)	0 (0.00%)	0 (0.00%)
VEG	VEG	152	6 (3.95%)	0 (0.00%)	1 (0.66%)	1 (0.66%)	2 (1.32%)	0 (0.00%)
BOK	BOK	145	0 (0.00%)	0 (0.00%)	0 (0.00%)	0 (0.00%)	1 (0.69%)	0 (0.00%)
1ST	1ST	142	7 (4.93%)	0 (0.00%)	8 (5.63%)	0 (0.00%)	0 (0.00%)	1 (0.70%)
BRK	BRK	129	0 (0.00%)	0 (0.00%)	0 (0.00%)	0 (0.00%)	0 (0.00%)	0 (0.00%)
OLN	OLN	106	0 (0.00%)	0 (0.00%)	0 (0.00%)	0 (0.00%)	0 (0.00%)	0 (0.00%)
PNS	PNS	83	6 (7.23%)	0 (0.00%)	0 (0.00%)	0 (0.00%)	0 (0.00%)	0 (0.00%)
SOCP	SOCP	82	0 (0.00%)	0 (0.00%)	0 (0.00%)	0 (0.00%)	0 (0.00%)	0 (0.00%)
VDN	VDN	77	0 (0.00%)	1 (1.30%)	0 (0.00%)	0 (0.00%)	0 (0.00%)	0 (0.00%)
STD	STD	69	0 (0.00%)	0 (0.00%)	0 (0.00%)	0 (0.00%)	0 (0.00%)	0 (0.00%)
EFPET	EFPET	57	0 (0.00%)	0 (0.00%)	0 (0.00%)	0 (0.00%)	0 (0.00%)	0 (0.00%)
DOE	DOE	54	0 (0.00%)	0 (0.00%)	0 (0.00%)	0 (0.00%)	0 (0.00%)	0 (0.00%)
LCV	LCV	30	0 (0.00%)	0 (0.00%)	0 (0.00%)	0 (0.00%)	0 (0.00%)	0 (0.00%)
VSN	VSN	29	2 (6.90%)	0 (0.00%)	0 (0.00%)	0 (0.00%)	1 (3.45%)	0 (0.00%)
ARV	ARV	21	0 (0.00%)	0 (0.00%)	0 (0.00%)	0 (0.00%)	0 (0.00%)	0 (0.00%)
BBN	BBN	19	0 (0.00%)	0 (0.00%)	1 (5.26%)	0 (0.00%)	0 (0.00%)	0 (0.00%)
2GU	2GU	15	0 (0.00%)	0 (0.00%)	0 (0.00%)	0 (0.00%)	0 (0.00%)	0 (0.00%)
CHD	CHD	14	0 (0.00%)	0 (0.00%)	0 (0.00%)	0 (0.00%)	0 (0.00%)	0 (0.00%)
2AI	2AI	13	0 (0.00%)	0 (0.00%)	0 (0.00%)	0 (0.00%)	0 (0.00%)	0 (0.00%)
2ST	2ST	5	0 (0.00%)	0 (0.00%)	0 (0.00%)	0 (0.00%)	0 (0.00%)	0 (0.00%)
1BD	1BD	4	1 (25.00%)	0 (0.00%)	0 (0.00%)	0 (0.00%)	0 (0.00%)	0 (0.00%)
1VE	1VE	4	1 (25.00%)	0 (0.00%)	0 (0.00%)	0 (0.00%)	0 (0.00%)	0 (0.00%)
1FS	1FS	3	0 (0.00%)	0 (0.00%)	0 (0.00%)	0 (0.00%)	0 (0.00%)	0 (0.00%)
2LE	2LE	3	0 (0.00%)	0 (0.00%)	0 (0.00%)	0 (0.00%)	0 (0.00%)	0 (0.00%)
2LL	2LL	3	0 (0.00%)	0 (0.00%)	0 (0.00%)	0 (0.00%)	0 (0.00%)	0 (0.00%)

Figure 2-4 Co-occurrence table: category vs. factory

The challenge with cotables is figuring out which numbers are interesting. It isn't always the ones you would think at first glance. To see why, examine the cell for ZZZ/heat bloom. The value of this cell seems large (15), so you might think there was an important relationship. But, it is also the case that this cell corresponds to a fairly large category in the taxonomy and a frequent factory in the database. Is the number in that cell actually more than we would have expected? This question can be answered mathematically.

Assuming no relationship exists that ties particular factories to particular taxonomy categories (an important if somewhat unrealistic assumption), we would expect to find around (X * Y) in a cell for a given factor and category, where X is the percentage of times a given factory occurs and Y is the percentage of times category Y occurs. Let's call this expected value: E. So, an exceptional value is something greater than E. This would be an event that occurs more often than we expect. That will be different for every cell in the cotable, assuming the number of calls for each factory and category differ.

If we pursue this line of reasoning a little further, we can get a relative significance for different values in the cotable. We can distinguish whether a 5 occurring in one cell is more interesting than a 10 occurring in a different cell. We do this with the Chi-Squared test.[10] This is a statistical test that calculates the likelihood of seeing any particular value in the cell of a cotable. The smaller this probability, the less likely the value, and the more interesting it is from a data mining perspective. When a very low probability value occurs, it suggests that our original assumption about no relationship existing between the taxonomy and the factory was incorrect. There actually may be a relationship, and that relationship may be indicated by the data. However, a correlation does not signify a definitive cause and effect between category and factory. It only tells us that there may be something worth investigating further.

To show significance, we shade the values of the cotable according to their calculated probability. This is much easier to read than a lot of small decimal floating point values.

Dark = Probability of 0.0.
Medium = Probability greater than 0.0 but less than 0.001.
Light = Probability greater than 0.001 but less than 0.5.

Now if we look at the "damage" column, and sort the rows by size of "damage," we see something interesting (see Figure 2-5).

Co-occurrence Analysis	Very High Affinity = ▪	Moderate Affinity = ▪	Low Affinity = ▪	No Affinity = □			
	damage	peanut	date	recipe	availability	reffered	voucher
SLO	107 (4.75%)	3 (0.13%)	45 (2.00%)	0 (0.00%)	8 (0.36%)	1 (0.04%)	6 (0.27%)
MEL	15 (1.26%)	0 (0.00%)	2 (0.17%)	5 (0.42%)	26 (2.19%)	2 (0.17%)	2 (0.17%)
ZZZ	12 (0.47%)	12 (0.47%)	21 (0.82%)	26 (1.02%)	59 (2.31%)	0 (0.00%)	16 (0.63%)
VEG	9 (5.92%)	1 (0.66%)	3 (1.97%)	0 (0.00%)	5 (3.29%)	0 (0.00%)	0 (0.00%)
OBL	6 (0.79%)	0 (0.00%)	10 (1.32%)	8 (1.05%)	19 (2.50%)	1 (0.13%)	0 (0.00%)
EFSN	6 (1.25%)	0 (0.00%)	2 (0.42%)	0 (0.00%)	0 (0.00%)	0 (0.00%)	0 (0.00%)
HAG	6 (3.45%)	51 (29.31%)	4 (2.30%)	0 (0.00%)	0 (0.00%)	0 (0.00%)	0 (0.00%)
1ST	6 (4.23%)	0 (0.00%)	2 (1.41%)	0 (0.00%)	0 (0.00%)	0 (0.00%)	0 (0.00%)
SOCS	5 (2.56%)	1 (0.51%)	3 (1.54%)	1 (0.51%)	2 (1.03%)	0 (0.00%)	1 (0.51%)
GAR	3 (0.99%)	0 (0.00%)	1 (0.33%)	0 (0.00%)	6 (1.99%)	0 (0.00%)	0 (0.00%)
Not assigned	2 (0.05%)	2 (0.05%)	15 (0.36%)	54 (1.28%)	443 (10.46%)	59 (1.40%)	81 (1.92%)
THO	2 (0.76%)	0 (0.00%)	3 (1.15%)	1 (0.38%)	49 (18.70%)	0 (0.00%)	0 (0.00%)
1GW	2 (1.20%)	0 (0.00%)	0 (0.00%)	0 (0.00%)	0 (0.00%)	0 (0.00%)	0 (0.00%)
PNS	2 (2.41%)	0 (0.00%)	2 (2.41%)	0 (0.00%)	4 (4.82%)	0 (0.00%)	1 (1.20%)
STD	2 (2.90%)	0 (0.00%)	0 (0.00%)	1 (1.45%)	0 (0.00%)	0 (0.00%)	0 (0.00%)
VSN	2 (6.90%)	0 (0.00%)	0 (0.00%)	2 (6.90%)	1 (3.45%)	0 (0.00%)	0 (0.00%)
KLN	1 (0.20%)	0 (0.00%)	7 (1.40%)	5 (1.00%)	6 (1.20%)	1 (0.20%)	1 (0.20%)
ERN	1 (0.40%)	0 (0.00%)	0 (0.00%)	0 (0.00%)	8 (3.17%)	0 (0.00%)	0 (0.00%)
VDN	1 (1.30%)	0 (0.00%)	1 (1.30%)	0 (0.00%)	3 (3.90%)	0 (0.00%)	0 (0.00%)
2GU	1 (6.67%)	0 (0.00%)	0 (0.00%)	0 (0.00%)	0 (0.00%)	0 (0.00%)	0 (0.00%)
2AI	1 (7.69%)	0 (0.00%)	0 (0.00%)	0 (0.00%)	0 (0.00%)	0 (0.00%)	0 (0.00%)
1FM	1 (50.00%)	0 (0.00%)	0 (0.00%)	0 (0.00%)	0 (0.00%)	0 (0.00%)	0 (0.00%)
PBO	0 (0.00%)	0 (0.00%)	2 (0.43%)	2 (0.43%)	16 (3.43%)	0 (0.00%)	1 (0.21%)
2MA	0 (0.00%)	0 (0.00%)	0 (0.00%)	0 (0.00%)	0 (0.00%)	0 (0.00%)	0 (0.00%)

| OK | Trend Examples | View Examples | Transpose | ☐ Date Display | Additional Taxonomy ▼ | Clear | Report |

Figure 2-5 Correlation between factory and damaged product

Clearly, the factory SLO has a significant correlation with "damaged" product. Here are some example cases for each of the co-occurrence events:

(#13995): ProductX - machine damage

(#14019): ProductX 37g machine damaged

(#13982): ProductX 6x54g machine damaged

(#14035): ProductX 7x62.5g machine damaged

(#14034): ProductX 5 + 2 machine damage

(#14018): ProductX machine damage

(#14736): ProductY 5x58g machine damaged

(#11082): ProductZ machine damage

(#10872): ProductZ 225g damaged in distribution

(#10873): ProductZ 225g damaged in transit

(#14021): ProductX x5 62.5g - machine damage confirmed

(#14005): "ProductX,6 pack, machine damage"

(#14023): ProductX multi-pack 5x62.5g machine damage

(#14078): ProductX big one rtnd end crimp damage

(#14032): ProductX 5 pack machine damaged squashed

There could be several reasons for this correlation. It could be the products produced at factory SLO are more fragile and, thus, are more likely than other products to be damaged. However, it could be something more serious; for example, it could be a quality control problem. One way to find out is to look at distribution of different products, by factory and category. In Figure 2-6, pie charts are shown in each cell to illustrate the distribution by factory of origin.

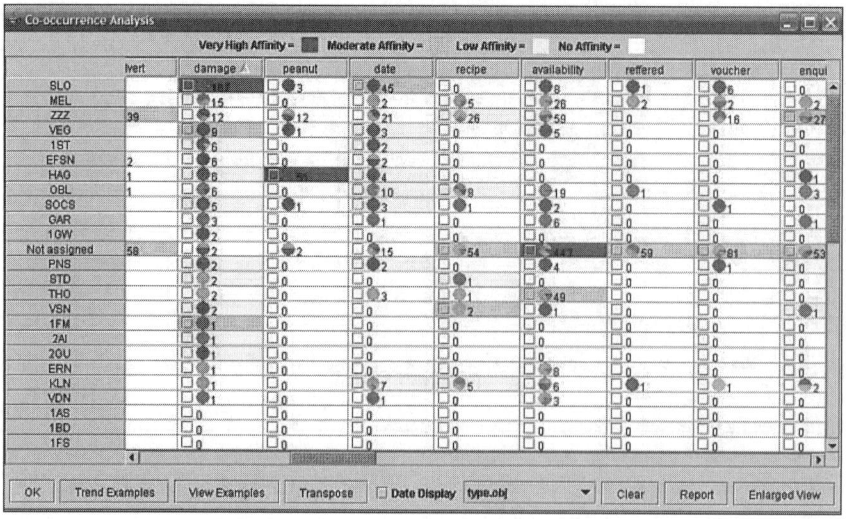

Figure 2-6 Co-occurrence between factory and category broken down by product type

It turns out that nearly all the factory SLO products are of food type "confectionary." If these products are more prone to damage, then the relationship could be explained. This points out the importance of not leaping to conclusions when a correlation is found. Correlations are not causes, but merely indicators of possible issues to be investigated.

Example 2: Customer Interactions with a Helpdesk

As mentioned in the introduction, we first developed and applied *Mining the Talk* techniques to improve the efficiency and quality of computer helpdesk services. Many of the analysis techniques and methods we developed were created to confront the challenges we faced in dealing with helpdesk problem tickets. A problem ticket is a record used to collect and track information related to an issue the customer is having with a product or service. Problem tickets describe the details of the problem along with what was done to solve it. They are typically authored by the person who takes the call from the customer.

The challenge is, given a large collection of problem tickets, find the low hanging fruit for possible automation, documentation, or problem prevention. In other words, find an issue that occurs often enough to justify making a change to reduce the cost of those calls. Like most *Mining the Talk* problems, the key step is to build a taxonomy containing meaningful categories of documents.

The first step in taxonomy generation from problem tickets is selecting the feature set. Text features are at the heart of any approach to analyzing unstructured information. Features are the means by which computers make sense of text. Every text mining technique described in this book boils down to counting. Features are the objects that get counted, and thus choosing them well is essential to making the statistics meaningful. In this example, we will describe in detail how features are created.

Creating Features from Text

The extraction of features from text is all done automatically by software. We cover the details here so that you have a mental model of what the software is doing for you so that it can be correctly interpreted. Much fundamental research and practice has laid the groundwork for this method of feature space generation, and there are many different methods and approaches that might achieve a similar result.[11]

Words are the first thing we count. For each problem ticket example, we first remove all punctuation, reduce all characters to lowercase, and then treat the example as a bag of words. Let's take a specific example to see how this works:

458051   Password failure unable to login to win2000. tried changing pw

This becomes:

{458051, password, failure, unable, to, login, to, win2000, tried, changing, pw}

Next, we use a few simplifying rules to remove some words that are unlikely to be helpful:

1. Remove any words that are numbers or that start with numbers. Typically numbers make poor features because they tend to be unique or are repeated only infrequently. Features that only occur once aren't useful for our purposes, because they don't help us to find similarities between examples.
2. Remove any non-content–bearing words. These are also known as *stopwords*.[12]

With numbers and stopwords removed, we are left with the following bag of words:
{password, failure, unable, login, win2000, changing, pw}

The next step is to identify which words are merely different words for the same thing, also known as *synonyms*. Synonyms can be found with domain dictionaries or automatically generated using stemming algorithms.[13] This leaves us with the following bag of words:

{password (2), failure, unable, login, win2000, changing}

When you look at the reduced form of this problem ticket, it looks like a fairly compact but intelligible version of the original. It's almost like the message one might have sent by telegraph—back in the days where text messages were expensive and every word was dear. In a sense, this is very much the case with *Mining the Talk*. Every word that we choose to turn into a feature is an important decision. We don't keep any words that are superfluous because they would simply add noise that obscure the signal we are trying to detect.

This is one kind of feature—individual words. The bag-of-words representation means they are unordered. We lose the context and keep only the occurrence. To help regain some of that context, we also create phrase features. We define phrases as all words that occur sequentially. Here are the two word phrases that occur in our password example:

{password_failure, failure_unable, unable_login, login_win2000, win2000_changing, changing_password}

We don't choose to create phrases longer than two words by default, because they would only add redundant information. For example, since password_failure and failure_unable occur together in the same example, this pretty much implies password_failure_unable. It is possible to conceive of a counterexample, but such examples are exceedingly rare, especially in short documents, and thus are not of much concern.

The next step in generating a feature space is pruning based on frequency of occurrence. There are two kinds of features we want to prune—those that occur too frequently and those that occur too infrequently. When words occur too frequently, they usually don't help in creating differentiable categories. Consider the extreme case where every example contains a particular word. In this case, knowing that an example has that word cannot help determine the category for that example. Therefore, we eliminate words that occur with high frequency, in practice 70% or more. This threshold is based on experience. Words that occur more frequently are usually poor features to define clusters.

What remains is the threshold for infrequency. Infrequent words are also not good features. Features that occur too infrequently will not help in creating differentiable categories. Take the extreme case where a feature only occurs once. Such a feature can at most help to categorize one example. One example is way too small to make an interesting category. In order to be helpful in analyzing problem tickets, a category must be significantly large to be considered low hanging fruit. An infrequent problem is probably not one that we want to spend time and money on to improve efficiency, because it is not likely to be a good return on investment.

Choosing a fixed threshold of infrequency to eliminate features is no simple matter. For some time, we tried to find a cutoff based on raw count (e.g., two or fewer occurrences of a feature in a data set result in elimination of the feature), or based on frequency (e.g., in a feature occurring in less than 1% of the documents gets eliminated). These approaches were problematic; for while they might work for a particular data set, but they were sub-optimal on larger or smaller data sets. Another approach was needed. Instead of looking for a fixed cutoff, we created a fixed number of features. For the goal of our analysis, this makes perfect sense. We want to create a reasonable number of categories no matter how large our data set. In other words, we don't want the number of categories to grow with more data. Since the number of features should be directly related to the number of categories, generating a sufficient number of features to generate a set number of categories proved to be a workable approach, no matter how many documents in the collection.

With our feature selection methodology understood, it only remains to find the right number of categories and features. We pick these to suit easy taxonomy editing. The number of categories that fits easily in an analyst's brain and on a single computer screen is around 30 (assuming one category per row and an average brain). Keeping the number of categories around this number allows the analyst to see all the categories at once in tabular form. This also turns out to be about the number of categories that can be readily looked at and evaluated in the space of about an hour. In one sitting, a 30-category taxonomy can be generated and thoroughly edited and comprehended.

For features, imagine we need one feature to differentiate every category from every other category. Each of the 30 categories then needs 29 different features to uniquely identify it. That leads to 870 total features needed. You could argue that this count should really be 435, since the same feature that differentiates category A from B, also differentiates category B from A. However, it's not so clear that we want to define a category purely as a negation of features that define other categories, so we do not rely on this simplification. Of course, not every feature the system comes up with is valuable, so we will double that number to be on the safe side, giving us 1740 features. We round up and conclude with the target at 2000.

Aside from being sufficient to model 30 categories, it turns out that 2000 features is not too large for a user to look at in less than an hour. This may seem to contradict our claim that an hour would be needed to look at 30 categories. But a single category requires more time to comprehend than a simple feature. The difference is that a category name is not a definition, but a description—and not necessarily an accurate description. To understand a category requires looking at a few examples and a summary of prevalent features. There may also be statistics such as cohesion and distinctness to be evaluated. Features are very different. Features are precisely defined by their name. Seldom does an analyst need to look at examples to understand what a feature means. In most cases, presentation of the features in alphabetical order is sufficient to edit the feature set for any anomalies. Figure 2-7 is an example of the Dictionary Tool in the IBM Unstructured Information Modeler.

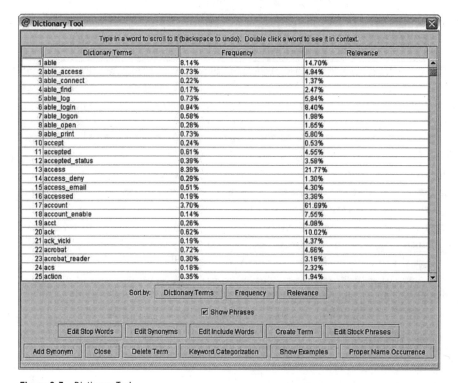

Figure 2-7 Dictionary Tool

How long did it take you to peruse this list of 25 features and determine which features you would preserve at this early stage? There are 80 more lists of this size to peruse to completely look at the entire feature space. This is not something you want to do for every analysis, but it is achievable when the ordinary methods of obtaining a good initial taxonomy continue to fail. The next section describes methods for editing and improving the feature space.

Editing the Feature Space

The ability to peruse the feature space provides the opportunity to correct problems. Two primary issues are detectable with a visual inspection of the feature in alphabetical order:

1. Features that need to be removed because they are not relevant to the purpose of the analysis.
2. Features that need to be combined, because their meaning is identical for the purposes of the analysis.

Removing spurious features helps generate better taxonomies by having categories reflect relevant topics to the business. In the example in Figure 2-7, the feature "ack_vicki" should be removed. It is based, in part, on a person's name and thus contains irrelevant information for the purpose of understanding the types of problems at the helpdesk.

Combining features, based on synonyms, creates a feature set that does not artificially bifurcate based on syntactic distinctions. In the preceding example, the words "account" and "acct" should be combined. This would prevent the taxonomy generation algorithm from creating different categories based on these features.

Feature edits can be remembered, by capturing them in synonym and stopword lists. *Stopwords* are lists of words that should not be included in the dictionary. Synonyms are list of words that are identical for purposes of feature space generation. The work of editing the dictionary is valuable for every future analysis in the same domain. Synonym lists can be generated automatically using a process known as stemming.[14] *Stemming* detects base word forms and the variations based upon prefixes and suffixes. For example, print is the base form of printer, printed, printing, and reprint.

Removing Stock Phrases

Stopwords are individual words ignored when creating a feature space. Another form of information that needs to be ignored is a *stock phrase*. Stock phrases are boiler plate or recurring structural text commonly present in unstructured information. In helpdesk logs, this occurs by convention, via cut-and-paste, or as a processing artifact.

For example, here are typical helpdesk tickets that exhibit several instances of stock phrases:

1. ```
   458052    10/20/00 2:34:15 AM 10/20/00 2:34:15 AM Lack of general
   information        [Recurring Description] ICE-SSPOC General information
   assisted customer [Recurring Initial Note] assisted user by providing
   general information needed [Notepad Comments] referred to boeing help
   desk seattle for ztoken pswd
   ```
2. ```
   458054    10/20/00 3:32:18 AM 10/20/00 3:32:18 AM Password failure
   [Recurring Description] ICE-SSPOC Single Password Reset [Recurring
   Initial Note] Single password reset. [Notepad Comments] reset imsm pswd
   ```
3. ```
   458107    10/20/00 5:41:11 AM 10/20/00 5:41:56 AM UNKNOWN CAUSE
   LS003535 73\65A\3\310. Loaded MS Project on customers machine via pcsi.
   Closing ticket.
   ```
4. ```
   458109    10/20/00 5:42:31 AM 10/20/00 5:43:11 AM UNKNOWN CAUSE
   LS003535 73\65A\3\310. Loaded NFS Maestro on customers machine via
   pcsi. Closing ticket.
   ```

You may notice from these examples that the following text is not the result of a person typing a description, but instead is an artifact of how the data was generated:

Recurring Description
Notepad Comments
Recurring Initial Note
UNKNOWN CAUSE

If we don't account for such features, they will almost certainly confuse the clustering algorithm. Regularized, non-content–bearing, semi-structured text of this form can often wreak havoc on text mining. Although a human reader can recognize such text for what it is, and ignore it, the text mining algorithm cannot. These phrases will statistically appear like prime candidates for building categories around. However, we know none of these categories is helpful from the perspective of understanding the problems occurring at the helpdesk.

One solution that might be proposed is to simply add the words from the phrases to the stopwords list, such as:

recurring
description
notepad
comments
initial

```
note
unknown
cause
```

This approach is an over compensation. There's nothing inherently wrong with the words themselves. They may be good inputs for generating categories in combination with other words. The word "initial" is especially noteworthy. It gets used in many different helpdesk contexts, such as "initial setup," "initial screen," and "initial login." Removing this word would result in too much useful information being tossed aside.

Instead, we use a list of stock phrases that can be automatically detected and tailored to each domain. This stock phrase list, like the stopwords and synonyms list, grows over time, gradually improving the performance of the analysis.

The Initial Taxonomy

The taxonomy in Figure 2-8 was generated from a collection of helpdesk problem tickets from a single location. The purpose of this analysis was to determine cost-effective ways to reduce call volume. This initial taxonomy was created using k-means clustering on a 2000-word feature space after stopwords, synonyms, and stock phrases were accounted for.

	Class Name	Size	Cohesion	Distinctness
1	password_failure	1241 (17.18%)	70.72%	72.98%
2	general_information & lack_gene...	439 (6.08%)	64.75%	87.74%
3	reboot	168 (2.33%)	62.27%	78.87%
4	hung & miss_process	249 (3.45%)	57.56%	78.87%
5	print	686 (9.49%)	56.31%	82.95%
6	loss_connectivity	134 (1.85%)	52.69%	77.14%
7	email	321 (4.44%)	51.97%	66.25%
8	account,quota	100 (1.38%)	50.72%	81.67%
9	software_usage	460 (6.37%)	49.50%	75.99%
10	userid,id	191 (2.64%)	47.56%	74.93%
11	incorrect	374 (5.18%)	46.40%	69.21%
12	log	114 (1.58%)	45.54%	59.42%
13	install	150 (2.08%)	44.40%	77.38%
14	outlook,personal	147 (2.03%)	44.04%	66.25%
15	server	194 (2.69%)	44.01%	66.86%
16	domain	65 (0.90%)	43.06%	57.50%
17	drive	141 (1.95%)	42.46%	70.29%
18	access	150 (2.08%)	41.14%	66.86%
19	file	507 (7.02%)	40.76%	65.26%
20	login,network	166 (2.30%)	40.58%	57.50%
21	netscape,open	129 (1.79%)	37.44%	61.63%
22	number,phone	120 (1.66%)	34.32%	59.23%
23	called	228 (3.16%)	34.16%	59.23%
24	hardware,service	366 (5.07%)	33.57%	70.95%
25	load,send	175 (2.42%)	32.86%	67.84%
26	win95,create,duplicate	210 (2.91%)	28.90%	61.63%
	TOTAL / AVERAGE	7225	50.89%	72.05%

Figure 2-8 Initial taxonomy

This table tells us a lot about the helpdesk in a very small space. We know right away, for example, that "password_failure" and "print" are the two biggest problems. But the picture is still very incomplete. Some of the categories are relatively clear from the category name, while others are not easily understood. For example, what is the "number,phone" or "called" category? We have more work to do to fully understand what is going on at this helpdesk. It will require more than just a good feature space and automated clustering. The best clustering is only as useful as it is relevant to the business. To get to a deeper level of detail, we need to add domain knowledge to the process by editing the taxonomy. It is perhaps the most critical step in *Mining the Talk*, and we describe it in detail in the next section.

Taxonomy Editing—Creating Categories That Mean Something

The taxonomy editing process has evolved over several years of practical text mining implementations.[15] Taxonomy editing is an interactive dialog between analyst and machine. The best way to begin is with a high-level overview of the process, followed by detailed examples.

The Dialog

The process of editing a taxonomy is first and foremost one of understanding. You cannot hope to improve what you don't understand. Categories of text examples can be understood in many ways: through examples, through statistics, through visualizations, by comparison with other categories, or by decomposition. Understanding leads to the desire for change—the need to make the categories match what you know about the domain. Only then can they be useful in making effective business decisions.

To see how this works, imagine the following dialog taking place between an analyst and a machine. The analyst is trying to edit the taxonomy to make it useful, and the machine is a collection of computer processes that reason over the examples using the feature space and raw text of the helpdesk logs.

```
Machine: I have created 26 categories from your collection of 7225 exam-
ples, with each example going into exactly one category. The biggest
category contains 17.18% of the data and the smallest contains 0.9% of
the data. Would you like to know more about these categories?
Analyst: Yes I would. Let's start with the simplest category to
understand.
Machine: OK. That would be "password_failure."
Analyst: Tell me more about that category. What's a good example of what
that category looks like?
Machine: "Password failure sl1001 password reset"
```

```
Analyst: Interesting. How many of the examples in this category contain
the word "password?"
Machine: "99.84%."
Analyst: Show me a good example of one that does not.
Machine: "UNKNOWN CAUSE reset node ha378112, okay now"
Analyst: OK. Move the examples that don't contain "password" into a new
category called "Miscellaneous."
Machine: Done.
Analyst: Now let's rename the category to "password reset."
Machine: Done.
Analyst: Now tell me about the next simplest category.
Machine: That would be "general_information & lack_general." Typical
example: "Lack of general information [Recurring Description] ICE-SSPOC
General information assisted customer [Recurring Initial Note] assisted
user by providing general information needed [Notepad Comments] Refer
customer to another Help Desk"
Analyst: Let's call that one "general info request." Are there any exam-
ples in this category that don't contain the phrase "general_
information?"
Machine: Yes, 20 examples have this property.
Analyst: Show me a typical one.
Machine: "Customer request General inquiry re Exchange. Advised."
Analyst: That's interesting. Put those examples aside in another cate-
gory for the time being; call it "deal with these at the end."
Machine: Done.
… and so on …
```

This dialog is a good example of what we mean by taxonomy editing. It shows how the mutual exchange of information occurs, and how the result of that exchange leads to modifications to the taxonomy—some permanent, others transient, but all capturing something the analyst knows about the domain.

Before we embark on a more detailed description of taxonomy editing in practice, let's stop for a moment and contemplate what we've just accomplished with the preceding dialog. The steps were so simple and straightforward, you might be somewhat unimpressed by the whole thing. But if you consider where we started and where we arrived and with how little was done on the analyst's part—it's really startling. Remember, each of the initial categories was created from a clean slate using automated clustering and only incorporating the minimal one-time effort on synonyms, stopwords, and stock phrases. For two different categories containing hundreds of examples each, the analyst was able to learn very precisely what each category contained and the salient features.

The analyst made adjustments to the two categories to correct defects that are perfectly reasonable when only considering the feature space, but completely wrong to someone with knowledge of the domain.

Considering all the steps in detail may make it seem like an arduous process, but in truth, with the right software, it took very little effort. In little more time than it took to read the dialog, an analyst could easily have accomplished the edits described using software that implements the *Mining the Talk* process. If we continue as prescribed for the remainder of the categories, what do we get for our investment of thirty to sixty minutes of effort? A fairly complete outline of what happened at this particular helpdesk during the week in question by using categories and statistics that aren't based on a preconceived notion of this helpdesk, or solely on random clusters from the data. These categories are compact fusions of data and experience, each one relevant to the business and validated by the information. When complete, we will have exactly what we set out to get: a meaningful description of the activity at this helpdesk in terms that are relevant to the business and can be reused in the future.

Let's take a look at the editing process in more detail. In the next section, we show the intricacies of each step in the editing process using real data from our helpdesk example case study.

Step 1: Selecting a Category to Edit

When faced with a complex problem, figuring out where to begin is often half the battle. We begin the editing process faced with many categories, each of them with a simple name that holds out the promise of simple and meaningful content. Unfortunately, this is not always the case. In fact, while some categories are relatively simple and straightforward to interpret, others will be more complex.

Why does this matter at all? If the analyst is eventually going to inspect each category, one might think the order in which the categories are studied should make no difference to the difficulty of the task or the end result. The explanation has as much to do with the way the mind learns as it does with text mining principles. After all, at its root, the *Mining the Talk* process is a kind of self-taught course in understanding the contents of a collection, with the analyst being the student. If you consider the typical course structure, they never begin with the most complex principle first. Instead, they begin with the simpler concepts, and then build up to the more complex issues. That natural progression from simple to complex is a practical approach to taxonomy editing as well; if we start with the simple categories, then by the time we tackle the complex categories, we will already have a store of knowledge about the domain stored in our brains to draw upon. The complex categories will be much less intimidating halfway through the process than they would have been at the beginning. More importantly, the decisions the analysts make in dealing with a complex category will be better informed, more accurate, and faster.

With simplicity established as an important measure to use in selecting categories, how do we actually measure it? What makes a category simple? In a word, homogeneity. A category where all the examples look alike is easy to understand. A category where all the examples are identical is trivial to understand—read one example and you are done, no matter how many times that example occurs. This is an important point: Size is not a reliable measure of complexity. As we saw in this example, the biggest category, "password reset," is also one of the simplest.

Homogeneity is reflected very well by our *cohesion* metric.[16] Categories that score high with this measure will have a significant number of examples with words in common. In the extreme, a category consisting of identical documents would have a cohesion value of 1.0. A category with no terms in common would have a cohesion value of 0.

Step 2: Viewing Typical Examples

The most straightforward approach to understanding a category is to read some of its examples. Relying solely on the category name is a dangerous practice, as it can be misleading or oversimplifying. At least a few examples need to be read, if only to validate the hypothesis that the category name implies. But which examples should be read, and in what order? It would be preferable to read the example that best communicates the essence of the category or the most typical example. How do we measure typicality?

The answer lies in the feature space by leveraging the cosine distance metric and the category centroid. Remember, the centroid is a model of the average document in a category. To find the most typical example, we measure the distance of each example to the centroid of the category and select the closest one.

In fact, we can have the computer calculate the distance of every document in the category to the category centroid and sort them in order of typicality (highest to lowest). The examples can then be presented to the analyst in this order, so that they can be perused systematically. Such a presentation prevents the problem of sample skewing, where the method used to select examples (even a random method) skews the interpretation of the set as a whole.

Of course, there is another, more subtle, kind of skewing that takes place using most typical sorting. Most typical sorting, used with no other category visualization techniques, tends to mislead the analyst as to the underlying variability of the category as a whole. This is analogous to what happens when a golfer calculates his handicap based only on his best games, ignoring the days when he plays poorly. The result is more wishful thinking than an accurate prediction of how the golfer will score in the future. Similarly, the peril with typical sorting is the analyst may not look deep enough to see beyond the typical areas of the category near the centroid to the outlying fringes, where things aren't nearly so neat and tidy. One way around this is to reverse the sorting and bring to the top the "atypical" examples. Although this is not an entirely unsound approach, it tends to be rather slow and imprecise. The methods in the following section are preferable for understanding the full range of what a category contains.

In practice, after reading a few such examples, the analyst has a pretty good idea of what a category is about. If the category is sufficiently cohesive and uniform (more on this in a moment) the analyst can move on without further ado. At this point, the experience and knowledge gained may be summarized by simply editing the category name to something that means (in as succinct a wording as possible) what the analyst now understands the category to be.

Step 3: Term Frequency Statistics

Up to this point, every step we have described in editing the taxonomy has relied on text and ordered tables as the main method of presentation. Also, there has so far been no real editing going on, other than possibly changing the category name, to reflect the analyst's better understanding of what the category contains. Now we move on to more visual descriptions and methods, which also allow more powerful kinds of editing to take place. The first, and most basic, visualization centers around the feature space and its relationship to the category. In a very real sense, we would like to visually show the analyst what the category centroid "looks" like (see Figure 2-9).

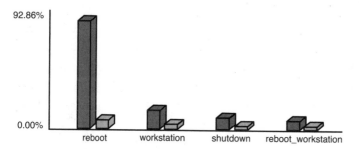

Figure 2-9 Centroid visualization

The preceding graph is one frame of a picture of a centroid illustrating how centroids can be charted. The actual centroid itself is 2000 floating point numbers. That's way too much information to convey succinctly with any degree of legibility. Instead, we try to focus on those numbers out of the 2000 that are most important, and then communicate the relevance of the value to the category. Selecting which of the 2000 features to display first is then the key problem. In general, higher frequency terms (those that occur more often in documents in the category) would be more preferable than lower frequency. There is one exception to this general rule. When a word occurs with equal frequency everywhere, as it does within the taxonomy, then it is no longer an interesting word in helping to understand the taxonomy, even if that word is frequent. In fact, one might even say that the relative importance of a word is not its in-category frequency at all, but the *difference* between the in-category frequency and the general frequency of the word overall.

This is what the bar chart in Figure 2-9 indicates. For each word, there are two bars. The bar on the left indicates the "in-category" frequency of the specified term, and the bar on the right indicates the overall frequency of the term in all of the data. The bars are then sorted in order of positive frequency difference, and the top four are displayed in order. This is how the preceding chart was arrived at for the category "reboot."

Such a chart tells us a lot more than a few typical examples about the overall composition of this category. The low frequency of the second most important word, "workstation," is a bad sign. This means that for this category, the only word that most of the examples share in common is "reboot." But reboot what and why? Unless the tickets say nothing else, this category is probably too broad, lacking a causal focus, and thus not very helpful from a business perspective.

So, now it's time to do some real editing. We can employ the visualization in the service of editing by making it interactive. Clicking on a bar (either one) should make a selection that incorporates the underlying examples that bar represents (either all examples with that feature, or all examples in the category containing that feature). Once selected, these examples can then be moved into an existing category, or into a newly created category.

Step 4: Untangling Relationships Between Categories

As the category editing process continues, there will naturally arise areas of overlap between categories. As much as possible we want to make sure the categories are distinct, well-defined entities so that any statistics we measure and conclusions we draw at the end will be equally well-defined and meaningful. To this end, it's important to be able to see any relationships between categories and make decisions about any adjustments that should be made to clarify intra-category differences. There are several tools we have come up with to measure and communicate how categories are related.

Distinctness

Distinctness is a measure of differentiation between categories. It is defined to be one minus the cosine distance between the category centroid and the centroid of the nearest neighboring category. Thus, the distinctness of a category that had the same centroid as another category would be exactly zero. The highest possible distinctness value would occur when the centroid of the category was completely different (contained none of the same features) than every other category. This would produce a value of 1.0.

In our helpdesk example, sorting by distinctness brings up the following category list (see Figure 2-10).

	Class Name	Size	Distinctness
16	domain	65 (0.90%)	57.50%
20	login,network	166 (2.30%)	57.50%
22	number,phone	120 (1.66%)	59.23%
23	called	228 (3.16%)	59.23%
12	log	114 (1.58%)	59.42%
21	netscape,open	129 (1.79%)	61.63%
26	win95,create,duplicate	210 (2.91%)	61.63%
19	file	507 (7.02%)	65.26%
7	email	321 (4.44%)	66.25%
14	outlook,personal	147 (2.03%)	66.25%
15	server	194 (2.69%)	66.86%
18	access	150 (2.08%)	66.86%
25	load,send	175 (2.42%)	67.84%
11	incorrect	374 (5.18%)	69.21%
17	drive	141 (1.95%)	70.29%
24	hardware,service	366 (5.07%)	70.95%
1	password_failure	1241 (17.18%)	72.98%
10	userid,id	191 (2.64%)	74.93%
9	software_usage	460 (6.37%)	75.99%
6	loss_connectivity	134 (1.85%)	77.14%
13	install	150 (2.08%)	77.38%
3	reboot	168 (2.33%)	78.87%
4	hung & miss_process	249 (3.45%)	78.87%
8	account,quota	100 (1.38%)	81.67%
5	print	686 (9.49%)	82.95%
2	general_information & lack_general	439 (6.08%)	87.74%
	TOTAL / AVERAGE	7225	72.05%

Figure 2-10   Category distinctness

As is the case here, the two categories at the top of the list (those with the lowest value) will always have the same distinctness value, since they must be the nearest neighbors of each other. In this case, "domain" and "login,network" are two categories with very similar themes. They both have to do with network access problems of one kind or another. Whether or not it makes sense to keep these as separate categories is a decision that needs to be made by the analyst. It all depends on how detailed the categorization needs to be, and how valuable the distinction is. For example, are problems relating to the domain of the network similar enough to each other and frequent enough to make a potentially interesting category for further tracking and study?

Category Deletion and Secondary Categories

Suppose we run across a category that we don't particularly find to be helpful. It may be based on features that don't represent a useful concept for the business to track or study. An example from the IBM managed helpdesk might be the category: "called." The most typical example for this category is the following:

```
Loss of connectivity LS004682: 73-270E\5\A6 Win2000: Customer gets into
desktop. Goes into Outlook unable to display folder. Inbox will not
open. Receives error message-Information Store cannot be open. Also
explored will not open. Called customer - he thought this ticket was
supposed to be sent to field initially. I was unable to tb2. Sending to
field. Customer requesting higher priority. Cust is calling back. He
needs a phone call with tech's eta. Called customer, left a vmx that I
would try and make it over in the morning. Customer called back, he feels
that service was 'unacceptable'. He called this ticket in early today
expecting service, did not get it, called back in and requested escala-
tion,,,,,,,someone called and said he would be out in am to assist.
Customer feels someone else should come out tonight and help him, he
needs very urgently to get to his email. wants escalated again and a call
back asap from problem management. ticket was assigned to WRIGHTAD,
track 4 placing in neo-slprobmgmt que, setting to impacting-1
```

Obviously this has nothing to do with any particular type of problem, but instead relates to a number of calls between customer and operator. Let us assume for a moment that the process of making phone calls to solve the problem is not significant to our analysis. It then makes no sense for us to retain this category. We could delete the "called" feature from the dictionary and recluster, but that would wreak havoc with any edits we had done thus far. There is another way to accomplish something similar, without having so drastic an effect. After removing the term from the dictionary, we could delete the centroid for this category, and let each of the examples in the category be placed in the category of the next nearest centroid—essentially having the machine put each example where it would have been, if the category had not existed in the first place.

There is a danger to this approach, however. What if most of the examples end up going to one particular category, instead of distributing fairly evenly? This creates the danger that we will not have gotten rid of the category at all, but simply moved the problem somewhere else. What's worse, we may have disrupted the cohesion of a perfectly good category in the process if all the deleted examples go to that category. To avoid this, we have developed a simple visualization in the IBM Unstructured Information Modeler called the Secondary Classes pie chart. It looks like this for the "called" category (see Figure 2-11).

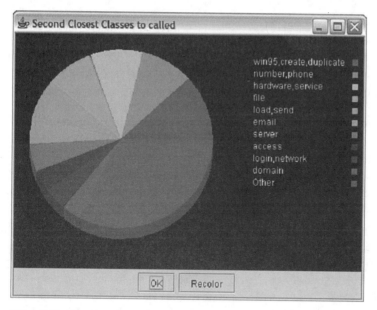

Figure 2-11 Secondary classes

It reveals precisely where the example will go if the "called" category is deleted. Furthermore, each individual slice can be selected, showing the analyst exactly what examples will be going to what categories. If the analyst sees a particularly large slice, this can be investigated to ensure that the examples being moved truly belong to the category in question. If not, the deletion can be done in a more piecemeal fashion, by selecting individual slices one at a time and moving the examples in them to where they do belong, leaving some selected slices behind to deal with later.

Scatter Plot Visualizations

All of the methods we have looked at so far focus on the categories as the primary concept and the features as secondary attributes describing them. This is useful, certainly, but there is also value in approaching the problem from the other direction—looking first at the feature space and then secondarily at the categories. Scatter plot visualizations provide a means of doing this, if we graph the position of each example as a point in the scatter plot and then label the points by their cluster membership. The resulting plot should show visually exactly how clusters relate to each other, and even provide greater detail about how examples are distributed within each category.

There is one small problem with this: A normal scatter plot has two dimensions, and our features space has 2000. But using a little creativity and a lot of geometry, this small problem can be overcome.[17]

Here is an example showing what we mean for a three categories helpdesk example (see Figure 2-12).

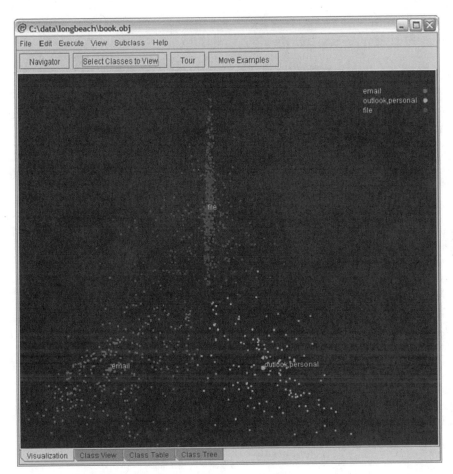

Figure 2-12 Scatter plot visualization

This plot is created by first observing the geometric principle that three points make a plane in any space, no matter its dimensionality. We choose three points to be the centroids of three categories of interest. We then project each document in the three categories onto that plane and record the position where it intersects. The result is the plot shown in Figure 2-12. The plot thus helps us to see both inter-category associations among the three selected categories, as well as intra-category subgroupings. For example, in the preceding "file" category, there seem to be three distinct kinds of documents: 1) those having something to do with email; 2) those having something to do with "outlook,personal;" and 3) those having nothing at all to do with either category. Clicking on points in the plot or selecting them with a selection window allows the analyst to investigate groups of examples readily and make any necessary adjustments to the taxonomy quickly and accurately.

The Finished Taxonomy

After we finish editing it, the taxonomy looks like this (see Figure 2-13).

C:\data\longbeach\final.obj	
File Edit Execute View Subclass Help	
Dictionary Tool View Selected Class Subclass	
Taxonomy Level: Root	
Class Name	Size
1 password reset	1367 (18.92%)
2 printing problem	689 (9.54%)
3 general info request	476 (6.59%)
4 software usage	429 (5.94%)
5 installation request	401 (5.55%)
6 email problem	353 (4.89%)
7 hardware problem	334 (4.62%)
8 process hung	311 (4.30%)
9 login problem	289 (4.00%)
10 incorrect configuration	279 (3.86%)
11 network connectivity	263 (3.64%)
12 corrupt file	260 (3.60%)
13 file and file system problems	256 (3.54%)
14 server problem	252 (3.49%)
15 ID request	196 (2.71%)
16 win95 problems	194 (2.69%)
17 Miscellaneous	165 (2.28%)
18 outlook problem	152 (2.10%)
19 personal folders setup	104 (1.44%)
20 netscape	86 (1.19%)
21 field service needed	80 (1.11%)
22 account quota exceeded	78 (1.08%)
23 reboot needed	56 (0.78%)
24 workstation problem	40 (0.55%)
25 novell client	39 (0.54%)
26 restore file	38 (0.53%)
27 admin access request	23 (0.32%)
28 shutdown	15 (0.21%)
TOTAL / AVERAGE	7225
Visualization Class View Class Table Class Tree	

Figure 2-13   Final taxonomy

This is much better than what we started with. First of all, the category names communicate most of what we need to know. More detailed reports can show typical examples for each category to help communicate the exact meaning of each category. Furthermore, every category is based on what type of problem was called in, not on the process for solving the problem (who called whom, when) or on which helpdesk operator took the call. This gives us what we need to make intelligent business decisions about where to spend resources at the helpdesk to reduce call volumes. For example, putting in automated web applications for password reset and printer driver installation or reboots has the potential to reduce call volume by as much as 28%. This figure can be multiplied by the cost of each call and the rate at which calls come in to compute the expected cost savings for implementing such a service. The business can then make an informed decision as to whether the benefits warrant the expenditure.

But do we really need *Mining the Talk* to get this result? It all looks so simple when you display it this way. Why not just ask each helpdesk operator to label each ticket as it comes in from a list of predefined categories? Wouldn't that be just as good? As it turns out, the helpdesk in question had tried this approach on this very account, as it had on all of its other accounts. Here is the result, which is fairly typical (see Figure 2-14).

	Class Name	Size
1	Customer request	1382 (19.13%)
2	Password failure	1138 (15.75%)
3	UNKNOWN CAUSE	726 (10.05%)
4	Software usage	607 (8.40%)
5	Lack of general information	434 (6.01%)
6	Incorrect configuration	361 (5.00%)
7	HARDWARE	352 (4.87%)
8	Hung/missing process	307 (4.25%)
9	Corrupt system or application file	240 (3.32%)
10	Loss of connectivity	178 (2.46%)
11	Customer created	167 (2.31%)
12	CUSTOMER RELATED	159 (2.20%)
13	Incorrect settings	156 (2.16%)
14	UserID lockout (intruder)	88 (1.22%)
15	Hardware failure	80 (1.11%)
16	Quota exceeded	64 (0.89%)
17	AMC ACTIVITY	57 (0.79%)
18	Network outage	51 (0.71%)
19	IBM GLOBAL SVCS SUPPORTED	42 (0.58%)
20	System/software limitations reached	42 (0.58%)
21	Corrupt data file	41 (0.57%)
22	Server outage	39 (0.54%)
23	New ID request	39 (0.54%)
24	Server related	35 (0.48%)
25	NETWORK	34 (0.47%)
26	Defect/known bug	31 (0.43%)
27	Security issues	30 (0.42%)
28	Old userID problems	29 (0.40%)
29	System software change	23 (0.32%)
30	Other	23 (0.32%)
31	Software incompatibility	21 (0.29%)
32	Outlook/Exchange migration	19 (0.26%)
33	Hardware configuration	19 (0.26%)
34	Needed routine maintenance	18 (0.25%)
35	Install problems	17 (0.24%)
36	Software push (IBM)	16 (0.22%)
37	Configuration problems	15 (0.21%)
38	Software push (Boeing)	15 (0.21%)
39	Incorrect context (Novell)	14 (0.19%)
40	Print queue stopped	14 (0.19%)
41	No NT Admin rights	11 (0.15%)
42	Lack of physical resources	11 (0.15%)
43	Boeing software load	10 (0.14%)
44	VRU error	10 (0.14%)
45	Incomplete mail configuration	9 (0.12%)
46	Firewall related	9 (0.12%)
47	Controller related	8 (0.11%)
48	Intranet navigation	7 (0.10%)
49	SERVERS	7 (0.10%)
50	Internet navigation	5 (0.07%)
51	Needed keyserved software	5 (0.07%)
52	Virus related	5 (0.07%)
53	Mail server out of disk space	5 (0.07%)
	TOTAL / AVERAGE	7225

Figure 2-14   Predefined taxonomy

Clearly there are a lot of problems with this. First, the "password" category has missed many relevant examples, which were probably classified as "intruder lockout" or "security issues." The printer category doesn't even exist. A large number of tickets are in fairly useless categories: "Customer Request," "UNKNOWN CAUSE," and "Customer Related." Many categories are so small as to be inconsequential. Another less-obvious problem is that categories are inconsistently applied by different helpdesk operators. This probably stems from the fact that the category definitions are imprecise. What is the difference between a "SERVERS" problem and a "Server-related" problem? If anyone ever knew, I doubt they still remember. This is fairly typical of what most call centers do, and we think it is one of the reasons that CRM (Customer Relationship Management) has something of a tarnished reputation in industry.

Deriving categories from the data is almost always more effective than putting them in place and labeling the data with them. *Mining the Talk* generated taxonomies are more flexible (can change when the data does), consistent (no multiple human interpretations), and adaptable (taxonomies can be tailored to different business needs).

Mining the Talk techniques have been used at many call centers for several years now to reduce call volumes, fix underlying problems, and monitor the quality of helpdesk response. Wherever it has been employed, the results of using these techniques have been universally perceived as a significant improvement over all other available analysis methods—so much so that we began to wonder what other types of problems might be solved with similar methods on other kinds of data. The results of that journey are described in the remaining chapters.

Summary

We have covered a lot of ground in this chapter, and we would like to now review what we consider to be the most important points for the reader to take away from it.

There is a fair amount of similarity between all Mining of Customer Interaction scenarios. The critical components that we see in every good example are the following:

- Business objectives defined up front.
- Significant amounts of data consisting of structured and unstructured elements.
- Taxonomies created automatically and refined via domain knowledge to match business needs.
- Analysis based on statistical correlations between categories and structured elements in the data.
- Generation of reports that highlight the most relevant correlations to business objectives, along with supporting examples and business case for changes to process.

With these points in mind, readers should be able to both recognize opportunities in their business where *Mining the Talk* could be used to improve customer interaction, and understand the basic outline of the process needed to achieve that improvement.

Endnotes

1. Such a tool is called the IBM Unstructured Information Modeler and is available from IBM alphaworks at http://www.ibm.com/alphaworks/tech/uimodeler.

2. In his paper entitled "Fundamentals of Taxonomy" [Hempel, C. G. (1965). *Fundamentals of Taxonomy. In Aspects of Scientific Explanation and Other Essays in the Philosophy of Science* (ed. C.G. Hempel), pp. 137–154. Glencoe, IL: Free Press.], Carl Hempel asserts the following about natural classifications (as opposed to artificial ones):

   In {natural classifications} those characteristics of the elements that serve as criteria for membership in a given class are associated, universally or with high probability, with more or less extensive clusters of other characteristics {reference}.

   This is a very old idea, going back to Aristotelian essentialism, or the idea that "things have essences." In science, behavioral or observable feature commonality among different things often leads scientists to group things into classes. Some of these groupings are *artificial*—for example, groupings of materials based on arbitrary ranges of their melting/freezing points. Such arbitrary groupings are rarely scientifically fruitful. Other groupings are *natural*, such as the division of the animal kingdom into fish, reptiles, amphibians, birds, and mammals. These *natural* groupings, for the most part, represent a hypothesis that there is some apparent or underlying structural equivalence shared by the members of that class. This hypothesis can then be tested, and if proven, lead to knowledge about the structure of the physical world. Thus, one purpose of a taxonomy is to help gain a greater understanding of the world around us. Taxonomies are not driven solely by data, but have purpose. This is an important principle that we shall come back to again and again as we *Mine the Talk*.

3. Here is an example of nine two-dimensional vectors plotted in a Cartesian coordinate system:

X	Y
7	4
4	6
7	6
7	5
9	2
3	9
8	3
8	8
0	0

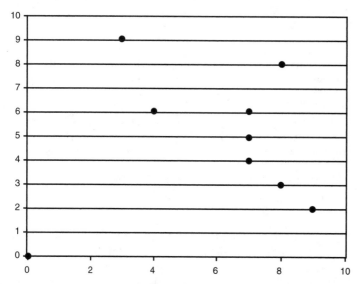

Figure 2-15   Points plotted in Cartesan coordinates

4. The reason can be seen if we compare the following three documents:

   A) I like bananas.

   B) I like bananas. Bananas like me. Bananas taste great.

   C) I like apples.

   Converting these documents to vector notation produces the following representation for each document:

Document	Bananas	Like
A	1	1
B	3	2
C	0	1

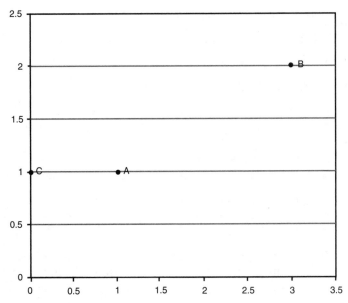

Figure 2-16 Documents displayed as points in dictionary space

And here are the Euclidean distances between each of the three points:

A←→B: SQRT((1*1) + (2*2)) = 2.24

B←→C: SQRT((1*1) + (3*3)) = 3.16

C←→A: SQRT((1*1) + (0*0)) = 1.0

Note that in this example, the two documents that seem most similar in terms of their text content (A and B), are not actually "nearest" to each other when measured by Euclidean distance. The reason A and B look so different is not because B is talking about a different subject, but simply because B is a longer document—the count of the words it uses is larger than A...thus making A seem more similar to C, a document with which it has nothing in common. So, straight Euclidean distance seems like a poor metric for our purposes, unless we can ensure that all documents are the same length, which normally we cannot.

5. The cosine of two vectors can be calculated using the following formula:

$$\cos(a,b) = \frac{a \bullet b}{\|a\| \cdot \|b\|}$$

In the previous example, this leads to the following values:

A←→B: (1*2 + 1*3)/(SQRT(2)*SQRT(13) = .981

B←→C: (0*3 + 1*2)/SQRT(13)*SQRT(1) = .555

C←→A: (0*1 + 1*1)/SQRT(1)*SQRT(2)= .707

Notice one oddity when using the cosine distance approach...the cosine "distance" actually increases as two points get closer (angle goes to zero). In fact, the cosine distance between two points that are the same is actually the maximum value: 1.0. With this understanding, A and B appear closest, C and A the next closest, and B and C the least similar. This is much more like our intuition about the documents.

The other extreme is similarly counter-intuitive. If two points are orthogonal—meaning, in this context, that they have no words in common—then the cosine distance between them is the minimum value: 0.0.

But aside from this unfortunate disconnect between the way we think about distance and the way cosine function works, in all other respects, the cosine distance is a reasonable approach to calculating how similar two documents are to each other.

6. Here is how the centroid looks graphically as an average of the three vectors in the previous example (see Figure 2-17).

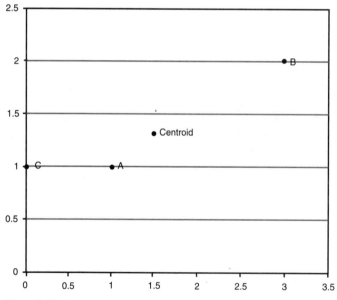

Figure 2-17 Centroid

The graph illustrates how the "centroid" got its name. The centroid represents the "center of gravity" of all the points in the document collection. As such, it represents a kind of summary of the features of the documents contained in that collection.

Now, clearly the centroid is far from being a complete description of the collection. Just like the batting average of a baseball player doesn't tell you anything about how well that player did in his last game, the centroid only gives us a tiny picture of the category as a whole and what it contains. But as a model, it serves to provide a means for comparing documents to collections. Here's how that works: We can take the centroid of any collection and compare it to another document (either in or out of the original collection that generated the centroid) and see how closely that document matches the model of the collection using our cosine similarity function.

A$\longleftrightarrow$Centroid: $(1*1.33 + 1*1.33)/(SQRT(2)*SQRT(3.55) = 1.0$

B$\longleftrightarrow$Centroid: $(3*1.33 + 1*1.33)/SQRT(13)*SQRT(3.55) = .784$

C$\longleftrightarrow$Centroid: $(0*1.33 + 1*1.33)/SQRT(1)*SQRT(3.55)= .707$

So A is the nearest to the centroid, which again matches our intuition for A being the most typical document of this cluster.

7. Duda, Richard O., and Peter E. Hart. 1973. *Pattern Classification and Scene Analysis.* New York: Wiley.

   Hartigan, John. 1975. *Clustering Algorithms.* New York: Wiley.

   Rasmussen, E. (1992). *Clustering Algorithms.* In Frakes, W. B. and Baeza-Yates, R., editors, *Information Retrieval: Data Structures and Algorithms*, pp. 419–442. Englewood Cliffs, NJ: Prentice Hall.

8. The authors are indebted to Dharmendra Modha for this cluster-naming scheme.

9. Here is a detailed description of the Intuitive clustering approach:

   1. Define a minimum size the smallest cluster can be. Don't select any words that occur less frequently, even if they are cohesive.
   2. Adjust the cohesion metric to take category size into account. Smaller clusters have a big advantage in terms of likelihood of being cohesive. We take this into account by adding an exponent to the denominator of the cohesion formula, like so:

   $$cohesion(T,n) = \frac{\sum_{x \in T} \cos(centroid(T), x)}{|T|^n}$$

   where T is the set of documents that contain a given term, centroid(T) is the average vector of all these documents, and n is a parameter used to adjust for variance in category size (typically n=0.9).

   3. Select the highest cohesion term and find all the documents that contain that term. Assign them to a cluster.
   4. Find the next most cohesive term and assign any documents not already assigned to a cluster to a new cluster based on this term. If the size of this cluster no longer meets the requirement, then skip this term.
   5. Repeat step 3 until a stopping criteria is met.
   6. Define a stopping point in terms of number of documents clustered. Usually this is around 90%. The remaining documents go into a "Miscellaneous" cluster.

7. When all done, find the centroid of each cluster and move each document to the nearest centroid (one iteration of *k*-means). This is to partially rectify any ambiguities for examples containing more than one cohesive term.
8. Name each cluster based on the cohesive term that generated it.

10. Press, W. et al. *Numerical Recipes in C*. 2nd Edition. New York: Cambridge University Press, 1992, pp. 620–623.

    Note: For small data set sizes, a test called Fisher's exact test may be more accurate. However, exact accuracy is not really at issue here. The point is only to find areas of *possible* significance. Even a rough approximation is usually sufficient for our purposes.

11. Salton, Gerard, and Michael J. McGill. 1983. *Introduction to Modern Informational Retrieval*. New York: McGraw-Hill.

    Salton, G. and Buckley, C. (1988). "Term-weighting approaches in automatic text retrieval." *Information Processing & Management*, 4(5):512:523.

12. Fox, C. (1992). *Lexical Analysis and Stoplists*. In Frakes, W. B. and Baeza-Yates, R., editors, *Information Retrieval: Data Structures and Algorithms*, pp. 102–130. Englewood Cliffs, NJ: Prentice Hall.

13. Honrado, A., Leon, R., O'Donnel, R., and Sinclair, D. *A Word Stemming Algorithm for the Spanish Language*. Seventh International Symposium on String Processing Information Retrieval (SPIRE 2000).

14. Ibid.

15. Spangler, S. and Kreulen, J. (2002). *Interactive Methods for Taxonomy Editing and Validation*. Proceedings of the Conference on Information and Knowledge Mining (CIKM 2002).

16. Here is a formal definition of cohesion:

$$cohesion(T) = \frac{\sum_{x \in T} \cos(centroid(T), x)}{|T|}$$

    where T is the set of documents in the category and *centroid(T)* is the average vector of all these documents. The cosine distance between document vectors is defined to be:

$$\cos(X, Y) = \frac{X \bullet Y}{\|X\| \cdot \|Y\|}$$

17. Dhillon, I., Modha, D., and Spangler, S. (2002). "Visualizing class structure of multidimensional data with applications." *Journal of Computational Statistics & Data Analysis* (special issue on Matrix Computations & Statistics) 4:1. November 2002. pp. 59–90.

3

Mining the Voice of the Customer

In the previous chapter, we looked at customer interactions as one kind of "talk" that we could mine for valuable business insights. This chapter discusses another source of information about the customer and a somewhat different approach to mining it. Instead of mining the business's interactions with the customer, we seek to hear what customers are saying about our company outside of those interactions. Every day our customers speak about us in numerous forums. The trick is to tap into this multi-threaded stream of consciousness and pick out what is relevant and then make sense of it. We call this approach mining the Voice of the Customer (VoC).

Market Research vs. Mining the VoC

The fundamental problem in market research, opinion surveys, or democracy for that matter, is this: How do you figure out what a lot of people are thinking? If you want to know what a particular group of people are thinking about a particular subject, you could simply ask each one of them that question and then listen carefully to their answers. But that usually doesn't work well for any target group of individuals larger than ten. When dealing with large populations whose opinions we want to grasp, we resort to a tool well established in politics: polling. Opinion polling in one form or another has been done for nearly 200 years. The most famous application of polling has been in predicting the outcome of elections. Historically, it has shown very mixed results. In 1936, a sample poll of 2.3 million possible voters indicated a preference for Alf Landon over Franklin Delano Roosevelt in the presidential race. FDR actually won by a significant margin. As it turned out, this poll was seriously flawed, probably due to a bias in the solicitation of poll respondents, who were primarily subscribers to a magazine called the *Literary Digest*.[1] Sample bias is a significant problem in getting accurate polling results. A poll taken on a skewed sample may be worse than useless—it may be downright misleading.

Mining the Talk to discover customer sentiment must also take this problem of skewed samples into account when interpreting unstructured mining results. After all, ultimately the information we mine doesn't come from reading the thoughts of a statistical cross section of customers. It comes from volunteered information, information collected directly from web logs, news articles, discussion groups, and other public forums. So as was the case in the 1936 election, the data comes solely from a self-selecting and motivated population that is not at all representative of the public at large.

What this means in practice is that we cannot use the principles of *Mining the Talk* to predict election results, or sales figures, or any kind of product preference. To do so would be almost certain to fail, because the comments that were mined would be very unlikely to represent the buying public in a fair and balanced way. To put it bluntly, the data would be skewed toward the "chattering class," which is to say, not necessarily anything like the "silent majority."

But the funny thing about data, especially unstructured text data, is that it almost always has something to tell you, especially if you have a lot of it. And we have a lot of talk out on the Web. Those people doing the talking are saying something—and it isn't just random noise. They are saying it with motivation, with purpose, and sometimes with great feeling. There's valuable insight there, and we can use our *Mining the Talk* approach to get at it.

And there are advantages to mining the Voice of the Customer as opposed to conducting standard market research or polling. Although it probably won't accurately predict elections, *Mining the Talk* can tell a business the answer to questions it didn't know to ask in a customer feedback questionnaire or a phone poll. Also, performing market surveys is becoming increasingly difficult and expensive as people in general become less and less available via home telephone.

Business Drivers for VoC Mining

VoC Mining is about understanding what's on your customer's mind. How is the business perceived—both positively and negatively? How do you compare, in your customer's mind, to your competitors? Why do they choose to do business with you instead of someone else? Obviously, obtaining such knowledge is critical to increasing, or even just maintaining, market share.

In addition to this general motivation, there are many more specific motivators that often spur business interest in specific VoC Mining applications. These include the following:

- Decreasing customer satisfaction scores on internal or external surveys
- Erosion of market share to competitive products or services
- Concern about brand image due to recent negative publicity surrounding specific events (e.g., product tampering, factory recall)
- Issues surrounding certain websites whose content reflects negatively on the company's image
- How a recent product or service offering is being perceived in the marketplace

The driving motivator is generally a need to quickly ascertain the thoughts of your customer base. Market surveys take time and budget that you may not have. VoC Mining is often the only practical approach to getting the customer insights you need to make the right decisions.

Characteristics of VoC Information

In contrast to customer interaction data sets, VoC information usually has far less structured and far more unstructured information. This will present additional challenges during the analysis phase. Also, VoC unstructured data tends to be longer and full of far more stuff that is unrelated to our analysis. This will create challenges during the Acquisition and Preparation phase. It will necessitate creation of structured data directly from unstructured using information extraction techniques or *annotations*. It will also necessitate the use of a text reduction technique called "snippetization"[2] to further improve data quality and relevance. Snippets and annotations will be discussed in greater detail later on in this chapter.

What Can VoC Mining Teach Us?

I've already mentioned some of the limitations of VoC data in terms of not originating from a statistically valid customer sample. But even without this feature, VoC information can be a rich source of insights about customers.

Our basic tool for getting at the useful information contained in this data stream is comparison. By that I mean comparing the text written by one connected set of individuals (a group) to another connected set of individuals (a different group). Within each group, the individuals doing the "talking" share some identifiable characteristic. This shared characteristic could be the time when the writing took place. Or it might be the subject being written about. Or it might refer to the company being criticized. Doing our analysis based on such comparisons within the existing sample allows us to draw some limited conclusions, at least about the population we are drawing from. These conclusions will be based specifically on the textual differences occurring between the different groups. These differences will then lead to hypothesis about what might be an underlying cause for them. The hypothesis can then be tested with additional data.

So what do we learn from these comparisons of different customer expressions in different populations? We seek to learn the underlying cause of this difference, in terms of something the company is doing wrong, or something the company should be doing but isn't. This knowledge can then be acted upon by working to change or enhance the customer's perception of the business.

Stages of the VoC Mining Process

The VoC Mining process shares many aspects with the process for mining customer interactions. But there are many important differences as well. In this section, we will describe the VoC Mining process in its entirety, focusing especially on those aspects that are unique to Mining the VoC.

Understanding of Business Objectives

For each analysis, the first step is to understand what the primary drivers are from a business perspective. Is there a known brand reputation issue? Has there been a recent erosion of market share? Are there any clues or theories as to why? Who are the people who monitor corporate reputation in the company and how do they do it currently? Who are the stakeholders? Who affects change when corporate reputation issues arise? The answer to these questions will shape what data is collected, how it is analyzed, and how that analysis is subsequently acted upon.

Demonstration of Capabilities

Ideally, the most effective demonstration of capability in the VoC Mining area is to take a particularly famous incident involving the company's products or brands and find historical data related to that incident. Using this data, we then demonstrate how this information might have been mined before, during and after the incident, to monitor public perception and take corrective action. If such data is not readily available, then using example analyses from other similar engagements will be the next most effective strategy. Demonstrating capabilities by using past scenarios that have similar character-istics to the situation at hand is the most effective technique to ensure that the initial analytic efforts will be properly focused, by helping to elicit from the stakeholders the kinds of analyses they will find most productive. You need to demonstrate what is possi-ble in order to give the stakeholders an understanding of what capabilities they can draw upon to meet the needs of their business.

Survey of Available Information

We have encountered two kinds of VoC information. Though they differ somewhat in the nature of their content, the analysis approach to both is virtually the same.

Customer Surveys

In a survey, a subset of customers are interviewed and asked a set of predefined ques-tions designed to elicit opinions about your business. They may be asked to provide an overall satisfaction score as well as specific scores for specific aspects of the relationship. Beyond this, they are often asked to provide feedback about specific issues that are trou-bling in the relationship or areas for improvement. The customer's answers may origi-nate in verbal or handwritten form, or be entered electronically. The structured data from this source is the numerical or categorical satisfaction scores, the date the survey took place, and the customer entity name and geographic location. The unstructured information is the free-form text responses given to questions that allow for open-ended answers.

The Global Information Space

Public information can include newspapers, periodicals, websites, blogs,[3] discussion forums, message boards, and so on. More and more such information is becoming readily accessible in analyzable form via web crawlers,[4] third-party vendors, or direct purchase of daily RSS feeds.[5] The stream of information is mind boggling in its size and diversity, but we can focus on just those articles or posts that refer to our company or its products. This results in a manageable stream of documents that can be readily mined over time. The structured information from this source is fairly limited, in part due to the fact that the information sources are typically unrelated to each other. However, certain structured information can usually be obtained from the originating source. For example, nearly all articles or posts will have a date associated with them. If not available, then the date the article was first crawled or downloaded can be used as an approximation. Some geographic information is also frequently available either directly from the news feed, or indirectly through the last part of the Uniform Resource Locator (URL) of the original website. The original query used to spot the article in the first place (brand or company name) can be a structured field value as well.

The unstructured information is the text content of the article, blog, or post. Typically, such documents are longer than the survey answers customers give to specific interviewer questions. Embedded in these long answers may be some additional structured information we can obtain via annotations.

Acquisition and Preparation

The acquisition and preparation process for VoC data is frequently more challenging than that for customer interaction information. This is due in part to having multiple data sources, each with its own layout. Also, the information collected is frequently formatted more for reading than for the purposes of analysis.

Collection

Customer survey responses are usually easy to obtain, since the survey is often commissioned by the company, although the perceived sensitivity of the data may restrict easy access. Collecting news articles on a given subject for a given time period is also relatively straightforward given the ready availability of services such as LexisNexis®. Collecting data from blogs or message boards presents a greater challenge. There are software tools (such as IBM's OmniFind®) that can crawl specific websites and save the contents of those websites locally for indexing and analysis. There are also services provided by companies to do this for a fee for specific queries. Even so, you may feel that the task of crawling the external Web is too daunting—after all, the Web is unimaginably big, so how can your company ever expect to analyze it? In fact, it is neither necessary nor desirable to mine the entire Web for any content related to your business. All we are looking for is a sample of sufficient size to learn what our customers are thinking. This task is typically not beyond the resources of the enterprise, nor will the costs be so prohibitive as to make the initial hurdle an unrealistic barrier to surmount.

Cleansing

Cleansing customer survey responses may prove to be something of a challenge because the data is often collected as pure text document templates summarizing an interview. These documents need to be parsed to filter out the question text and to put each response in the appropriate context. Structured information associated with the interview, such as company name and geographic location, may need to be inferred or derived from other sources and then combined with the text information during the ETL process.

Cleansing news articles and web data requires stripping out the HTML tags that provide formatting information about how the document should be displayed, and leaving behind the text that represents the content of the article. It may also involve extracting date information from the article text. URLs may also need to be parsed to obtain relevant information about the original website and inferred geographic location of the content.[6]

Annotation

Annotations are what we call features that are derived from text, instead of the text itself. In a way, synonyms (discussed in Chapter 2, "Mining Customer Interactions") are a simple form of annotation, in that a word that occurs in the text may get translated into another word. So, for instance, "pw" may become "password." This is just what annotations do—they create new features from words occurring in text based on rules or translations that are known ahead of time. Annotations can be created in many different ways: from tables, from dictionaries, from rules, from mathematical models, from machine learning approaches, and so on. In this chapter, we will discuss one way that has worked exceptionally well for *Mining the Talk*, because of its general flexibility and robustness. This is to create annotations from *regular expressions*.

> A **regular expression** (abbreviated as **regexp** or **regex**, with plural forms **regexps**, **regexes**, or **regexen**) is a string that describes or matches a set of strings, according to certain syntax rules. Regular expressions are used by many text editors and utilities to search and manipulate bodies of text based on certain patterns. Many programming languages support regular expressions for string manipulation. For example, Perl and Tcl have a powerful regular expression engine built directly into their syntax. The set of utilities (including the editor sed and the filter grep) provided by Unix distributions were the first to popularize the concept of regular expressions.[7]

What regular expressions provide for us is the ability to represent nearly any kind of text sequence that can be represented as a dictionary of string patterns. As we shall see in a moment, this covers a lot of ground—although it doesn't cover everything.

The syntax we use for creating regular expressions is based on the Java 1.4 specification.[8] We recommend this syntax for its simplicity and its power, though other schemes may be equally effective.

Mining the Talk employs regular expression to create features by employing domain-specific dictionaries when the features space is first created. An example of such a regular expression dictionary is shown here:

```
DateString=\d/\d\d/\d\d
PriceString=\$\d+\.\d\d
PlanetString=Mercury|Veunus|Earth|Mars|Jupiter|Saturn|Uranus|Neptune
IBM=IBM|International Business Machines|big blue
```

The first line creates a feature called DateString whenever it sees something like 9/27/06 anywhere in the text of an example (\d = any digit). The second line creates the term PriceString whenever it sees something like $23.05. The third line creates the term PlanetString whenever one of the names of the planets appears in the text. And the last line creates the term IBM whenever any of the identified names for the company are used.

Note that annotations get created in addition to other words and phrases that might occur in the text frequently enough to warrant it. One difference, though, is that the annotation becomes a feature in the dictionary even if it only occurs once in the entire data set. It does not have to meet the minimum occurrence threshold to be included; to put it another way, the minimum occurrence threshold is always 1.0 for an annotation. It is assumed that if the analyst goes to the trouble of defining an annotation, it must be important.

Creating the Initial Taxonomy

Creation of the taxonomy is the first step in breaking the analysis problem down into manageable chunks. For mining VoC data, we build our categories around snippets of the documents rather than using the full documents.

When collecting data off the Web, one must remember that originally the data was not created for any purpose related to your business. Therefore, it is bound to contain a great deal of extraneous information, no matter how good the original query used to collect it. Web information is seldom broken up into discrete packets, each containing one thought. In many cases, the vast bulk of the data will be completely irrelevant to the subject we are interested in studying. This is because a discussion page or a blog may contain a single reference that matches a query, while the bulk of the page is about something else entirely.

The solution to this problem is a way of breaking up the text stream into relevant packets called "snippets." *Snippets* are small chunks of text of limited size that contain some selected query. This text is then extracted out of the larger document—like a paragraph "snipped" out of the newspaper. A snippet may be defined as a certain number of words before or after the selected query, a single sentence containing the query, or some number of surrounding sentences to a sentence containing the query. Snippets provide two advantages over complete documents. First, they are almost always focused on the topic of interest, and second, they usually contain no more than one discrete concept. An example later in this chapter will show the value of taxonomies created via snippets compared to those created from full documents.

Refining the Taxonomy

In the taxonomy refinement phase for VoC, the taxonomy edits are less about capturing domain knowledge and more about clearing away the clutter and debris that web data (even snippet web data) and news feeds will inevitably contain. A certain amount of conceptual disambiguation must be done to ensure that each category's content is clear to the analyst and as much as possible represents a single concept. Also, no matter how good your cleansing process, some stuff that is extraneous to the voice of the customer will inevitably find its way in. In fact, a large majority of the data may be this stuff. Refining the taxonomy gives you a quick way to locate the extraneous content and filter it out before performing deeper analysis.

The second point to note here is there may be more than one way to create categories to get at the comparisons that will be relevant to the business purpose of the analysis. As we will see in the examples, multiple taxonomies can be created based on the following:

- Words or other indicators of customer satisfaction/dissatisfaction
- Mentions of business name or products, or competitor's business name or products
- General discussion topics
- Specific topical issues that are deemed important to the business to monitor.

Creating taxonomies around multiple dimensions in this way will be critical to obtaining insights from information that may not represent a statistically valid sample of your customers.

Analysis for Insight

Once a meaningful set of taxonomies are created and refined, the next step is to look for any correlations between categories of different taxonomies or between categories and other structured data elements. This would include the following:

- Looking at the evolution of categories over time to spot emerging trends or unique events that influence customer perception.

- Looking for high co-occurrence between a category and a structured field value such as customer satisfaction score to detect any underlying systemic causes of dissatisfaction.

- Looking at differences across companies to see how the customer may perceive your businesses strengths and weaknesses compared to the competition.

Each of these correlations may indicate an area for further investigation. Not all of these correlations will be relevant, but looking at specific examples for each correlation will help determine whether the correlation actually corresponds to an interesting, aggregate customer opinion about your business.

Reviewing Results with Stakeholders

The report for a VoC analysis should include both high-level statistics and graphs to show overall trends and correlations, as well as the text of specific examples to allow the customer's own voice to speak for itself. Often we find in these presentations that it is the quotes from actual customers that are far more compelling and persuasive than any graph or chart can be. It's almost as if the customers have joined the meeting, adding their own opinions to the mix. The great thing about VoC data is that it's firsthand. It's not filtered by a representative of the business who is summarizing what the customer said. This makes the actual text quotations that much more valuable. They capture emotion as well as content. Such first-hand customer voices can be wonderful idea generators for the business.

Making VoC Mining an Ongoing Concern

Once the initial analysis bears fruit, the stakeholders will often wish to monitor the publicly available data sources on a continuing basis. This requires that a process be put in place of continuous collection, analysis, and reporting of VoC issues.

Setting Up the VoC Process

The overall process for the VoC monitoring system consists of the following components: information acquisition, data storage, automated querying, analysis, and report generation. The diagram in Figure 3-1 illustrates this flow.

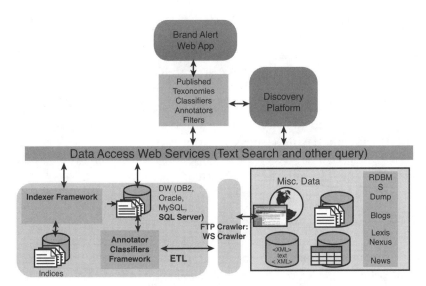

Figure 3-1 The ongoing VoC monitoring system

Information moves from multiple sources into a data warehouse where it is collected, cleansed, and indexed. From there, queries are generated on a regular basis. Information matching the queries is analyzed using text classifiers based on taxonomies designed to recognize specific issues. The level of significance needed to create an "alert" condition is configurable. The results of this analysis are displayed in a web application, which selects example text from documents that match the alerted incident. A discovery platform is provided for refining the taxonomies, helping to capture new critical issues as they arise over time and add these to the existing models.

Creating Specific Pattern Classifiers to Monitor as Alerts

The taxonomies created during the refinement phase will often have specific categories identified as being critical ongoing concerns for the business. The data contained in these categories can be used as a training set to create text classifiers.[9] Alternatively, the analyst can design annotation filters that can be used to capture those documents that match certain predefined patterns. In either case, these patterns or classifiers can then be applied to incoming data and used to automatically categorize all posts that are found and create reports showing any interesting trends or co-occurrences.

Measure Effectiveness and Refine

The accuracy of the text classifiers or annotation filters needs to be monitored over time to ensure that they continue to work as expected. Terminology and descriptive language tends to evolve and change over time, and patterns that work well at one point in time may fail later on. They may fail either by matching incorrect examples or missing examples that should have been flagged. Monitoring can be accomplished by periodically sampling the data stream and having a subject matter expert carefully look at the examples that are not being flagged. If mistakes are being made, the expert would then try to determine if those mistakes can be recognized with any general pattern.

Expand the Application

Success in one area of the business will often lead to additional application ideas. Leverage the success stories in one domain to encourage greater analysis of newsfeeds, blogs, and web data for other issues of concern to the business. Go beyond brand and corporate name queries to include queries around issues that are of potential concern to the enterprise. These might include environmental issues, political issues, business climate, protests, and boycotts. There's really no limit to the different issues that can be studied that will give valuable insight into the mind of current and potential customers.

Making It Real: Detailed Examples

Now for those readers who are interested, we would like to go to a much deeper level of detail, in order to describe just how *Mining the Talk* works in practice on VoC data sets. The detailed examples in this section will especially focus on snippet analysis and various forms of trend and co-occurrence analysis, assuming other aspects of the methodology are already understood, or will be covered more thoroughly in subsequent chapters.

Insurance Industry Landscape Analysis

The first example shows how we can use general web data collected in an industry to find comparative differences between companies in that industry. This text analysis was done on discussion forums relating to the insurance industry.

In the co-occurrence table in Figure 3-2, we show the breakdown of comments by topic and by the insurance company being talked about. The topics were generated via automated taxonomy creation over snippets created around particular insurance company names. The insurance company names themselves were used as the other dimension. By splitting up the data in this way, we can look at the different topics across the different companies and highlight any areas of unusually high co-occurrence. What's unusual here is the high number of claim stories involving Insurance 1. When we look inside at the examples behind this cell, we see the following:

Class	Class	Size	Insurance 1	Insurance 2	Insurance 3
claim st...	claim stories	453	(highlighted)	9 (1.99%)	0 (0.00%)
Miscella...	Miscellaneous	3988	14 (0.35%)	28 (0.70%)	4 (0.10%)
questio...	questions about a possible ...	591	11 (1.86%)	4 (0.68%)	0 (0.00%)
insuran...	insurance claimants as a gr...	523	7 (1.34%)	7 (1.34%)	0 (0.00%)
process...	processing claims	674	5 (0.74%)	9 (1.34%)	0 (0.00%)
house i...	house insurance	166	5 (3.01%)	1 (0.60%)	1 (0.60%)
car insu...	car insurance claim	411	2 (0.49%)	9 (2.19%)	0 (0.00%)
police r...	police report	382	2 (0.52%)	0 (0.00%)	0 (0.00%)
property	property damage	220	2 (0.91%)	2 (0.91%)	0 (0.00%)
paid cla...	paid claims	149	2 (1.34%)	3 (2.01%)	0 (0.00%)
Not Rel.	Not Related	1504	1 (0.07%)	7 (0.47%)	0 (0.00%)
fraudule...	fraudulent claims	808	0 (0.00%)	1 (0.12%)	0 (0.00%)
forms	forms	387	0 (0.00%)	0 (0.00%)	0 (0.00%)
paymen...	payment of claim	338	0 (0.00%)	13 (3.85%)	0 (0.00%)
free adv...	free advice / tips	191	0 (0.00%)	1 (0.52%)	1 (0.52%)
health i...	health insurance	163	0 (0.00%)	0 (0.00%)	0 (0.00%)
internati...	international claims	130	0 (0.00%)	4 (3.45%)	0 (0.00%)
adjuster	adjuster	116	0 (0.00%)	1 (0.97%)	0 (0.00%)
injury	injury	103	0 (0.00%)	0 (0.00%)	0 (0.00%)
surveys	surveys	98	0 (0.00%)	0 (0.00%)	0 (0.00%)
denied...	denied claims	82	0 (0.00%)	4 (4.88%)	0 (0.00%)
claimants	claimants	78	0 (0.00%)	2 (2.56%)	0 (0.00%)
UNUM	UNUM	78	0 (0.00%)	0 (0.00%)	0 (0.00%)
deny	deny	70	0 (0.00%)	4 (5.71%)	0 (0.00%)
settled	settled	65	0 (0.00%)	0 (0.00%)	0 (0.00%)
pictures...	pictures for insurance claim	46	0 (0.00%)	0 (0.00%)	0 (0.00%)
submit...	submit a claim	33	0 (0.00%)	0 (0.00%)	1 (3.03%)
world tr...	world trade center	32	0 (0.00%)	0 (0.00%)	0 (0.00%)
Total	Total	11870	83	115	8

Figure 3-2 Insurance company vs. topic

Favorable Comments:

- YAY! For those who have been following and/or care about the disposition of my claim with Insurance 1, here's the good news: Insurance 1 not only declared my car a total loss, they estimated the value of my car better than the actual payoff value of my car! With the extra money as down payment, I was able to get myself into a new car today!

- So I'm going with Insurance 1 for pricing and because they were nicer, which goes a long way with me.

- The people at Insurance 1 have been surprisingly helpful. Car crashes are usually less boring than this.

- In fact, the lady who side-swiped me was uninsured. Insurance 1 handled it like a breeze. Within a week, my car was in the shop being fixed, they had paid my deductible, and the claim was settled.

- I left town shortly following the wreck and had to deal with my insurance company over my cell phone. (I'm not looking forward to this bill!) Actually, it turned out to be pretty easy. She gave me a fake phone number, but kudos to Insurance 1 for doing a little research and getting her number. Turns out she's under Insurance 1, as well. She admitted fault, and I took my car to Stuart's.

Unfavorable Comments:

- This was right after my car had been smashed by a cellular blonde in an SUV, and I was haggling with idiots from Insurance 1 Insurance Company who wanted to give me a pittance for my prized Plymouth. [Insurance rant begins here:] The man handling my claim was an idiot and very unprofessional. He claimed that my vehicle had been damaged by hail storms, which was ludicrous since it had never been in a hail storm. He and everyone at Insurance 1 I spoke to over the phone treated me like …

- I had one personal experience where I was hit while sitting at a light. Someone slid into me on the ice. Insurance 1 insured the other vehicle. For awhile, they actually balked at paying…said I was partly at fault…but never offered an explanation of how that could have been true. They paid though…but reluctantly.

- Due to an ice storm that left me with no power for 5 days, I lost all my food. I filed a claim with Insurance 1, and they have caused more stress than the actual incident. Since I failed to give a change of address, they are denying the claim, stating that as a technicality, I would have still lost the food at the old place because there was no power there either. They have called me all week while I was trying to work. This is the second time I've had a serious issue with them, and it's now time to look for a new company.

- …Insurance 1 wouldn't extend the rental period so I'd have a way to look for a new car, until I went ballistic…on them. The "fair replacement value" they determined that they'd give me was a good $3500 below what you'd find on a used car lot for the same thing.

What's interesting about this is how the analysis focuses attention on the issues that make this insurance company unique in these consumer's minds. It's not the insurance product itself, but stories about filing claims that make up most of the internet chatter. And this company is more or less alone in this regard. Now this doesn't imply that most customers of Insurance 1 feel this way, or that they should necessarily change their business practices as a result of this simple analysis, but it does point to possible areas for further study. The insurance company in question might begin to investigate its claims filing process and see if internal data verifies what the web data is showing. If so, then specific actions might be taken to reduce the customer dissatisfaction in this area that is leading to bad publicity on the Web. The web data could then be monitored to see if the actions were having the desired effect over time.

Analyzing Customer Surveys: The Good, the Bad, and the Ugly

Here's another example of how breaking things down into categories and then studying the differences in the text content between categories can be enlightening. These customer survey results came from interviews conducted with corporate customer representatives concerning their satisfaction level with a vendor's level of service. The survey was designed to elicit from the respondents a ranking on a scale from 0–10 (10 being most satisfied) and then asked them to give any additional comments concerning service. Here is a summary of the results (see Figure 3-3).

Very High Affinity = ■ Moderate Affinity = □ Low Affinity = □ No Affinity = □						
Count /	GOOD -High Sat	GOOD-8	GOOD-Low Sat	BAD-High Sat	BAD-8	BAD-Low Sat
responsiveness 1640	108 (0.6818876)	91 (2.2117)...	55 (0.0625816)	52 (1.4764268E-4)	41(0.1576...	60(0.039568342)
understanding 1221	112 (3.246178E-5)	70 (4.6334...	41 (0.109238505)	34 (0.025247475)	22 (1.0)	40 (0.35003543)
relationship 1142		130 (8.85E-...	92 (1.4808864E-31)	24 (0.6596919)	22 (1.0)	32 (1.0)
PE 1109			96 (1.9838844E-37)	14 (1.0)	16 (1.0)	29 (1.0)
team 937	127 (2.7660183E-20	86 (5.8270...	66 (1.0399268E-17)	15 (1.0)	23 (0.3413...	23 (1.0)
management 521	29 (1.0)	25 (0.2572...	29 (2.5755868E-5)	10 (1.0)	13 (0.4414...	24 (0.014338523)
trust 223	26 (0.0010804741)	23 (4.7709...	12 (0.010380429)	2 (1.0)	4 (1.0)	5 (1.0)
communication 217	18 (0.23712859)	14 (0.0457...	7 (0.5898068)	5 (0.6845307)	5 (0.76959...	13 (0.00506619...
flexibility 168	8 (1.0)	5 (1.0)	3 (1.0)	4 (0.6673447)	5 (0.37995...	15 (1.9094796E-...
help 159	10 (1.0)	3 (1.0)	11 (7.414188E-4)	3 (1.0)	4 (0.65961...	10 (0.008702437)
slow 121	2 (1.0)	0 (1.0)	5 (0.3053311)	8 (1.7109407E-4)	2 (1.0)	12 (2.6767245E-...
incidents 87	3 (1.0)	3 (1.0)	3 (0.6383051)	5 (0.009405486)	2 (0.85601...	8 (3.5467301E-4)
teamwork 85	14 (1.2561401E-4)	12 (8.4366...	5 (0.06198177)	1 (1.0)	4 (0.07883...	4 (0.30050975)
Total 24342	1545	938	643	469	493	692

| Trend Examples | View Examples | Report | OK | Filter | Enlarged View |

Figure 3-3 Satisfaction level vs. sentiment

We divide the comments into categories based on their overall satisfaction level:

0–7 = Low Sat
8 = 8
9–10 = High Sat

Then we further break down the information based on whether the specific comment was positive or negative. This is done via a sentiment annotator that utilizes a dictionary to create the term "GOOD" or "BAD" based on synonyms for these sentiments. Here are the regular expressions we used to detect positive and negative sentiments from that data set:

```
GOOD=good||great |outstanding|excellen|thank|works well|working
well|very well|quite well|go well|done well|going well|goes
well|responded well|responds well| so well|
nice|optimistic|pleased| praise
BAD= bad | poor | terribl| awful | complain| irritat| angry |
frustra| difficult| dissatisf|critic| lack| reform |wrong
```

Taking the numeric score plus the sentiment together gives us the six columns shown in Figure 3-3 that match all the combination of overall satisfaction with positive and negative comments. The rows represent individual taxonomy categories.

What the highlighted areas of significance reflect is that both high and low satisfaction customers tend to focus on the relationship with the Project Engineer (PE), while low satisfaction customers tend to say positive things about teamwork and management. A lack or responsiveness is mentioned significantly for high and low satisfaction customers, while a lack of flexibility is significant for low satisfaction customers. This kind of breakdown helps the service provider to see where to spend effort in maintaining high satisfaction, and in improving low satisfaction scores.

Whatchamacallit[10] Coffee

In this example, we use web information to better understand how a company is perceived by the public at large and how this perception is trending. Snippets are a useful tool for focusing on just the data that is most relevant to the company we want to study.

Say we are Whatchamacallit coffee and we want to understand more about how our image is perceived on the Web. We do a query and extract a random set of web pages that mention the phrase "whatchamacallit coffee." We download the text of these pages and create a taxonomy using text-clustering techniques to understand what we have found. Here is what such a taxonomy might look like (see Figure 3-4).

	Class Name	Size	Cohesion	Distinctness
1	book	6554 (3.09%)	80.42%	61.88%
2	journals	928 (0.44%)	76.32%	69.99%
3	gifts	17932 (8.45%)	72.58%	57.22%
4	amazon.com	8322 (3.92%)	63.82%	51.79%
5	stock purchase plans	21908 (10.32%)	60.24%	48.27%
6	hotel	4220 (1.99%)	55.98%	50.87%
7	wireless networks	7943 (3.74%)	52.85%	41.07%
8	financial news	11310 (5.33%)	48.99%	29.66%
9	forums	5651 (2.66%)	50.27%	56.14%
10	church publications	1482 (0.70%)	49.74%	39.70%
11	vacations	1432 (0.67%)	44.15%	51.80%
12	food,restaurant	7519 (3.54%)	39.96%	36.52%
13	music,play,show	8999 (4.24%)	37.26%	20.05%
14	event,school,information	9255 (4.36%)	36.02%	29.71%
15	shop,locate,park	10163 (4.79%)	36.10%	29.71%
16	Miscellaneous	9830 (4.63%)	34.74%	34.24%
17	news	25707 (12.11%)	43.94%	29.66%
18	blogs	53101 (25.02%)	43.55%	20.05%
	TOTAL / AVERAGE	212256	49.47%	35.37%

Figure 3-4 Taxonomy at the page level

This high-level breakdown is all we can really expect text clustering to do for us at this page level, because the individual pages have so little in common with each other and so much other data extraneous to our original query. To get beyond this high-level taxonomy using text-clustering approaches, we need to change the documents we are clustering. We focus the data on snippets that surround the name of the company: "Whatchamacallit." Our definition of a snippet is the sentence that contains the word "Whatchamacallit," plus the previous sentence and the succeeding sentence.

Now if we look at sentence-level snippets for "whatchamacallit coffee" across data from categories most likely to hold consumer comments (such as forums and blogs), we see a much different, more detailed picture of what some people are saying about the company (see Figure 3-5).

D:\data\whatchamacallit\nodups\relevant\blogs\snippets\nodups\final.obj		

File   Edit   Execute   View   Subclass   Help

| Dictionary Tool | View Selected Class | Subclass | Merge Classes |

Taxonomy Level: Root

	Class Name	Size	Trend
20	gift cards	509 (0.98%)	10/1/02
16	fast food	726 (1.40%)	9/6/02
7	today I went to whatchamacallit	1429 (2.76%)	8/29/02
26	money	426 (0.82%)	8/29/02
4	home away from home	2511 (4.85%)	8/26/02
19	free coffee	570 (1.10%)	8/22/02
32	closed	300 (0.58%)	8/13/02
25	whatchamacallit locations	452 (0.87%)	8/12/02
2	social gathering place	2777 (5.36%)	8/3/02
18	tea	589 (1.14%)	8/3/02
17	finding a whatchamacallit	704 (1.36%)	7/31/02
14	lattes	869 (1.68%)	7/29/02
1	Miscellaneous	23044 (44.51%)	7/26/02
30	seattle_best	302 (0.58%)	7/26/02
21	smashing windows whatchamacallit	494 (0.95%)	7/24/02
3	working at whatchamacallit	2698 (5.21%)	7/21/02
13	walking to whatchamacallit	979 (1.89%)	7/21/02
28	building a whatchamacallit	343 (0.66%)	7/19/02
9	mocha	1095 (2.11%)	7/17/02
24	whatchamacallit on every corner	459 (0.89%)	7/15/02
5	meet at whatchamacallit	1853 (3.58%)	7/14/02
22	jobs at whatchamacallit	483 (0.93%)	7/14/02
12	mornings	981 (1.89%)	7/3/02
33	canadian labor	177 (0.34%)	7/1/02
15	local issues	812 (1.57%)	6/27/02
6	store openings	1440 (2.78%)	6/18/02
8	globalization	1203 (2.32%)	6/8/02
10	cups	1048 (2.02%)	6/2/02
27	espresso	403 (0.78%)	5/27/02
23	local~business	477 (0.92%)	5/3/02
11	seattle	982 (1.90%)	4/23/02
31	fair~trade	302 (0.58%)	3/12/02
29	employee	339 (0.65%)	12/19/01
	TOTAL / AVERAGE	51776	

| Visualization | Class View | Class Table | Class Tree |

Figure 3-5 Taxonomy at the snippet level

This comment summary immediately goes from being bland to eye popping. It's as if a door has been opened and we stepped into a room of chatty customers, each one begging us for our attention. Here's just a smattering of some of the more interesting comments in each category:

1. Association with fast food:
   - Everywhere you look, you see a [fast food restaurant] and Whatchamacallit.
   - [Fast food restaurant], Whatchamacallit—you name it, they're here.
   - Afterwards, we wandered up and down Market, went to the Metreon, went to [fast food restaurant], and then went to Whatchamacallit.

2. Home away from home:
   - Whatchamacallit here i come!!!!! woohoo—my new home away from home.
   - It's the familiarity of Whatchamacallit that provides that "comfort of home."
   - Tasty finds Whatchamacallit, my home away from home it seems, has a couple of new offerings.

3. Social gathering place:
   - These are people i've trained with; people i have Whatchamacallit trips with; people i have lunch with; people i play halo and puzzle fighter with; people i have crazy, hilarious, industry-related, disgusting, and heart-felt conversation.
   - Many middle-aged normal-looking people, like the people you'd see at Whatchamacallit.
   - When people you love (such as the people I was with at Whatchamacallit) help you to realize certain things, it's good.

This clustering of snippets, along with the typical examples for each cluster, are enough in this case to achieve our objective: namely, to get some ideas of how Whatchamacallit coffee is perceived on the Web. Even without having a statistically valid sample of Whatchamacallit customers, we at least have some interesting ideas about how to focus on the positives ("home away from home" and "social gathering place") and combat the negatives ("Whatchamacallit on every corner," may indicate marketplace saturation).

Events in the Time Stream

Another kind of analysis uses the time dimension to split up the data into categories and then analyzes the differences between text in the time categories to discover how actions by the company are perceived by the public.

Here is an example of web chatter around a particular insurance company (see Figure 3-6). The clustering again is created based on snippets centered around the insurance company's name.

Class Name	Size /	Trend
13 Miscellaneous	3940 (43.79%)	10/2/02
11 working for Insurance1	1013 (11.26%)	7/4/02
2 job cuts	857 (9.52%)	7/29/03
10 claims	745 (8.28%)	5/15/02
5 agents	463 (5.15%)	8/29/02
8 collective farming	443 (4.92%)	11/1/00
6 car insurance stories	332 (3.69%)	7/21/02
3 stadiums	256 (2.85%)	1/5/03
4 like a good neighbor...	248 (2.76%)	7/17/02
12 unrelated documents	206 (2.29%)	4/8/02
9 legal news	199 (2.21%)	5/28/02
7 monthly payments	153 (1.70%)	2/16/02
16 human generated catastrophe	76 (0.84%)	4/26/03
1 charity	33 (0.37%)	3/19/03
14 favorable comments	25 (0.28%)	2/8/02
15 unfavorable	9 (0.10%)	4/6/03
TOTAL / AVERAGE	8998	

Figure 3-6   Snippet taxonomy around insurance company

The trend charts in the right-hand column are created using a special process that helps to indicate how each snippet category's occurrence over time differs from the overall occurrence of the snippet data as a whole. This process starts by sorting the data chronologically. It then divides the data into brackets of contiguous time, each with equal size. We then create line graphs for each category by plotting what percentage of each category's information occurs in each of the brackets. The average date for each category is then calculated by converting the date of every example in the category to an integer and calculating an average. This average is then converted back into an "average" date. The line graph and the average are displayed together for each category as a kind of date summary (mean and distribution).

"Why do all this?," you may ask. Why not simply plot the trend lines with a standard x-axis that is linear in time, with the origin being the earliest data point and the other end being the most recent? The problem is that this displays poorly when the underlying distribution of the data is not evenly distributed over time. Web pages are a good example of such data. We often see the number of web pages with recent dates far outnumber those with older dates. This creates the "hockey-stick" effect, whereby all categories appear to be trending upward about equally. Such displays give too much weight to a very small sample of old data, and too little weight to the much greater amount of more recent data. By sorting the examples chronologically and taking equal-size buckets to represent each time interval on the X-axis, we avoid this problem and also fairly compare the time distribution of each category against every other. We essentially take the underlying distribution into account in our display of each individual category, thus maximizing the information content of that display.

Such a display can help us to see upward trends, such as that for the "job cuts" category. It will also help us to see spike events that take place at a certain point in time and then dissipate. A good example of this kind of phenomenon can be seen in the "human-generated catastrophe" category (see Figure 3-7).

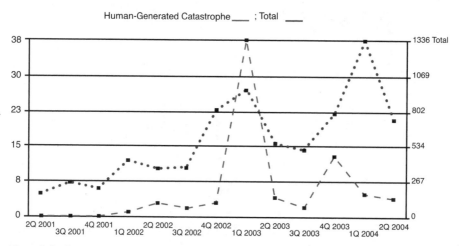

Human-Generated Catastrophe ___ ; Total ___

Figure 3-7 Human-generated catastrophe category over time

The trend chart in Figure 3-7 shows a spike occurring in this data during the first quarter of 2003. Notice that the spike for human-generated catastrophe (dashed line) is much more pronounced than the spike for the overall comments about Insurance 1 (dotted line). A look at a typical example for this time period shows what event caused this sudden spike in customer talk on this obscure topic:

> As if the potential for nuclear reactions from North Korea and Iraq weren't enough, Insurance 1's automotive insurance unit informed customers last week that [human-generated catastrophes] won't be covered by their car policies. The insurer has begun alerting customers that it won't cover the fallout [from such events].

Notice how the indication of an event of interest comes despite not having a statistical sample from which to draw conclusions. So although it would be pretty meaningless to say that X% of Insurance 1 customers on the internet are upset about the human-generated catastrophe issue, it is meaningful to note that during a certain period of time, a significantly higher number of Insurance 1 customers were talking about this issue than at any other period of time.

Summary

We have shown that mining VoC information is a powerful tool for finding out what our customers think about us. Although it certainly lacks the rigor of a well-designed poll with a statistically representative sample, we are able to harness the data that is freely available and detect the answers to questions that a pollster or survey taker may never think to ask.

In understanding the mood of the buying public, as in many areas, the painful truth is we don't always know what we don't know. *Mining the Talk* to hear the Voice of the Customer alerts us to issues that may need further study to understand whether or not the issue will seriously impact our business. This may tell us painful truths that we don't always want to hear about ourselves. But the Voice of the Customer is very often constructive as well. More often than not, our customers really want us to serve them better. They are telling us how to do it, if only we would listen.

Endnotes

1. See the Wikipedia article: http://en.wikipedia.org/wiki/Literary_Digest.

2. D. Gruhl, L. Chavet, D. Gibson, J. Meyer, P. Pattanayak, A. Tomkins, and J. Zien. "How to build a WebFountain: An architecture for very large-scale text analytics," *IBM Systems Journal*, v.43 n.1, pp. 64–77, January 2004.

3. A blog is short for "web log," and refers to a personal journal or diary that is published by individuals on the Web.

4. A web crawler is a software program that collects web content in a systematic manner. This content can then be stored or indexed for later use in search engines or text analysis programs.

5. RSS ("Really Simple Syndication") is a general format for newsfeeds on the Web. See the Wikipedia entry: http://en.wikipedia.org/wiki/RSS.

6. A URL (Uniform Resource Locator) describes the location on the network of a web page. The following link describes how the country where the network server is located can be inferred from the URL: http://www.bitmedia.com/cc/url1.htm.

7. Wikipedia: http://en.wikipedia.org/wiki/Regular_expression.

8. http://java.sun.com/j2se/1.4.2/docs/api/java/util/regex/Pattern.html.

9. Text classifiers are models that identify the category of a text example based on training data. Text classifiers can be generated automatically from taxonomies. A description of how to generate classifiers from training data is outside the scope of this book, but here are a few good references on the subject:

Manning, Christopher D., and Hinrich Schütze. 1999. *Foundations of Statistical Natural Language Processing.* Cambridge: MIT Press.

McCallum, Andrew, and Nigam, Kamal. *A Comparison of Event Models for Naïve Bayes Text Classification*, AAAI-98.

Mitchell, Tom M. 1997. *Machine Learning.* New York: McGraw-Hill.

10. Here, as in many places in the book, the name of the actual target company has been cleverly disguised. It is difficult in these litigious times to get permission from lawyers to use actual names of existing companies in print.

4

Mining the Voice of the Employee

In this chapter, we show how *Mining the Talk* methods can be used to play a critical role in organizational communication. Employee talk can be an inexhaustible resource for innovative ideas and process improvements. Mining the Voice of the Employee is a critical step to letting that voice be heard.

Business Drivers

The problems of how to foster valuable dialog in a large hierarchical organization are well known. In his autobiography, Thomas J. Watson Jr. refers to the tremendous challenges that were involved with IBM's rapid growth in the 1960s. It was always Watson's goal to keep the lines of communication open between employees and management as the company increased exponentially in size.

> *I knew exactly the attitude I wanted to cultivate in ordinary IBM employees. I wanted them to feel a proprietary interest, and to have some knowledge of each other's problems and goals. I also wanted them to feel they had access to top management and that no one was so far down the chain of command they couldn't be kept aware of where the business was heading. As the hierarchy grew to include five, six, and seven layers of command, this became a huge challenge. I was constantly looking for ways to maintain a small company attitude. One of the surprising things we learned was that to overcome the problems of change, we had to increase communication within IBM far out of proportion to our growth rate. —Thomas Watson Jr.*[1]

This challenge has not gone away since Thomas Watson Jr. served as IBM President. Fortunately, new tools have become available since Watson's time that make it possible for an organization to greatly increase the bandwidth of communication between management and employee and among employees across disparate parts of an organization. The internet and email have allowed each employee to have a much greater degree of access to information than ever before. But there still remains the problem of how to distill and summarize all the "organizational talk" into something management, or any individual employee, can utilize to understand what's going on in the company—using that information to make their own contribution to the communication stream or to take individual actions that are in harmony with the corporation's aspirations. This is where *Mining the Talk* can become a key enabler of organizational communication—by synthesizing and organizing the information generated by a large number of employees into a coherent structure.

Mining the Talk can be employed to understand many streams of employee feedback, including emails sent to corporate officers or suggestion boxes, survey results, blogs, and personal websites. But there is one form of employee communication that is currently unique to IBM that we want to focus on in this chapter. It is called a "Jam," and it is just what Thomas Watson Jr. would have wished for when he faced those early corporate communication challenges.

The Jam: Taking Corporate Communication to a New Level

The Jam we refer to is an Internet- or intranet-based discussion and idea-stimulation vehicle.[2] More formal than a chat room, participants work together to create a vision, and build consensus on actionable ideas on a variety of topics. The purpose is to try to create a collaborative environment where ideas can flow freely and where conclusions can achieve widespread buy-in.

A Jam is typically organized into a handful of separate "forums," each on a different subtopic related to the overall Jam topic. The Jam is continuous and for a limited time period, usually between 48 and 72 hours. During the event, participants can come and go into the Jam as often as they like. Participants who register at the site can make original posts, or reply to existing posts. The posts are labeled with the participant's name (no anonymous contributions). Some Jam participants may simply read the existing posts, while others will enter posts without reading anyone else's thoughts. Most participants will both read what's already in the Jam as well as make their own contributions. As the Jam continues over time, "themes" emerge from the communication stream. These themes, detected by our *Mining the Talk* techniques, are posted back to the Jam periodically, along with typical comments for each theme, allowing participants to see, at a glance, what is being said.

Moderators in each forum can highlight "hot topics" as they emerge in the discussion. Participants can also use full-text search to browse for posts on a certain subject or for posts that particular individuals have contributed. Finally, posts can be emailed by Jam participants to others to encourage new contributions.

The process of Jamming at IBM has evolved over several years. At first, it involved no text mining technology at all, but used only human facilitators and participant "idea-rating" to help analyze the event as it was happening and communicate information back to participants. This system suffered from the inevitable problem of early ideas usually getting the most votes. With the introduction of text mining techniques into the more recent Jam events, every individual participant in the Jam is given the necessary information to "hear" the Jam as a whole.

Stages of Mining the Jam

A Jam is unlike any other *Mining the Talk* engagement because of the nature of the event. Jams take place in a fixed window in time, and the data is constantly changing and evolving during that time period. Normally an analyst would set aside at least a half day to do a complete analysis and report on a significant new data set. In a Jam, a single analyst may have to do multiple analysis across 4–8 forums in the space of four to six hours. Of course, this necessitates doing more automated taxonomy generation and less refinement, and routinizing the entire process as much as possible.

Understanding Business Objectives

Each Jam is not just about having a conversation. The Jam is also focused on achieving a specific organizational objective. Some issue is being discussed around which consensus needs to be built. The objective of Jam mining, therefore, is to capture and communicate the themes and topics of the discussion in order to enable consensus. Understanding specifics of the stakeholder's objectives for the Jam will help the analyst to determine which categories are most important to highlight in refining the taxonomy and generating reports.

Data Feed

Since Jams require *Mining the Talk* in real time, some preparatory work is required to ensure that data from the Jam can be regularly obtained at predefined intervals, without disturbing the underlying Jam infrastructure. Typically, we have obtained incremental data from the Jam on an hourly basis. This data contains not just the text of each post but structured information as well, including the poster's email address, work location, the forum the post was submitted to, and the date/time of the post.

If the Jam takes place in multiple languages, then it is important to segregate the data into those different languages. This can either be done by having each poster self-identify the language of the post, or by using text classification[3] to segregate the posts by the language of its content.

Taxonomy Generation

Taxonomy generation is the key driver of Jam theme reports. Creating categories directly from the information helps to describe exactly what is taking place in the conversation at a meta-level. Over the years, different text-clustering techniques have been employed, and the one that seems to suit Jam Mining the best is the Intuitive clustering algorithm described earlier in Chapter 2, "Mining Customer Interactions." This algorithm identifies specific words and phrases around which topics of conversation appear to center. These categories then become the basis for regular reports that are generated throughout the Jam and after the Jam.

Taxonomies are generated both per forum and overall across the entire Jam. The Intuitive clustering approach easily scales to keep up with Jams (thousands of posts), generating taxonomies in a matter of minutes using ordinary PC hardware.

Taxonomy Refinement

Taxonomy refinement is needed to remove categories that would not contribute to better understanding of the conversation or to the objectives of the discussion. Examples of categories that would not help understanding would be those built around terms that are too generic to be useful, such as "business" or "information." Categories that might not contribute to the objectives of the discussion would be any that center around local issues not germane to the discussion or those that talk about the process of Jamming as opposed to the topic under consideration (e.g., "Hey, jamming is really cool! Let's do these events more often.").

Because the Jam is taking place in real time, there is less time than usual available for detailed taxonomy refinement. In general, it is not necessary at this stage that the taxonomy be perfect. As long as it captures the main topics of the discussion, it serves the purpose. After the Jam is complete, more careful taxonomy refinement can be done to ensure that no useful concepts in the discussion are missed.

Looking for Trends

In addition to taxonomies, term trend analysis is an important tool to identify any emerging topics that may not be captured as categories. Such trends are detected by comparing term occurrence in a recent "slice" of the data to term occurrence in the collection as a whole. Any terms that show significant co-occurrence with the recent time slice are flagged for further investigation by the analyst.

Reporting Back to the Jam

At regular intervals (every 4–6 hours), reports are generated for each forum and for the overall Jam. These reports contain both the overall activity for the forum and also details on any recently occurring themes. The themes (which correspond to categories in the taxonomy) are described by a name (which may be automatically generated from the cluster-naming approach described earlier and which may be edited by the analyst) and by a set of "typical" example posts. The reports contain links that take the reader back into the Jam at the relevant point in the conversation.

Summary Report of the Entire Event

At the end of the Jam, a set of reports are generated that summarize what took place. These contain categories of posts for each forum, along with complete lists of the posts within each category. Such reports provide an invaluable tool for the post-Jam analysis teams to use in coming up with specific action items and recommendations based on the Jam discussion.

Categorization of the posts helps the post-Jam analysis teams to organize the reading of the posts in a logical fashion, so that no one person has to read all of the content for a forum. Automatic ordering of the posts within a category based on the "most typical" measure (described in Chapter 2) helps readers see all posts on a specific topic quickly and summarize each concept without having to worry that they are missing related material that exists elsewhere.

Making Jams a Part of the Business

IBM has been holding at least one corporate-wide Jam a year from 2000–2006. The feedback from these events has been very positive, and the Jams have been a key part of creating a new corporate values statement, making concrete policy changes that implement those values, and targeting new areas for corporate investment. Recently, IBM has begun helping other organizations sponsor their own similar events.

Case Studies

We will focus on two Jam events that took place in August 2003 and December 2005, respectively. ValuesJam was a 72-hour event in 2003 involving IBM employees exploring the company's fundamental business beliefs and values. Habitat Jam, sponsored by the UN Habitat Initiative, the government of Canada, and IBM, was an open discussion on the Internet about the future of cities and finding solutions to critical worldwide urban issues. During this 72-hour event, over 15,000 posts were generated from participants in 120 different countries.

ValuesJam

ValuesJam was a 72-hour global brainstorming event on the corporate intranet, held July 29–August 1, 2003. IBMers described their experiences and contributed ideas via four asynchronous discussion forums. The purpose of *Mining the Talk* for the Jam was to generate forum "topics" that allowed participants to identify themes as they emerged in each forum—and in the Jam overall. Total posts for this event were in excess of 8,000 over the course of the event, with one of the largest forums containing more than 3,000 posts.

Analyzing discussion forum data to produce concepts of interest presents several challenges that an interactive text mining approach is well suited to address. First, the forum analysis must produce categories that are meaningful, and each category must not contain a significant number of extraneous or misclassified examples. Second, each category of posts must be given a concise yet meaningful name. Third, when presenting a category of posts, a set of representative examples are needed to further explain the meaning of the category, and direct the user to the appropriate point in the discussion. Finally, the categories need to evolve with the discussion, adding new categories over time as appropriate to incorporate the new topics that arise, without losing the old categories and thus the overall continuity of the discussion topic list. Clearly a completely automated solution is impractical given these requirements, and a manual approach requiring a set of human editors to read over 8,000 posts in 72 hours and classify them is prohibitively expensive. *Mining the Talk* is thus an ideal candidate for this application. During ValuesJam, different experts in each forum used our tools to develop themes for that forum, and a single primary analyst helped coordinate the analysis as a whole.

Here is a detailed example of how *Mining the Talk* was used to make sense of the conversation in one of these forums and communicate that information back to the dialog (see Figure 4-1). The first taxonomy generated for discussions in the largest forum of ValuesJam was created on 1,308 posts representing 20 hours of discussion.

Taxonomy Level: Root			
	Class Name	Size	Cohesion	Distinctness
1	loyalty	92 (7.03%)	55.95%	93.26%
2	basic beliefs	91 (6.96%)	55.67%	85.50%
3	respect for the individual	98 (7.49%)	49.32%	47.51%
4	values of ibmers	10 (0.76%)	47.48%	73.79%
5	stock price	47 (3.59%)	46.38%	78.87%
6	management	24 (1.83%)	43.59%	72.32%
7	sharing	18 (1.38%)	39.07%	87.45%
8	dealing with change	43 (3.29%)	38.96%	75.96%
9	valuing diversity	32 (2.45%)	38.88%	80.17%
10	question,term	11 (0.84%)	38.69%	79.64%
11	customers	137 (10.47%)	38.30%	63.98%
12	integrity,buy	49 (3.75%)	37.86%	63.98%
13	individual,post	49 (3.75%)	34.67%	47.51%
14	ethic,well,quarter,examples	30 (2.29%)	34.42%	78.28%
15	set,welcome_valuesjam	53 (4.05%)	33.62%	68.24%
16	care,trust	73 (5.58%)	31.46%	71.74%
17	live,exist	59 (4.51%)	31.14%	68.72%
18	year,team	94 (7.19%)	31.09%	69.19%
19	agree,goal,high	38 (2.91%)	30.79%	65.63%
20	believe,day	50 (3.82%)	30.65%	68.72%
21	world,specific,develop,ebu...	49 (3.75%)	30.36%	71.74%
22	comment,treat,family	52 (3.98%)	30.15%	72.49%
23	lead,quality,key	50 (3.82%)	29.93%	76.56%
24	Miscellaneous	59 (4.51%)	19.60%	65.63%
	TOTAL / AVERAGE	1308	38.05%	68.34%

Figure 4-1 Categories sorted by cohesion

We begin by sorting the categories created via text clustering by their cohesion scores. This gives us a useful order in which to tackle the problem of quickly under-standing the taxonomy, category by category, and making necessary adjustments. We view each category in detail, making adjustments and giving the category a new name if appropriate. Occasionally, we find categories that are formed based on words that are not relevant to the content of the post, such as for the "question,term" category in Figure 4-2.

By viewing the secondary classes, we can determine where the examples will go when the centroid for this category is removed (see Figure 4-3).

Seeing that they will distribute themselves evenly throughout the taxonomy, we can feel safe in deleting the centroid without ill effect.

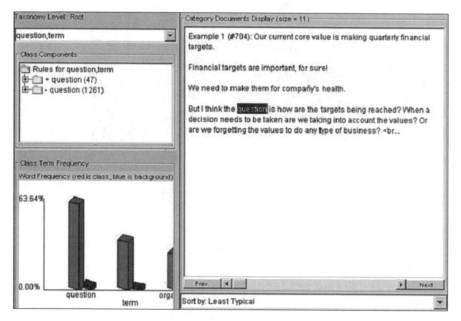

Figure 4-2 Detailed view of "question,term" category

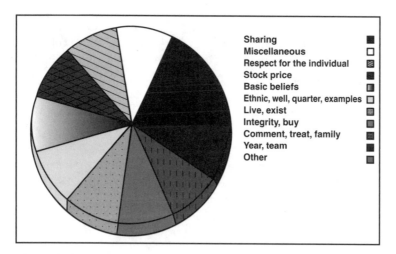

Figure 4-3 Secondary classes for "question,term"

The Miscellaneous category requires special attention. Frequently, individual dictionary terms can be used to extract a common set of examples from a Miscellaneous category and create a separate category. For example, here is a category centered around the word "trust." Clicking on the red "trust" bar in the graph in Figure 4-4 will cause all examples in Miscellaneous that contain the word "trust" to be selected. This subset can form the basis of a new category called "trust."

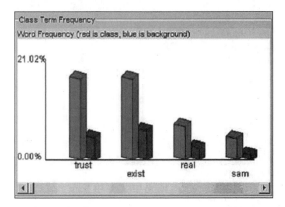

Figure 4-4   Term model for the Miscellaneous category

After a series of such editing decisions are made by the analyst, the resulting categorization emerges (see Figure 4-5).

Taxonomy Level: Root

	Class Name	Size	Cohesion	Distinctness
1	loyalty	93 (7.11%)	55.42%	82.47%
2	basic beliefs	97 (7.42%)	53.78%	65.36%
3	respect for the individual	100 (7.65%)	47.74%	49.61%
4	values of ibmers	20 (1.53%)	37.94%	72.56%
5	stock price	52 (3.98%)	43.70%	76.78%
6	management	48 (3.67%)	31.99%	62.70%
7	sharing	30 (2.29%)	31.49%	64.47%
8	dealing with change	49 (3.75%)	38.09%	76.32%
9	valuing diversity	34 (2.60%)	38.98%	77.77%
10	customers	151 (11.54%)	37.26%	64.09%
11	integrity	49 (3.75%)	40.40%	64.09%
12	individual values	60 (4.59%)	31.79%	49.61%
13	ethics	21 (1.61%)	44.87%	81.11%
14	caring	41 (3.13%)	39.88%	71.57%
15	live your values	42 (3.21%)	36.81%	74.16%
16	historical comments	116 (8.87%)	29.15%	67.79%
17	global values	51 (3.90%)	29.92%	68.53%
18	leadership	34 (2.60%)	39.42%	76.76%
19	Miscellaneous	127 (9.71%)	16.13%	62.70%
20	quality	15 (1.15%)	50.05%	77.80%
21	trust	29 (2.22%)	46.72%	71.44%
22	existing values	34 (2.60%)	34.43%	72.30%
23	measure	7 (0.54%)	48.15%	82.00%
24	behaviour	8 (0.61%)	49.23%	78.67%
	TOTAL / AVERAGE	1308	38.06%	67.37%

Figure 4-5   Edited taxonomy

Using our *Mining the Talk* methodology and supporting technology, this entire process required about a half hour's work by the analyst. Now we can use this information to generate reports to the ValuesJam participants. The resulting web page report is shown in Figure 4-6.

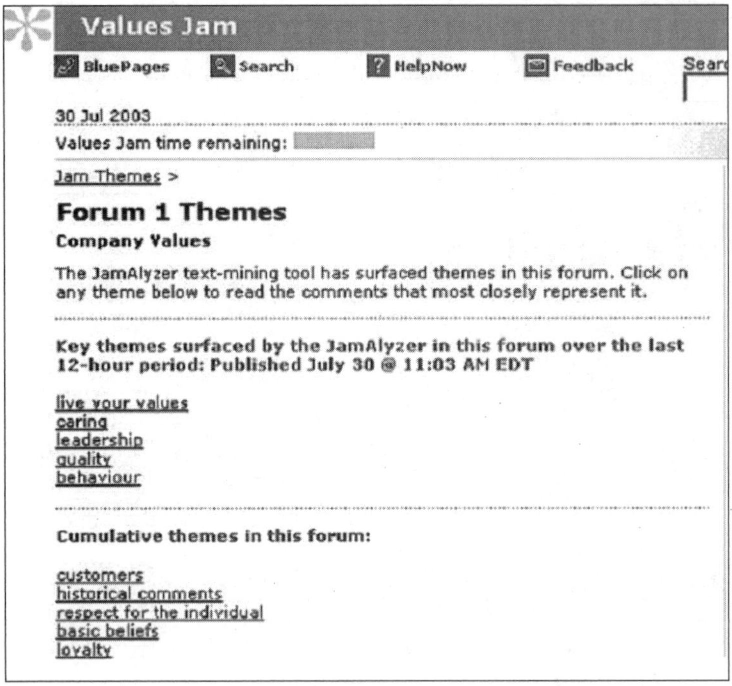

Figure 4-6 Jam themes published to Jammers

Selecting any of the preceding links would take the user to a display of 10 of the "most typical" comments for that theme. This process was then repeated for each of the remaining forums and for the Jam as a whole. The entire reporting operation took about 3–4 hours.

As the Jam progressed, new topics naturally emerged. To identify these, the Trends analysis described in Chapter 6, "Mining to See the Future," was especially valuable. A good example of this came late in the Jam when a breaking news story about a court case relating to IBM pensions had an impact on the discussion.[4]

We observe that the word "pension" occurred 51 times overall, and 11 times in the last 10% of the data. A Chi-Squared test indicates a low probability of this event ($P=0.0056$). A view of the trend line for this keyword shows the spike (see Figure 4-7).

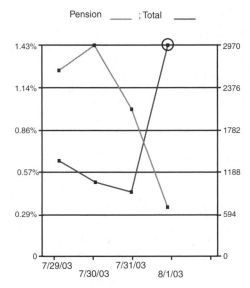

Figure 4-7 Pension issue over time

Mentions of "pension" had been decreasing as a percentage of the total posts, but on the last day there was a sharp increase. Looking at the text for these examples quickly revealed the cause, and thus a new category was created centered around this word and the examples that used the word in a context related to the news event.

Our approach showed itself to be very capable of supporting real-time analysis of a discussion among thousands of users. A survey including 1248 respondents done after ValuesJam indicated that 42% of participants used the theme pages to enter the Jam. Those who used this feature found it to be both important and satisfactory (72% important, 61% satisfactory "top two box" scores). Only 10% of those who used the feature were dissatisfied.

The final result of ValuesJam was a new values statement for IBM based on the employee comments and subsequent analysis and rewording by executives. Here is the values statement for IBM that resulted from this event:

Dedication to every client's success.
Innovation that matters—for our company and for the world.
Trust and personal responsibility in all relationships.

You can see categories from the taxonomy in Figure 4-5 that contributed to each of these values. The "customers" category had many examples that talked about the importance of customer focus to IBM's values. For example:

> *"Our Business Is Your Success"*
> *If we have a maniacal focus on our customers and their success and LIVE this principle, we will not only attract strong customer loyalty and high customer satisfaction, but gain significant marketshare and respect in the industry WAY BEYOND technology leadership. Our customers buy products and services from us to solve business problems...they are trying to be successful in their business endeavor. If we are committed to and make them succeed at that goal, then we have succeeded. This, in turn, will lead to repeat business and will foster stronger referenceability in the industry.*
> *This can't be talk, however; it needs to be action and a very deep desire to do what is right for the customer during their time of need. We have to be smart about how we act, but if we act with the customer's interest at heart, we will not only gain their business, but their trust. Once you've gained a customer's trust long-term, the rest is easy...but you've got to *live it* every day!*

The "trust" category and the "ethics" category were reflected in the values statement as well, including this comment:

> *Trust & Integrity—I believe that fundamental to a lot of IBM's practices today is the trust and integrity that IBMers share. In a workplace as large, diverse, and globally present as IBM, the ability to maintain trust and integrity will continue to help IBM stay ahead of others. Everything we value and believe in would have little significance without the trust and integrity expected of each one of us in this workplace.*

Finally, the "leadership" and "dealing with change" categories spoke to the area of innovation. Here is a sample comment in this space.

> *Draft values—relative to excellence through innovation—I like the first draft list of commitment to the customer, integrity that earns trust—I think these both are key. I think a nuance that's missing from excellence through innovation is the notion of value of innovation for customers and society... "Innovation that makes the world a better place." We're lucky enough to work for a company that can make a difference for mankind—I value that every day I come to work.*

So ultimately, categories generated using our techniques led directly to IBM's current values statement. We take great pride that *Mining the Talk* played an important role in creating the values code that has become an integral part of IBM's DNA.

Habitat Jam

In Habitat Jam, we exposed the Jam technical infrastructure to a non-IBM audience for the first time. The purpose of the Jam was to identify topics for discussion at an upcoming World Urban Forum. Habitat Jam was a 72-hour event that included participation from 120 countries. Posts were submitted in both French and English across seven forums. During the event, text analysis was done three times a day for each of the seven forums and three times a day for the Jam as a whole. The English forums were all done by a single analyst using the intuitive clustering techniques described in Chapter 2. Despite the fact that nearly twice as many themes were generated in the same time period for this Jam as for ValuesJam, the post-event survey indicates the quality (as measured by importance and satisfaction scores) did not degrade. We attribute this partly to the use of intuitive clustering to generate the themes. A post-event survey was conducted following the Jam (n=1374 respondents). The results shown in Figure 4-8 indicate that the Jam theme was both the most important and the most satisfactory discovery tool available during the event.

(RANDOMIZED LIST) *Values in Cells Are Means*	FREQUENCY OF USE 3 = Used often (TOP) 2 = Used a few times 1 = Used once 0 = Did not use	IMPORTANCE 5 = Very important (TOP) 4 = Somewhat important 3 = Neither important nor unimportant 2 = Somewhat unimportant 1 = Very unimportant	SATISFACTION 5 = Very satisfied (TOP) 4 = Somewhat satisfied 3 = Neither satisfied nor dissatisfied 2 = Somewhat dissatisfied 1 = Very dissatisfied
a- Habitat Jam search tool - The search utility on the site.	1.6	4.1	3.4
b- Jam Alert - Notices posted on the Jam home page and forum pages; usually news or featured links.	1.0	3.4	3.3
c- Jam Themes - pages open the Jam site where central themes are displayed overall and by forum.	**2.1**	**4.2**	**3.8**
d- "Web Mail" - the ability to send or receive Jam posts as e-mail to or from other participants.	0.6	3.4	3.0

Figure 4-8   Post-Jam survey results

The user feedback scores from these and other Jams, with different audiences and topic areas, all show that Jam themes generated by *Mining the Talk* are the most frequently used tool for navigation and discovery—even more so than text search. The overall satisfaction was also higher for Jam themes than for any other Jam tool. Although there is still room for improvement, these results indicate that our *Mining the Talk* approach gave significant value to discussion participants. It has also been used heavily for post-Jam analysis to study what exactly was said and to help summarize the results for organizations to use in building consensus and communicating direction.

The result of this Jam was an agenda that focused the conference on the ideas, interests, and needs of the participants. Here is a quote from the World Urban Forum website posted in April 2006, just prior to the conference:

> *Over three days, from December 1–3, tens of thousands of people got online to discuss issues of urban sustainability. People from 191 countries registered for the Jam and shared their ideas for action to improve the lives of people living in slums, to improve the environment in cities, address issues of finance and security, governance, and the future of our cities.*
>
> *The Jam was extraordinary because it was global and reached out to people who wouldn't otherwise be able to participate in the World Urban Forum next June. It was also extraordinary because we heard from people who don't often have a voice, especially women and youth in developing countries. Thousands of women in India participated in the Jam through moderators who went out into communities to seek their views. In the Philippines, women who had never before seen a computer were provided training and a Yahoo account so that they could participate. In Kenya, people lined up for hours to have access to computers so that they could have their say. An extraordinary number of people participated who are blind and deaf thanks to technology that made accessibility a priority.*
>
> *The results of the discussion from the Jam will be part of a lasting legacy as the content is analyzed and included into the World Urban Forum agenda. Habitat JAM is an example of how we can combine innovation with our values of social inclusion and equality. As one of the Jammers said, "technology can be a powerful tool of communication and inclusion."*

My own personal experience in mining the Habitat Jam data as it came in was one of profound wonder and excitement. The fact that an electronic discussion facilitation and analysis process worked well for a company of computer geeks, like IBM, was absolutely no guarantee that it would work at all for participants in the developing world. In fact, the same phenomenon occurred in Habitat Jam that we saw occur in all of the IBM Jams. People immediately took to the idea of being able to share ideas across time zone, cultural, and geographic boundaries, and in every case, they found the *Mining the Talk* results to be by and large a valuable part of that experience. The success of this event and the role our approach played in that success were a significant factor in our decision to write this book.

The Future of Jamming and *Mining the Talk*

The process of Jamming and the use of our approach to facilitate online discussion are still in their infancy. Each Jam we do at IBM is a new experience in which we learn more about how *Mining the Talk* can be used to facilitate online discussion. Some of the techniques that we have begun to experiment with in this space are near neighbors, sentiment analysis, and visualizations.

Near Neighbors

One of the things Jammers and those who analyze data from Jams often want to do is find related ideas to a given post. Using the cosine distance metric to measure similarity between different posts, we can display the most related posts for any selected post. In the future, we might even be able to design the Jam application to take advantage of this feature by observing the post as the user types it in and moving to the appropriate context in the Jam to receive that comment. Another application for this functionality might be to suggest "birds-of-a-feather" sessions or "Mini-Jams" between participants who have similar interests.

Sentiment Analysis

In addition to topical themes, it would be useful to detect emotions or opinions in the Jam data and report on the findings. Annotators can be created to detect features such as the following:

- Agreement or disagreement
- Positive opinions ("good idea," "cool")
- Negative opinions ("I hate that," "we don't do that very well")
- Feasibility assessments ("that's impossible," "no way")
- Frustration or anger
- Enthusiasm or encouragement

These features can in turn be used to look for correlations between sentiments and themes to draw some conclusions about overall rating of ideas, or to locate particularly "hot topics" of discussion.

Visualizations

In some Jams, we have tried making scatter plots and other forms of text visualization available to the Jam participants as the Jam is taking place. These have been mostly well received by participants, but performance and scalability for these heavily trafficked events have been a problem. We will continue to work on ways to help participants better "see" what is going on in the complex, multi-threaded discussion.

Summary

We have demonstrated the value of using text mining techniques to facilitate and enhance large-scale electronic dialogs. It is interesting to observe that while the computer does not take part directly in the discussion in the same way as a human participant, it is still playing (in conjunction with the human analyst) a critical role in generating content that furthers the discussion. In fact, the computer is playing a role in the Jam conversation that might be played by a human being in a much smaller conversation—the role of facilitator and moderator—helping to ensure that all points of view are heard and taken into account by all participants.

The planned future direction of our work is to continue to minimize the amount of human analyst effort required. This will require more precise text category naming strategies, as well as intelligent pruning techniques for removing categories that are not meaningful or helpful in summarizing a topic area. Perhaps the conversation participants themselves might be enlisted to provide feedback on categories that might be used to adjust the text categorization algorithms. Social bookmarking[5] information could be integrated into the taxonomy as well.

Inevitably, computers are becoming a greater and greater participant in our conversations. Through *Mining the Talk*, they can tell us things that humans would find difficult or even impossible to discover on their own about just what is being said. We hope the reader will take away from this chapter a sense of what Mining the Voice of the Employee enables in terms of meeting the challenges of large-scale organizational communication.

Endnotes

1. Watson, Thomas J. Jr., and Peter Petre. 2000. *Father, Son & Co: My Life at IBM and Beyond*. New York: Bantam.

2. P. Hemp and T. A. Stewart. "Leading Change When Business is Good." *Harvard Business Review*, December 2004, pp. 60–70.

   K. Dave, M. Wattenberg, and M. Muller. "Flash Forums and ForumReader: Navigating a New Kind of Large-scale Online Discussion." CSCW'04, Vol. 6, Issue 3, November 6–10, 2004, Chicago, IL, pp. 232–241.

   Spangler, S. and Kreulen, J. (2005). "Interactive Methods of Taxonomy Editing and Validation." In Kantardzic, M. and Zurada, J., editors. *Next Generation of Data Mining Applications*. Pages 495–524. Piscataway, NJ: IEEE Press.

3. Johnson, D. E., Oles, F. J., Zhang, T., and Goetz, T. (2002). "A decision-tree-based symbolic rule induction system for text categorization." *IBM Systems Journal*, 41:3, pp. 428–437.

   McCallum, Andrew and Nigam, Kamal. *A Comparison of Event Models for Naïve Bayes Text Classification*, AAAI-98.

4. Walsh, M. W. "Judge Says IBM Pension Shift Illegally Harmed Older Workers." *New York Times*, August 1, 2003. http://query.nytimes.com/gst/abstract.html?res= F00B14F73E5A0C728CDDA10894DB404482.

5. Social bookmarking is a process that allows users to store lists of interesting sites and share those lists with the community at large. See Wikipedia, "Social Bookmarking," at http://en.wikipedia.org/wiki/Social_bookmarking.

5

Mining to Improve Innovation

At first glance, it might not seem like *Mining the Talk* has much to do with business innovation. We usually think of innovation as springing spontaneously from a brilliant idea coming from an individual. Although this is often the case, innovation also comes from collaboration. More and more companies are finding that to innovate effectively, they need to partner with other organizations that have enabling technology.[1] Furthermore, even when innovations happen internally, bringing them to market often requires a detailed assessment of existing intellectual property space, research consensus surrounding related technology, and consumer receptiveness to the novel approach. *Mining the Talk* can help summarize all the information relevant to a new product introduction, enabling the business to make informed decisions about when a given innovation is "market ready."

Up to this point, we have focused on mining informal communications. Primarily, these have been more or less conversational in tone, similar to the ordinary give and take of everyday speech. Now we embark on more formal territory. In this section, we describe methods for mining technical descriptions or research articles in a very specific subject area. This type of "talk" is more like a lecture than a dialogue. Even though far more detailed and precise than the more informal documents we dealt with earlier, the documents in this section are still reasonably short and speak about one topic only. So, many of the same methods we used before will still apply here. Plus, we will add a few others that make sense in order to get the maximum value out of this very rich form of data.

Business Drivers of Innovation Mining

There is no single business driver of Innovation Mining that applies to all companies. Each company's innovation strategy is somewhat unique. Here are a few of the business drivers of Innovation Mining that we have come across:

- Having a set of research innovations that are "sitting on the shelf" because they lack a partner with the requisite enabling infrastructure that would allow them to succeed.

- The need for strategic market intelligence related to the technology landscape in order to look for possible "white space" where new innovation may succeed.

- Wanting to understand whether a given "new" technology is actually new or whether something similar has been done in the past by other businesses or research entities.

- Needing better sources of competitive intelligence—the desire to understand and counteract your competitors' innovation strategy.

- Locating who the experts are in a particular subject area, either within your own company or within the technical community at large.

These are just a few examples of how businesses can use readily available information to help enhance innovation, if only they can *Mine the Talk*.

Characteristics of Innovation Information

As was mentioned before, innovation information is not exactly like customer interaction or VoC information. These documents are more formal in nature—much more like a lecture than a conversation. Repositories of patents and research articles are publicly available data sources that can be mined for surprisingly detailed and comprehensive information on a wide array of technical subjects. To understand the process for mining such data, one must first understand how it is structured. We will begin with patents, such as those applied for and granted by the United States Patent & Trademark Office (USPTO).

A patent for an invention is the grant of a property right to the inventor, issued by the Patent and Trademark Office. The term of a new patent is 20 years from the date on which the application for the patent was filed in the United States or, in special cases, from the date an earlier related application was filed, subject to the payment of maintenance fees. U.S. patent grants are effective only within the U.S., U.S. territories, and U.S. possessions.

The right conferred by the patent grant is, in the language of the statute and of the grant itself, "the right to exclude others from making, using, offering for sale, or selling" the invention in the United States or "importing" the invention into the United States. What is granted is not the right to make, use, offer for sale, sell, or import, but the right to exclude others from making, using, offering for sale, selling, or importing the invention.[2]

Patents are focused documents that talk in detail about one specific idea. They are a special kind of "talk" that is designed to describe a particular invention for the purpose of claiming exclusive rights to the invention. By law, the description must be complete enough that anyone "skilled in the art" of the technical subject area of the invention could reproduce the invention from the text and drawings in the patent.

A patent document has a somewhat structured format. Each patent document contains the same set of sections. These are as follows:

1. **Title**—The title of the patent.
2. **Abstract**—A concise statement of the technical disclosure including that which is new in the art to which the invention pertains.
3. **Claims**—Define the invention and what aspects are legally enforceable. The specification must conclude with a claim particularly pointing out and distinctly claiming the subject matter that the applicant regards as his invention or discovery. The claim or claims must conform to the invention as set forth in the remainder of the specification, and the terms and phrases used in the claims must find clear support or antecedent basis in the description so that the meaning of the terms in the claims may be ascertainable by reference to the description. (See 37 CFR § 1.58(a).)
4. **Body**—The main section of the patent that describes the invention in detail along with any examples and figures.
5. **References**—Also known as prior art. Contains pointers to previous patents or publications that are related to the invention.

In addition, each patent has certain values associated with it:

1. **Assignee(s)**—The owner of the patent.
2. **Inventor(s)**—One who contributes to the conception of an invention. The patent law of the United States of America requires that the applicant in a patent application must be the inventor.

3. **Main Class**—Patents are classified in the U.S. by a system using a three-digit class and a three-digit subclass to describe every similar grouping of patent art. A single invention may be described by multiple classification codes. The first three-digit class is also called the Main Class.

4. **Subclass**—The second three digits in the classification.

5. **Filed Date**—The date the application was received by the patent office.

6. **Publish Date**—The subsequent date on which the patent office published the patent application.

7. **Grant Date**—The date the patent was granted by the patent office.[3]

Since 1977, over four million patents and applications have been published in electronic format. An electronic copy of this data can be purchased from the U.S. Patent Office. For companies who are serious about Innovation Mining, this is a worthwhile investment.

Research articles, such as those found in Medline,[4] are structured in a similar fashion to patents, containing information such as publication date, title, abstract, authors, and references. Less formal data, such as that found more generally on the Web, may also be of use to gain insight as to public receptiveness or market readiness for a potential new product or service.

What Can Innovation Mining Teach Us?

Mining the Talk for Innovation is all about discovering hidden business relationships. For large organizations, these hidden relationships might easily exist internally, but every organization may have hidden external relationships whose potential is just waiting to be revealed. *Mining the Talk* for Innovation is also about how your company's innovation fits into the overall business ecosystem. What are the roadblocks, such as patents or other research, which might pre-date yours and be considered equal or superior? How receptive is the market likely to be to your innovation?

Getting a clear picture of how your company and its products fit into the business landscape is the primary driver of Innovation Mining. One way to do this is by taking the documents that describe the company's products or inventions and comparing them to similar documents from related companies or organizations. Using *Mining the Talk* techniques, we can leverage text models generated for our company and the other business entities to locate interesting areas of overlap or similarity. These in turn may lead to knowledge or insight about the business that result in pursuit of some new product, research direction, or joint venture.

The Innovation Mining Process

The Innovation Mining process expands upon the framework we've already described to leverage unstructured information in the organization. The taxonomy creation and editing steps remain much the same, but more work is done both before the taxonomy is initially created and after editing of the taxonomy is complete. This is due to the fact that the data sets we are looking at are more extensive and generally more complex, and also because more detailed kinds of analysis are needed to discover all the potential hidden relationships that might exist between our company and other business entities. We therefore require a further refinement of our *Mining the Talk* methodology that we refer to as Explore, Understand, and Analyze. This is a process that utilizes the power of both SQL query to database and indexed search via a search engine in order to locate potential data of interest. That's the Explore. It then pulls the unstructured text content for the matching records into a taxonomy in order to allow the user to make sense out of what was found. The user looks at the categories and adjusts them using the methods we have outlined previously for visualizing and editing taxonomies. That's the Understand. Finally, the taxonomy is compared to other structured fields in the database using co-occurrence table analysis and trend analysis. That's the Analyze. Put it together, and you have a powerful method for discovering useful insights from patents, or any other data that is relevant to innovation (see Figure 5-1).

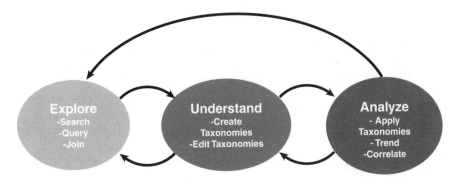

Figure 5-1   The Explore, Understand, Analyze process

Understanding of Business Objectives and Hidden Business Concerns

Understanding objectives is always the key first step in any *Mining the Talk* endeavor, and never more so than in Innovation Mining. Many factors come into play when considering possible business partnering relationships. There are usually historical issues such as previous agreements (or disagreements) between the companies. Then there are issues around the competitive landscape. For example, it may not make sense to partner with a company if this might raise anti-trust concerns. Companies, which analysis says may be perfectly good partnership candidates, may not actually be possible partners for reasons that are extraneous to the data. Furthermore, the available information is not always what it seems on the surface. Patents that were originally assigned to one company are later sold or licensed to others, and the publicly available information does not always reflect this. Some patents or technologies may be off limits for other internal strategic reasons. All of this information may be closely guarded and difficult to come by. Finding out as much as you can about the technology licensing environment as early as you can will save much wasted effort down the road.

Demonstration of Capabilities

One of the wonderful properties about the innovation information we discuss in this chapter is that it is both public and very strategic. This means that for almost any company with a significant history and technical track record, we can use *Mining the Talk* principles to quickly generate a taxonomy of their patent portfolio and compare this taxonomy across the landscape of their competition. One example of such a landscape would be a taxonomy of patents drawn from a selected industry with a structured co-occurrence table built from the assignee information from each patent. In almost every case, I have found the results of this analysis to communicate something important to the primary stakeholders about their business—often something they either did not know, or something they thought that only they could know. Although this survey type analysis may not lead immediately to business impact, it does serve to make the stakeholders aware of the power of the technology when applied to this data, and gets them thinking about other applications in this space. Other analyses that can be done from such a collection include recent trends (what technologies are emerging in the industry) and white space analysis (what technical areas are not being concentrated on by any of the major players). Such a demonstration helps generate specific ideas around how Innovation Mining can be used most effectively to suit a given organization's business objectives.

Survey of Available Data

Aside from patent data, there are other public sources of information that are useful to mine for innovation. In health care and life sciences, there is the Medline database of research abstracts. This can provide a wealth of information on the latest studies and results in medicine and human health. Other databases of research publications are available from various research and technical associations such as the ACM or IEEE. In addition, many companies have internal databases related to invention disclosures, trade secrets, and research publications.

Data Cleansing and the ETL Process

Because of the amount of data involved and the complexity of the content, the ETL process for building a data warehouse for Innovation Mining is a serious endeavor. Documenting all the details of the best practices for achieving clean data in this area could be the subject of another book, but suffice it to say that the data cleansing effort required for the U.S. patent corpus alone can be quite extensive. As an example, the assignee field for this data contains many inconsistencies and changes over time. In the long run, such problems need to be addressed. In the short term, the information can be put into a data warehouse in rough form and then refined gradually as time goes on, while still using it to generate value prior to achieving the desired state of cleanliness.

Explore—Selecting the Collection

Explore is the first stage of the Innovation Mining process. Its purpose is to locate the specific documents that are relevant to a given *Mining the Talk* exercise. In previous chapters of this book, the Explore was essentially ignored because it was fairly obvious. For example, in the case of mining customer interactions, the Explore phase would have encompassed the extraction of all customer interactions for a given product over a given time period. For Voice of the Customer Mining, the Explore phase would have corresponded to finding all customer comments around a specific brand or company name. In both of these cases, the selection of what information to mine is readily apparent.

The Innovation Mining Explore process may be much more involved. It makes use of multiple database queries and/or text index searches in combination. The problem is to identify documents that are both on topic and in the correct context. By on topic, we mean that they are relevant to the subject area under consideration (for example, we don't want railroad patents getting mixed in with our *train*ing methodology analysis). By correct context, we mean assigned to our company and also not expired, as an example.

The basic operation of the Explore process is a *search* or *query*. A search is a keyword string that matches some word or phrase in the text of the document collection. All matching articles are returned and put in a result *collection*. A query is a database operation that returns all articles that match the value of a structured field. These are also returned and put in collections. These collections can then be further refined using additional queries or searches. Multiple collections can be merged by intersection or join operations to create additional collections. The final result is a single collection of documents whose unstructured information can be extracted and analyzed during the Understand phase.

Understand

The purpose for creating and refining the taxonomy in Innovation Mining is the same as in the other *Mining the Talk* applications—to create categories that mirror the underlying business purpose of the analysis. However, since innovation is very much a discovery oriented process, taxonomy refinement may not require much category editing at all. It is only important that each category in the taxonomy be an actual meaningful concept that can be understood and will be useful during analysis.

The knowledge gained in this phase may lead to the conclusion that some data is extraneous or that other data is missing from the collection created during the Explore phase. Any categories that are discovered during the Understand phase that are irrelevant to the subject of interest may be eliminated by removing the data corresponding to those categories from the taxonomy object. Additional data may need to be added if it turns out that while looking at categories, a possible new keyword query is discovered that might add significant relevant material.

This return to the Explore phase may be an iteration that is repeated several times.

Analyze

The Analysis phase is a search for relevant trends and correlations between the taxonomy in comparison with structured information (or other taxonomies). In addition to looking for correlations between categories in a taxonomy and structured field values such as *assignee*, we would also look for correlations between structured field values and specific words or phrases in the unstructured text. This finer-grained analysis technique can detect specific concepts that are not frequent enough to be categories on their own. Correlating dictionary terms over time can lead to discovery of emerging technologies in a given industry. This in turn may lead to new categories being created in the taxonomy (returning to the Understand phase).

As in other types of *Mining the Talk*, any correlations or trends that are discovered must be illustrated with typical examples from the document collection, in order to discern and verify the underlying cause of the co-occurrence.

Presenting Results to Stakeholders

Results for Innovation Mining consist of reports showing the company's position in the technology landscape. This includes high-level summaries showing counts of patents or research papers in a given field in comparison to other companies, with these counts broken down by key technologies. Beyond such high-level statistics, summaries of the most interesting patents or research documents in specific areas of interest should be shown, with the most relevant language from the document highlighted. In the case of research articles, an aggregate summary of research conclusions in a given area may be sufficient. In the case of patents, specific patents and even specific claims within patents may need to be specified. The key in every presentation is to go as deep as necessary in bringing out the relevant data to validate your conclusions.

Making Innovation Mining an Ongoing Concern

The ongoing analysis of innovation information is the key to realizing the full innovation potential of the organization. We have developed the following process flow to illustrate roughly how Innovation Mining should be done across many different data sources and combined to produce a focused analysis to take to potential innovation partners (see Figure 5-2).

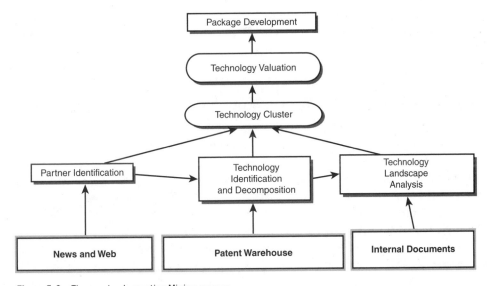

Figure 5-2 The ongoing Innovation Mining process

In this ongoing process, data is analyzed as it emerges from news articles and newly released research on the Web. When significant new approaches or events happen that are flagged to be of interest (such as a hot new technology or a dispute over technology ownership issues in a field related to the business), then a technology decomposition and identification process takes place that mines the patent literature to find documents that are related to the technology in question. This might include both patents and pre-granted patent applications. Internal research documents and invention disclosures within the company are then mined in combination with patents from other companies to fill out the technology landscape picture. All of these inputs are then combined into a cluster of patents and/or technologies whose individual value is then assessed, based on factors such as patent citation, internal rankings, estimates of discoverability, and typical licensing value for technologies in this area. Finally, a formal package is put together for presentation to the potential technology partner to make the case for a joint venture or licensing agreement of some kind.

To do such Innovation Mining on an ongoing basis requires, first of all, continuous updating of public data sources, such as U.S. patents or Medline research articles. The fees, infrastructure, and overhead required for such ETL processes are not negligible, so the organization will need to consider whether there is enough justification from the potential benefits to incur this ongoing cost. Vendors who supply this information for a reasonable fee may be the answer.

Beyond the data issues, the issue of becoming an ongoing part of the organization's innovation process is important. Innovation Mining needs to be inserted as a regular part of the invention disclosure and evaluation process (i.e., the process in each company for writing and submitting patents). In addition, patent licensing or technology partnership groups in the organization should leverage Innovation Mining analytics whenever such arrangements are under consideration.

The Innovation Mining Process in Action: Finding the Most Relevant Patents in a Large Portfolio

The best way to make the Innovation Mining process clear is with a specific example using patents. In this fictional scenario,[5] we show how to compare two patent portfolios. Imagine that IBM wants to see what intellectual property it owns that might be potentially useful to companies in unrelated industries. One example of such an industry would be medical equipment suppliers. So we begin by finding a significant set of patents related to medical equipment. This can be done with search queries, but the danger of this approach is that we might miss significant areas of the space, by not knowing exactly what terms to query with. A better way is to pick one or more major companies in the industry and retrieve all of their patents. This should provide us with a good cross-section of patents in the industry.

We use structured queries and unstructured searches against the text abstract field and the major class code field in the patent data warehouse to create a collection that is generally relevant to the medical equipment subject area. We then look at the assignee field counts for the patents in this collection to find a single company that is broadly representative of this area. Finally, we use a structured query against this assignee name (and its variations) to find all the patents owned by this company. This resulting collection is 1,942 patents in size.

This gives us a starting place to begin mapping out the medical equipment technology space. In some cases, we might wish to refine this collection further by looking at the patent grant date and removing older patents from consideration, but for now let's simply assume we are finished *exploring*. Next, we move on to the Understand phase.

Creating a Taxonomy

We use text clustering to create a taxonomy of patents. In this case, we use k-means clustering. Intuitive clustering also works, but has fewer advantages over k-means in the patent space. One reason is that patents are longer documents that contain more words, with each word generally occurring in more examples, and multiple times in each example. This makes the cohesion metric somewhat less powerful.[6]

The text we use as input for clustering is usually a concatenation of title, abstract, and claims. These fields give us the primary gist of the patent, without adding potentially extraneous detail that is prior art or background information. It is important to include the claims, because they are the legal definition of the patent, whereas the title and abstract may not necessarily contain all the important key elements.

The taxonomy we create for the medical equipment supplier is to help us to model their IP space to find patents in IBM's portfolio that might be relevant to the medical equipment supplier's business (see Figure 5-3).

	Cluster Name	Size
1	tube	74
2	acid,compounds	48
3	filter	44
4	wall	66
5	contained	105
6	base,formed	36
7	membrane	48
8	valve	72
9	extending	56
10	positioned,formed	41
11	tubing	82
12	extending,port	47
13	solution	92
14	hemoglobin	36
15	assembly,adjacent	75
16	composition	82
17	cells,circuit	37
18	light,control	37
19	locate,axis	43
20	signal & output	68
21	binding,molecular	29
22	material	82
23	patient	44
24	catheter & distal	94
25	fluid & flow	200
26	blood	211
27	chamber	142

Figure 5-3   Initial medical equipment supplier taxonomy

Editing the Taxonomy

The purpose of editing is to better understand what technologies make up the medical equipment supplier's portfolio and to make sure that text clustering has done a reasonable job in creating meaningful categories that will help us to define the medical equipment supplier's business. It is not necessary to have deep expertise in the domain in order to rename categories or make other adjustments that help to make the categories more meaningful.

In the editing process, we view each of the categories in order of decreasing cohesion, renaming them as we go to names that make more sense. For instance, the category in Figure 5-4, originally named "extending,port," we rename to "sealing and closures," based upon looking at most typical patents in the category and also at summary term statistics for the category.

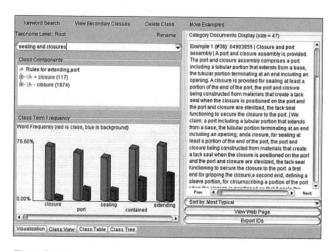

Figure 5-4 Renaming a category

When we discover that two categories are similar, we merge them into one. Similar categories can be found by sorting on the Distinctness metric. In the example shown in Figure 5-5, we can see that the "chamber" and "fluid & flow" categories are the least distinct. They have the same distinctness score because distinctness is based on distance to nearest category, and these two must be nearest to each other.

Some classes may be deleted if they have no clear theme. The "contained" class in this taxonomy is one example. Before deleting, we check to be sure the documents in the category will be sent to the correct location. The chart in Figure 5-6 indicates the percentage of documents that will be sent to each of the other remaining classes. Each slice of the pie chart is selectable, and we can look at a display of typical patents that represent that slice to determine its content. This helps the analyst to verify that the results of the class deletion will be reasonable.

Taxonomy Level: Root

Class Name	Size	Cohesion	Distinctness ▽
15 chamber	142 (7.13%)	47.00%	46.49%
18 fluid & flow	200 (10.05%)	42.73%	46.49%
8 contained	105 (5.27%)	50.24%	47.87%
23 wall	66 (3.31%)	40.70%	47.87%
6 sealing and closures	47 (2.36%)	51.10%	51.94%
13 valve	72 (3.62%)	49.03%	53.72%
19 base,formed	36 (1.81%)	42.61%	54.59%
26 assembly,adjacent	75 (3.77%)	36.57%	54.59%
12 extending	56 (2.81%)	49.16%	58.00%
5 blood	211 (10.60%)	51.39%	58.43%
4 tubing	82 (4.12%)	51.90%	59.69%
20 locate,axis	43 (2.16%)	42.46%	61.12%
11 tube	74 (3.72%)	49.25%	61.58%
10 membrane	48 (2.41%)	49.50%	61.75%
27 positioned,formed	41 (2.06%)	36.29%	61.90%
2 filter	44 (2.21%)	62.26%	62.89%
24 patient	44 (2.21%)	40.10%	63.98%
14 signal & output	68 (3.42%)	47.89%	64.63%
16 light,control	37 (1.86%)	44.69%	64.63%
22 cells,circuit	37 (1.86%)	41.62%	64.83%
17 material	82 (4.12%)	44.04%	66.48%
21 binding,molecular	29 (1.46%)	42.11%	67.26%
25 acid,compounds	48 (2.41%)	38.71%	67.26%
7 solution	92 (4.62%)	50.49%	68.66%
9 composition	82 (4.12%)	49.96%	69.82%
3 catheter	94 (4.72%)	52.51%	69.93%

Visualization | Class View | Class Table | Class Tree

Figure 5-5 Merging classes based on distinctness

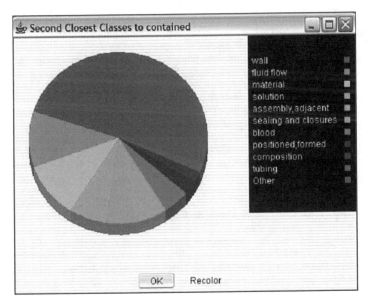

Figure 5-6 Secondary classes for "contained"

The resulting taxonomy after editing looks like the one in Figure 5-7.

	Class Name	Size	Cohesion	Distinctness
1	hemoglobin	36 (1.81%)	66.88%	83.39%
2	filter	45 (2.26%)	62.01%	58.58%
3	catheter	97 (4.87%)	51.63%	69.23%
4	tubing	86 (4.32%)	50.79%	59.30%
5	blood	217 (10.90%)	50.85%	58.46%
6	sealing and closures	53 (2.66%)	50.11%	44.18%
7	solution	99 (4.97%)	49.78%	69.37%
8	composition	84 (4.22%)	49.32%	69.82%
9	membrane	49 (2.46%)	48.95%	59.70%
10	tube	77 (3.87%)	48.32%	59.44%
11	injection	62 (3.11%)	47.33%	57.03%
12	valve	82 (4.12%)	46.39%	51.74%
13	signal detection	68 (3.42%)	47.89%	64.06%
14	optical detectors	40 (2.01%)	43.90%	85.11%
15	plastic films	93 (4.67%)	42.90%	62.82%
16	web films	56 (2.81%)	38.64%	63.24%
17	protein binding	29 (1.46%)	42.11%	67.26%
18	cells	38 (1.91%)	41.28%	64.06%
19	containers	132 (6.63%)	39.08%	44.18%
20	patient monitoring	19 (0.95%)	44.40%	48.61%
21	acid compounds	48 (2.41%)	38.71%	67.26%
22	fluid flow	357 (17.93%)	38.77%	50.87%
23	centrifuges	22 (1.10%)	55.90%	67.21%
24	pump	26 (1.31%)	46.45%	48.61%
25	Miscellaneous	76 (3.82%)	31.48%	51.19%
	TOTAL / AVERAGE	1991	45.55%	58.22%

Figure 5-7   Fully edited taxonomy

This completes the Understand phase.

Applying the Medical Equipment Supplier Taxonomy to IBM's Portfolio

Now that we "understand" what it means to be a medical equipment patent, we can use that understanding to find similar patents in IBM's portfolio. This is a really powerful idea. The concept is to use the category models we have generated for the medical equipment supplier portfolio and apply these to a different set of data: the IBM portfolio. We use a centroid classification model[7] for the taxonomy to classify each IBM patent into the "nearest" medical equipment supplier category. The cosine similarity metric is used to measure the distance between every IBM patent and every medical equipment supplier centroid (having first converted each IBM patent to the feature space of the medical equipment supplier centroids). Then each IBM patent is classified into the category of the closest medical equipment supplier centroid. Figure 5-8 shows the result of this classification process.

Notice that there are over 40,000 patents and applications in the IBM portfolio. This is far more than we could comb through individually to find patents of interest to the medical equipment supplier (even using search, how would we know which terms to search for?). Of course, this results in far more patents in each category that actually should exist. The classification model is only as good as the training set used to create it, and since the domain of IBM's patents is, for the most part, far different than the field of the medical equipment supplier's patents, it is no surprise that many of IBM's patents fall into categories they should not. However, it is also true that if we look in each category and view those patents that are "nearest" to each of the medical equipment supplier centroids, we should find those patents that are "most similar" to the medical equipment supplier's, and thus the ones that are most relevant.

Taxonomy Level: Root			
Class Name	Size	Cohesion	Distinctness
1 plastic films	6738 (16.33%)	36.18%	82.62%
2 solution	333 (0.81%)	34.49%	69.37%
3 tube	105 (0.25%)	32.82%	59.44%
4 signal detection	11851 (28.72%)	32.30%	64.06%
5 composition	681 (1.65%)	31.69%	69.82%
6 filter	319 (0.77%)	29.80%	58.58%
7 membrane	63 (0.15%)	29.28%	59.70%
8 cells	4539 (11.00%)	24.64%	64.06%
9 optical detectors	3631 (8.80%)	23.36%	65.11%
10 fluid flow	800 (1.94%)	22.03%	50.67%
11 valve	108 (0.26%)	20.52%	51.74%
12 sealing and closures	284 (0.69%)	20.37%	44.18%
13 acid compounds	464 (1.12%)	19.46%	67.26%
14 Miscellaneous	3409 (8.26%)	19.41%	51.19%
15 web films	2191 (5.31%)	19.12%	63.24%
16 centrifuges	931 (2.26%)	17.51%	67.21%
17 containers	850 (2.06%)	14.74%	44.18%
18 catheter	198 (0.48%)	14.49%	69.23%
19 tubing	13 (0.03%)	13.83%	59.30%
20 injection	239 (0.58%)	13.31%	57.03%
21 protein binding	589 (1.43%)	10.73%	57.26%
22 patient monitoring	518 (1.26%)	9.21%	48.61%
23 pump	2217 (5.37%)	8.59%	48.61%
24 blood	145 (0.35%)	8.31%	58.46%
25 hemoglobin	11 (0.03%)	5.81%	83.39%
26 Other	36 (0.09%)	0.00%	100.00%
TOTAL / AVERAGE	41263	26.17%	61.18%

| Visualization | Class View | Class Table | Class Tree |

Figure 5-8 Medical equipment supplier taxonomy applied to IBM's portfolio

Examining each category, we find individual IBM patents that are most related to the medical equipment supplier's business by focusing on the patents nearest to each category centroid (see Figure 5-9).

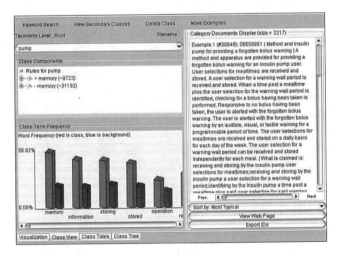

Figure 5-9 IBM patents in the "pump" category

The patent shown in the figure is the "Most Typical" IBM patent in the medical equipment supplier "pump" category. This is a very surprising patent to find in the IBM portfolio. Listed next are some other surprises we found.

Most Typical from the <u>Valve</u> Category

Patent number: 6432135

Title: Torsion heart valve

Abstract: A rigid leaflet blood check valve uses a torsion wire suspension to suspend the leaflet. The leaflet is non-contacting with the housing. Complete washout of all valve parts in blood contact exists. This eliminates areas of blood stasis which exist in valves employing conventional pivot bearings. Relative motion, wear, and washout problems have been eliminated in the valve.

Most Typical from the <u>Blood</u> Category

Patent number: 5360445

Title: Blood pump actuator

Abstract: An implantable blood pump actuator uses an efficient direct drive voice coil linear motor to power an hydraulic piston. The motor is immersed in oil and has but one moving part, a magnet which is attached to the piston. The piston is supported using a linear double acting hydrodynamic oil bearing that eliminates all wear and will potentially give an infinitely long life. There are no flexing leads, springs to break or parts to fatigue. A total artificial heart embodiment is very light, small, and as efficient as present prosthesis. The motor uses two commutated coils for high efficiency and has inherently low side forces due to the use of coils on both the inside and outside diameters of the magnet. The motor is cooled by forced convection of oil from the piston motion and by direct immersion of the coils in the oil. The highly effective cooling results in a smaller lighter-weight motor.

Amazing what kinds of things turn up in IBM's portfolio! Imagine how difficult it would be to find these patents using search techniques alone, given limited knowledge of the medical equipment domain. Searching on the phrase "medical equipment" would not have revealed any of these. By creating powerful models to do the sifting for us, we have created a kind of surrogate text reader that knows what we want (because we taught it from examples) and goes out and finds it for us. This is the power of the *Mining the Talk* approach. The taxonomy generation and editing phase lets the user interact with the text to derive a taxonomy that captures a combination of data plus knowledge. The text information provides the substance—the concrete examples of what actually exists out in the world. The knowledge provides the motivation—what do you want to learn from the data and how do you want to apply it? Without knowledge, data is meaningless. Without data, knowledge is abstract and theoretical. The *Mining the Talk* approach leverages both to provide value that neither can supply alone.

The results of such analyses can be monetized in many ways. There is the possibility of licensing or outright sale of patents owned in a technology that is not currently being developed by the organization. Another approach is to partner with a company doing similar work in the space to leverage each other's strengths—one company does the product development, while the other takes the product to market, for example.

Research for a New Product: Mars Snackfood Division

In 2005, a research team in the Mars company came to us with an interesting problem. They had a new product they were about to introduce called CocoaVia®. CocoaVia® is a line of chocolate-based products that maintain healthy serum cholesterol levels and promote healthy circulation. It is based on a novel technology for making chocolate products from uniquely processed cocoa that allowed the product to retain:

> …natural plant extracts clinically proven to reduce bad (LDL) cholesterol levels up to 8%. All **CocoaVia®** Brand snacks also have a guaranteed 100 mg of naturally occurring cocoa flavanols, like those found in red wine and green tea. Studies indicate that flavanols in cocoa and certain chocolates have a beneficial effect on cardiovascular health. —*CocoaVia.com*

The questions that Mars had for us were: 1) How was this product likely to be perceived in the marketplace?; 2) What claims could they reasonably make about its health benefits that would resonate with current consumer trends?; 3) What were their competitors doing in this space?. As it turns out, each of these questions could be answered by analyzing the talk from three different data sources. Here is how we accomplished it.

Marketplace Analysis (Web Data)

Understanding marketplace perception can best be answered by looking at what people were saying about the health benefits of cocoa on the Web. To get at this, we start with a set of snippets (see Chapter 3, "Mining the Voice of the Customer," for a description of how to create snippets) around the term "chocolate," extracted from web pages. We then cluster these snippets into categories and edit the categories to create a taxonomy, and add a time-based analysis of the categories to create the display shown in Figure 5-10.

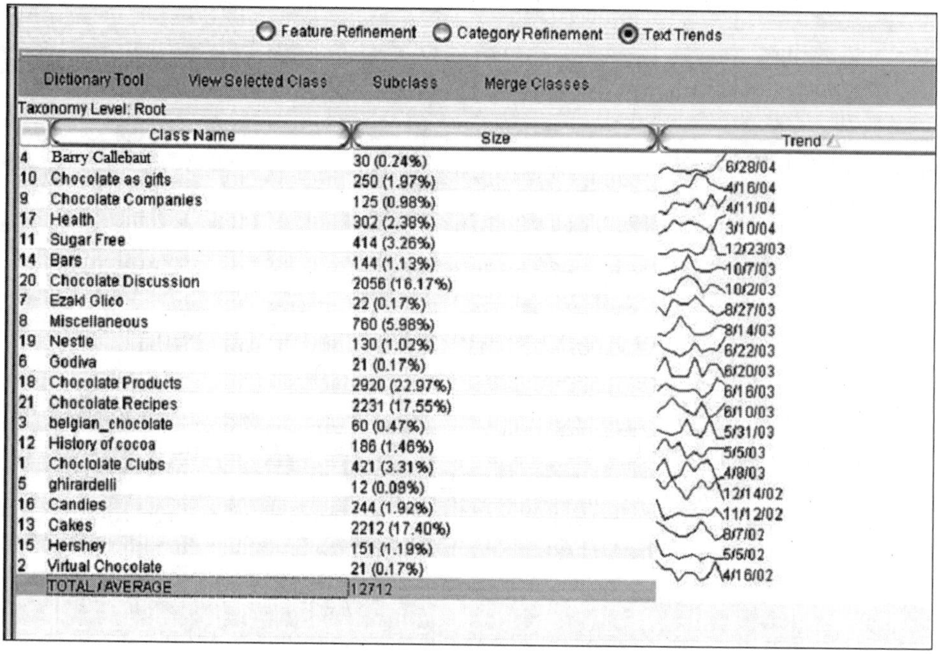

Feature Refinement | Category Refinement | Text Trends

Dictionary Tool | View Selected Class | Subclass | Merge Classes

Taxonomy Level: Root

	Class Name	Size	Trend
4	Barry Callebaut	30 (0.24%)	6/28/04
10	Chocolate as gifts	250 (1.97%)	4/16/04
9	Chocolate Companies	125 (0.98%)	4/11/04
17	Health	302 (2.38%)	3/10/04
11	Sugar Free	414 (3.26%)	12/23/03
14	Bars	144 (1.13%)	10/7/03
20	Chocolate Discussion	2056 (16.17%)	10/2/03
7	Ezaki Glico	22 (0.17%)	8/27/03
8	Miscellaneous	760 (5.98%)	8/14/03
19	Nestle	130 (1.02%)	6/22/03
6	Godiva	21 (0.17%)	6/20/03
18	Chocolate Products	2920 (22.97%)	6/16/03
21	Chocolate Recipes	2231 (17.55%)	6/10/03
3	belgian_chocolate	60 (0.47%)	5/31/03
12	History of cocoa	186 (1.46%)	5/5/03
1	Choclolate Clubs	421 (3.31%)	4/8/03
5	ghirardelli	12 (0.09%)	12/14/02
16	Candles	244 (1.92%)	11/12/02
13	Cakes	2212 (17.40%)	8/7/02
15	Hershey	151 (1.19%)	5/5/02
2	Virtual Chocolate	21 (0.17%)	4/16/02
	TOTAL / AVERAGE	12712	

Figure 5-10 Trends in chocolate web page snippets

We select the Health category as being especially relevant to the new product and create a trend chart. We can use our Chi-Squared co-occurrence analysis to detect correlations between contiguous time intervals and words/phrases in the dictionary. These correlations are then shown as labels in the trend chart (see Figure 5-11).

Each term label is followed by a number in parenthesis indicating the support for that word or phrase during that time period. Words shown on the chart are co-occurring significantly with the Health category during the time period where they are displayed. The interesting thing to note here is the movement away from mentions of sugar_free chocolate toward words like "heart" and phrases like "health_fitness." This is a positive indication that the CocoaVia® product (which is not sugar free) may be filling a recent consumer need. The next chart reveals this more clearly (see Figure 5-12).

Web mentions of "sugar free" and "chocolate" are actually on the decline, in stark contrast to "health" chocolate mentions. Looking at the posts that underlie these trends shows snippets corresponding to both consumers, newspapers, and other product advertisements. So, from the standpoint of public/marketplace acceptance of healthy chocolate, it appears that CocoaVia® is on track to hit a receptive marketplace.

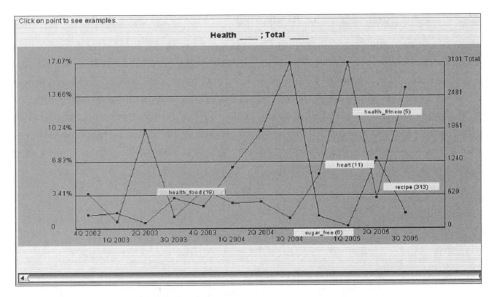

Figure 5-11   Health trends related to chocolate

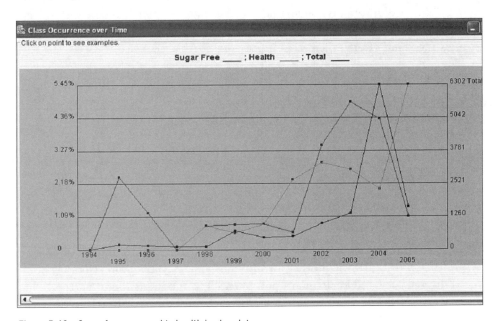

Figure 5-12   Sugar free compared to health in chocolate

Health Benefits Analysis (Medline Abstracts)

Understanding what health benefits can be claimed is best answered by looking at Medline research abstracts, because Medline consists of scientific, peer-reviewed journals. (Medline is an indexing service for research in medicine and related fields provided by the U.S. National Library of Medicine.) For this analysis, we did a query on "polyphenols" (the substance the CocoaVia® product contains that contributes to health). We then did a snippet clustering around the word "conclusion" in order to focus on just the final result of each study. The resulting taxonomy revealed several relevant study results for Mars:

- Olive oil and red wine antioxidant polyphenols at nutritionally relevant concentrations transcriptionally inhibit endothelial adhesion molecule expression, thus partially explaining atheroprotection from Mediterranean diets. (http://www.ncbi.nlm.nih.gov/entrez/query.fcgi?cmd=Retrieve&db=pubmed&dopt=Abstract&list_uids=12615669)

- Our experiments are the first demonstration that dietary polyphenols can modulate in vivo oxidative damage in the gastrointestinal tract of rodents. These data support the hypothesis that dietary polyphenols might have both a protective and a therapeutic potential in oxidative damage-related pathologies. (http://www.ncbi.nlm.nih.gov/entrez/query.fcgi?cmd=Retrieve&db=pubmed&dopt=Abstract&list_uids=11131367)

- A slight reduction in saturated fat intake, along with the use of extra-virgin olive oil, markedly lowers daily antihypertensive dosage requirement, possibly through enhanced nitric oxide levels stimulated by polyphenols. (http://www.ncbi.nlm.nih.gov/entrez/query.fcgi?cmd=Retrieve&db=pubmed&dopt=Abstract&list_uids=10737284)

- Cocoa powder and dark chocolate may favorably affect cardiovascular disease risk status by modestly reducing LDL oxidation susceptibility, increasing serum total antioxidant capacity and HDL-cholesterol concentrations, and not adversely affecting prostaglandins. (http://www.ncbi.nlm.nih.gov/entrez/query.fcgi?cmd=Retrieve&db=pubmed&dopt=Abstract&list_uids=11684527)

- Both clinical and experimental evidence suggest that red wine does indeed offer a greater protection to health than other alcoholic beverages. This protection has been attributed to grape-derived antioxidant polyphenolic compounds found particularly in red wine. (http://www.ncbi.nlm.nih.gov/entrez/query.fcgi?cmd=Retrieve&db=pubmed&dopt=Abstract&list_uids=11831110)

Clearly substantial clinical evidence exists to support the idea that polyphenols have health benefits. It seems then reasonable for Mars to communicate these potential health benefits of the CocoaVia® products in their marketing.

Competitive Analysis (Patents)

We look at patents to understand the competitive landscape using the Explore-Understand-Analyze method. For this analysis, we first collected all patents that mention polyphenols in the text. Next we created and edited a taxonomy, making sure that we created a category around patents that were related to process of interest—namely that of preserving polyphenols in cocoa during processing. We then created a co-occurrence table showing the relationship between assignees for the polyphenol set and subject areas. The result is shown in Figure 5-13.

		Very High Affinity = ■	Moderate Affinity =		Low Affinity = □		No Affinity = □		
	Size	Archer Daniels Midland	BATTELLE MEMORIAL	MEIJI SEIKAKA...	Mars	N/A	NESTEC, SA	PACIFIC FIM M...	PROCTER + GAMBLE
preserve polyphenols in cocoa	45	0 (0.00%)	0 (0.00%)	1 (100.00%)	41 (45.56%)	3 (20.00%)	0 (0.00%)	0 (0.00%)	0 (0.00%)
antineoplastic	34	0 (0.00%)	0 (0.00%)	0 (0.00%)	34 (37.78%)	0 (0.00%)	0 (0.00%)	0 (0.00%)	0 (0.00%)
extraction of polyphenols	7	0 (0.00%)	0 (0.00%)	0 (0.00%)	5 (5.56%)	2 (13.33%)	0 (0.00%)	0 (0.00%)	0 (0.00%)
extract_compounds from cocoa	4	0 (0.00%)	0 (0.00%)	0 (0.00%)	4 (4.44%)	0 (0.00%)	0 (0.00%)	0 (0.00%)	0 (0.00%)
beverage products	8	0 (0.00%)	0 (0.00%)	0 (0.00%)	3 (3.33%)	1 (6.67%)	1 (100.00%)	1 (100.00%)	2 (100.00%)
postprandial	2	0 (0.00%)	0 (0.00%)	0 (0.00%)	2 (2.22%)	0 (0.00%)	0 (0.00%)	0 (0.00%)	0 (0.00%)
extraction of sterols using solvent	3	0 (0.00%)	0 (0.00%)	0 (0.00%)	1 (1.11%)	2 (13.33%)	0 (0.00%)	0 (0.00%)	0 (0.00%)
chocolate storage	4	0 (0.00%)	2 (100.00%)	0 (0.00%)	0 (0.00%)	2 (13.33%)	0 (0.00%)	0 (0.00%)	0 (0.00%)
preservation of flavanoids	4	0 (0.00%)	0 (0.00%)	0 (0.00%)	0 (0.00%)	4 (26.67%)	0 (0.00%)	0 (0.00%)	0 (0.00%)
cosmetic	3	2 (100.00%)	0 (0.00%)	0 (0.00%)	0 (0.00%)	1 (6.67%)	0 (0.00%)	0 (0.00%)	0 (0.00%)
Total	114	2	2	1	90	15	1	1	2

Figure 5-13 Assignees vs. subject area for polyphenol patents

Mars has 41 of the 45 patents in the space of preserving polyphenols in cocoa. Mars seems to have a significant competitive advantage in this key technology. A closer look at the four competitive patents did not reveal any concerns. So from this standpoint as well, it would seem that the product launch should be a go.

In fact, Mars did subsequently launch the CocoaVia® product line, and it is still available in stores today as of the writing of this book.

Summary

Innovation Mining is a powerful tool for discovering relationships in the business ecosystem. The examples we've shown serve to illustrate how *Mining the Talk* enhances corporate innovation, enabling monetization of technology that might otherwise sit on the shelf. A new product or device that only sits in the lab is not truly innovative. It's only when that product or device finds the right development partner or consumer that true innovation takes place. *Mining the Talk* helps to find the right home for technology and products by exploring the space around them and finding the right development partner or market niche—a crucial component for successful innovation.

But good Innovation Mining is also not a trivial exercise. It requires direct access to significantly large, dynamic data sources and expertise in using all of the *Mining the Talk* techniques we have outlined so far. Creating an ongoing mining process for innovation requires a significant investment, but the potential rewards in greater leverage of corporate technology into new products and services far outweighs the cost.

Endnotes

1. Gassmann, O., and Enkel, E. (2004). "Towards a Theory of Open Innovation: Three Core Process Archetypes." Paper presented at the R&D Management Conference 2004, Lisbon.

2. http://www.uspto.gov/web/offices/pac/doc/general/whatis.htm.

3. http://www.uspto.gov/patft/help/helpflds.htm.

4. http://medlineplus.gov/—A service of the U.S. National Library of Medicine.

5. We use a fictional scenario here because actual patent licensing or assignment arrangements that we have used *Mining the Talk* technology to facilitate are considered confidential IBM information.

6. After all, in the extreme worst case, where every word occurs in every patent, every word has exactly the same cohesion score. Although this is hardly ever the case, it does show that cohesion as a metric eventually breaks down when the documents become long and the words used in each become less differentiated. This is more the case with patents than with shorter documents, such as problem tickets.

7. The centroid model is only one text classification model that could be applied here. It is usually the best one to use because it models the way that k-means created the categories in the first place.

6

Mining to See the Future

Contributors to This Chapter:
Larry Proctor and Ray Strong

We have seen techniques for *Mining the Talk* being used to tackle a wide range of challenging problems in industry. To this point, though, all of our analysis has essentially been a study of the past, of what has been said before in order to understand what people are communicating. Basically, this is a historical analysis. In this chapter, we shift our focus from understanding the past, to showing how *Mining the Talk* techniques can be used to gain insight into how events may unfold in the future.

How Can Unstructured Data Help Us to See the Future?

"History has a habit of repeating itself," or so the saying goes. Most patterns that occur in data tend to recur over time. If we can spot these patterns as they begin, then we can predict how they will play out. This is the essence of *Mining the Talk* to see the future. Occurrences of categories in unstructured data taxonomies plotted against time are used to make educated guesses about how often examples will fall into that category in the future, and this leads to conclusions about the underlying generators of those examples. We call this approach "Future Mining." While in general, mining cannot predict unforeseen events, it can help to estimate the scope and duration of events that have already begun to occur, or identify the scope of future events based on analyzing similar past events. If we catch events early enough—before they have already begun to have a strong effect on the organization—then we can use what we know from past events to predict how they might affect the organization in the future, as the event unfolds. The organization can then determine how to take actions to mitigate risk or take advantage of an opportunity in the marketplace.

Business Drivers of Future Mining

Organizations today exist in complex, constantly changing ecosystems. Understanding how this ecosystem will evolve in the future is a necessity for survival. The ability to monitor many sources of information to detect "weak signals" allows a business to get the jump on the competition and exploit opportunities as rapidly as possible. It is also equally important to detect threats to the business as soon as possible, to give the organization the maximum time to respond to these threats in an effective manner. These are some of the motivators that cause us to undertake Future Mining.

Characteristics of Future-Oriented Data Sets

In any organization's ecosystem, there are many types of events that occur as weak signals. The process of detecting weak signals starts with the identification of content sources and their authority level. The authority level of the content will help to determine the importance of the signals. The following chart is a guideline of how to evaluate various types of content (see Figure 6-1).

Clearly, when modeling the future, the organization must consider the authoritativeness of the content. Generally, the more the analysis is based on authoritative sources, the more it can be trusted. However, less authoritative sources are often the earliest indicators of events that will someday be of major importance to the organization. In summary, modeling the future effectively requires all of the information sources.

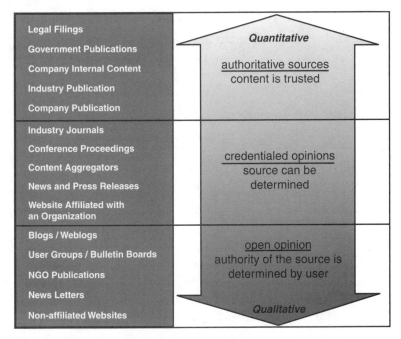

Figure 6-1   Source authoritativeness

Stages of Mining to See the Future

The process of Mining to See the Future is much the same as Mining for Innovation. The difference is that it often relies more heavily on detecting the same event in multiple sources and linking up the multiple threads across time to verify any trend detected in a single source.

Understanding the Business Objectives

The Business Objectives are a key input to both the Explore and the Understand phase. Without these objectives, we are basically shooting in the dark when it comes to where to look for the weak signals that might be relevant to the business. Some example business objectives would be the following:

- Discover any recent news events that might have an impact on my industry.
- Find the next disruptive technology that will affect my market.
- Find those products that my customers are going to be most excited about in the immediate future.

A focused objective helps determine the selection of data as well as the analysis strategy.

Demonstration of Capabilities

There is always the danger in making the case for Future Mining that one may sound like a prophet or a charlatan. Therefore, it's important to highlight realistic capabilities with concrete real-world examples. One technique that has been effective for us in customer engagements is to find a disruptive event relevant to the business that happened some time in the recent past. This can either be the introduction of a new technology or some seismic shift in the consumer environment caused by external events. Then mine the data surrounding that event to show how Future Mining techniques could have been used to detect the event when it was just a tiny wave on the way to becoming a tsunami. Of course, this kind of after-the-fact prognostication falls short of a true capability demonstration, but it still serves to illustrate what is possible to do with a Future Mining approach.

Survey of Available Data

The data sources used for Future Mining are very similar to ones employed for Mining for Innovation. They tend to be more extensive, however, because of the greater need to detect weak signals and the further need to verify those weak signals across multiple sources to ensure their validity.

Here are a few of the possible data sources that can be used for Future Mining:

- Legal filings
- Government publications (e.g., patents)
- Industry journals
- Conference proceedings
- Newsfeeds
- Websites
- Blogs (web logs)
- User groups/bulletin boards

This is not a complete list, nor is each and every source listed a requirement. The analysis objectives and resources of the business will determine how much and which data sources should be included.

One further note about patent data in this context: It is possible to purchase pre-grant data[1] from the U.S. patent office (or from the European patent office), and this is a good source of early information about where technology is heading before it actually becomes patented.

Data Cleansing and ETL

The sheer number and variety of different data sources makes collecting, transforming, cleansing, and storing the data in a warehouse a truly challenging undertaking. Fortunately, the good news is that you don't have to wait for all of the data to be in place and completely cleaned up before you can begin extracting value from it in terms of Mining the Future. Also, structured information for this application is far less important than text. This is due to the fact that we are looking for emergent phenomenon, whereas structured information tends to document well-established events. Primarily, only one structured field is absolutely essential to get right—that is the creation date of each document. Without this information, trending—and thus Future Mining based on past trends—would be impossible.

The Taxonomy Generation and Analysis Process

Mining the Future uses the same process for generating taxonomies that was used in Mining to Improve Innovation. The typical strategy is to Explore each individual source to select the relevant information from that source. Partitioning of the examples is done through snippetization. Breaking the examples into snippets around a suitable keyword or phrase is usually a desirable practice (see Chapter 3, "Mining the Voice of the Customer"), as it helps keep the focus around the topic of interest and avoids too much extraneous noise preventing the weak signal from being detected.

Once snippets have been extracted, a taxonomy is created using Intuitive clustering. The taxonomy is then edited by the analyst using the techniques described earlier in this book. Finally trend analysis is used very heavily in Future Mining to analyze the evolution of both categories and features over time and then extrapolate these trends into the future. Each data source is analyzed separately with this process, and then these separate results are used to verify (or qualify) the case for the conclusions.

Publish Results

Results for Mining the Future typically begin with trend charts showing the detected event as it manifests itself across various data sources. Example snippets from these data sources are also critical so that the stakeholder audience can fairly estimate the relative weight to put on each detected event and determine the best course of action to take in response.

Avoid making definitive claims about what WILL happen in the future. The output of Future Mining is not so much a prediction as it is a warning (or, in the case of a diminishing trend, an assuagement) about possible future concerns.

Making Future Mining an Ongoing Concern

To do Future Mining on an ongoing basis requires, first of all, continuous updating of all the relevant data sources. The fees, infrastructure, and overhead required for such continuous ETL processing are not negligible, so the organization will need to consider whether there is enough justification from the potential benefits to incur this ongoing cost. Once again, vendors who supply this information for a reasonable fee may be the answer.

Beyond the data issues, the issue of becoming an ongoing part of the organization's strategic planning process is important. Future Mining needs to be recognized as a regular part of the strategic thinking in the organization. To reach this level of acceptance will require tangible benefits documented from specific Future Mining successes within the organization.

Examples of *Mining the Talk* to See the Future

The best way to understand Future Mining is to see how it works in practice. This section describes four examples of how mining of unstructured information sources has been used to See the Future. These examples illustrate the wide array of innovative techniques employed by advanced practitioners of the art of *Mining the Talk*.

The Effect of Bird Flu on Pet Food Sales—By Larry Proctor

In this example, we look at an event with a large pet food company who was trying to assess the future impact on their ecosystem of a cat dying in Germany from the NH51 "bird flu virus." The National and International Press ran this story in early March of 2006. Excerpts from the press reports paint a potential significant impact to the pet food industry.

Germans ditch their cats after bird flu death[2]

Berlin—Hundreds of German cat-owners have dumped their pets at shelters since the country recorded the first case of a cat dying of bird flu in the European Union, the German animal welfare society said on Thursday.

"Nationwide, several hundred cats have been left with us. People are scared their cats have bird flu," a spokesperson for the group, Jan Pfeifer, told AFP.

"We do not want to give more exact figures because we do not want people to think that there is good reason for this and spread more panic."

"We have had endless phone calls from people wanting to give away their cats immediately. Some are even ready to have them put to sleep," spokeswoman Alexandra Diezermann said.

"It is particularly bad in Bavaria," she added, referring to the southern state that is one of five in which bird flu has been detected since mid-February.

We can tell from our content models that this story came from "authoritative sources," so this is something that we assume to be authentic, but also historical. What we don't know is how this story will evolve. Will the buzz about the event increase or subside? Will this event spread to other geographies? Will this affect the sales of pet products? To understand these future impacts, we need to look beyond historical sources like news media and look at less-credentialed opinions to try to discover any emerging trends or patterns on how this event is evolving. To accomplish this, we will start by analyzing "open opinion" content. Open opinion content is the richest form of early trends, but it's also like listening to a radio program with lots of static; it is very hard to understand what is being said clearly. To bring clarity to the chatter, we use snippet analysis techniques to identify the key topics based on a data sample of content from blogs and bulletin boards using the query "bird flu" for a three-month period starting when the story was first reported in the mainstream press.

We begin the discovery process by letting the system automatically classify the snippets into a "Bird Flu Landscape" using intuitive clustering techniques followed by analyst refinement. This result (see Figure 6-2) is a taxonomy of major themes of what people are talking about, with the associated size and trends for each theme. Using this landscape, we attempt to address the questions of "how will this story evolve?," and "will the buzz about the event increase or subside?." When we are looking for trends, it's desirable to be able to compare the trend against something you already know or something that is constant for all of the trend comparisons. Since we are interested in the event involving cats, we will select the "Cats" category, which contains snippets about cats and "bird flu." We will use "Pandemic" as an anchor since this category better represents the overall trends associated with bird flu. The system will automatically show the trend of all the documents. Figure 6-3 represents the trend comparison.

Dictionary Tool	View Selected Class	Subclass	Merge Classes

Taxonomy Level: Root

	Class Name	Size	Trend △
1	Bird flu is a hype	37 (1.05%)	4/3/06 2:45 PM
5	Preparation	21 (0.60%)	4/1/06 5:45 PM
12	Pandemic	183 (5.19%)	3/30/06 4:31 AM
15	Scared	61 (1.73%)	3/28/06 1:40 PM
17	Fear	242 (6.86%)	3/28/06 10:13 AM
13	Spread of avian flu	315 (8.93%)	3/26/06 2:27 AM
7	Poultry	137 (3.88%)	3/26/06 7:04 PM
20	Misc. Dups.	1076 (30.50%)	3/25/06 8:01 AM
10	Spreading to Humans	169 (4.79%)	3/25/06 12:23 AM
16	Health	129 (3.66%)	3/24/06 9:26 PM
6	Effect of spread of bird flu	87 (2.47%)	3/24/06 3:34 PM
14	Infecting People	105 (2.98%)	3/24/06 1:06 PM
4	People death	58 (1.64%)	3/23/06 4:10 AM
18	Reported Cases	60 (1.70%)	3/22/06 5:11 AM
9	Outbreaks	94 (2.66%)	3/21/06 2:12 PM
2	Swan	80 (2.27%)	3/21/06 1:34 AM
19	Wild Birds	118 (3.34%)	3/19/06 9:10 PM
3	Spread in Asia	47 (1.33%)	3/18/06 6:54 AM
11	h5n1	211 (5.98%)	3/18/06 5:56 AM
8	Cat	298 (8.45%)	3/15/06 10:16 PM
	TOTAL / AVERAGE	3528	

Visualization	Class View	Class Table	Class Tree

Figure 6-2 "Bird flu categories"

Before we start analyzing the trends, it is important to know how to read the trend chart. The vertical axis on the left represents the percentage of the category as compared to the total number of documents (for example, the number of documents for Cat on 3/05/06 was 116, and the total number of all documents was 620, so Cat represents 18.71% of all the documents for this period). The axis on the right represents the total number of all documents. Looking at the trends, we see some interesting results. Point number 1 represents the period when the story first was reported; it dominated the conversation around bird flu. Point 2 in the chart shows that over the previous numbers of weeks, the Cat topic, which had been losing momentum, had sprung to life again. Taking a closer look by viewing example documents, we see that the emphasis has shifted away from personal issues about how to protect cats to more of an institutional issue, where groups are doing studies to understand how cats will participate in the overall chain of spreading bird flu. Here are some of the snippets from this period of time:

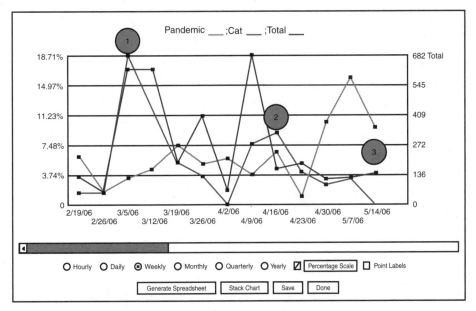

Figure 6-3 Document trends

4/9/06: Final / The Truth About Cats, Dogs, and Bird Flu—A group of European scientists criticized world health agencies last week, saying not enough had been done to monitor cats, dogs, and other animals that might transmit avian flu virus. Their concern is that if the virus spreads in more species, this will increase the risk that it will change into a form that could be easily transmitted to people.

4/09/06: Did you see this... A scientist with the UN's Food and Agriculture Organization is setting up a study aimed at trying to determine if cats are playing a role in the spread of the H5N1 avian flu virus.

4/09/06: Did you hear about the restrictions on farmers in the surveillance zone that are likely to be in place for at least the next three weeks? They are worrying about bird flu's impact on pet owners, particularly as it is known that cats can catch and carry the virus. I heard animal charities are urging owners this weekend not to abandon their pets because of the disease, after seeing this happen in affected areas of France and Germany... you better keep your cat indoors.

Point 3 reflects the fact that Pandemic is growing at a disproportionate rate to the number of all documents, where the trends in Cat is gradually diminishing to the point where on 5/14/06, it is zero. This gives part of the answer to our questions "how will this story evolve?," and "will the buzz about the event increase or subside?" It appears that the initial flurry of buzz about cats and bird flu has subsided, but the real issue of the future is monitoring the Scientific and UN studies on how cats will influence the chain of infections between birds and humans. This will require additional monitoring of some authoritative sources, like Medline (medical journal abstracts).

Using Geography Spread to Predict the Future

One of the early indicators of future impact for a given event is to understand how wide and fast the event has spread. To accomplish this, we need to look at a number of factors: where, how fast, and what is being said.

In Figure 6-4, we tracked who was talking about the spread of bird flu via cats. One interesting observation was that initially, this seemed to be mostly isolated to Germany, with some spill over to Austria, which occurred in the first month of the event. It then took another six weeks for any major mentions in France.

Figure 6-4 Geography spread of Pandemic and Cat

Using Blogs to See the Future

Blog and bulletin board sources can provide leading indicators of possible future events. In Figure 6-5, we see where the system identifies "movies" as one of the topics being discussed along with "bird flu." Looking at the trends of "movie," it was apparent that not only was it an anomaly, but it also had a significant spike during the same time frame as "pandemic."

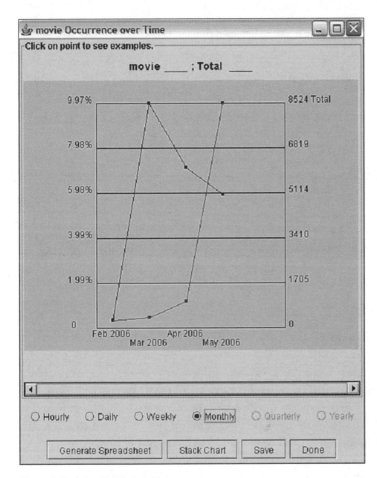

Figure 6-5 Avian flu trends in blogs

This is a good example of a "weak signal" since it appears to have limited direct connections with the death of the cat incident, but has some association to bird flu and pandemic. Taking a look at the following snippets can give some idea of the topic:

(http://blondesense.blogspot.com/2006/05/that-damn-flu-movie.html)

ABC will air "Fatal Contact: Bird Flu in America," a made for TV movie Tuesday evening, May 9 (8:00 pm EST). There is likely to be a heightened response from the general public following its airing; therefore, APIC reached out to governmental agencies in developing the following message points as they relate to the airing of this movie.

INFORMATION ON AVIAN FLU IN RESPONSE TO ABC MOVIE

The ABC Movie "Fatal Contact: Bird Flu in America" is a movie, not a documentary …

(http://crofsblogs.typepad.com/h5n1/2006/05/us_government_b.html)

The uproar over tonight's movie has even prodded the U.S. government into creating a page [visit http://pandemicflu.gov/news/birdfluinamerica.html] about <u>Fatal Contact: Bird Flu in America</u>. It even points out that it's not a documentary.

Meanwhile, the National Chicken Council has supplied a list of negative reviews of the movie, and half the current stories on NewsNow's avian flu page seem to be about the movie.

Awareness of this movie by the pet food company might lead the company to take proactive steps to head off any deleterious effects from negative publicity specifically related to bird flu and pet food. This might be nothing more than pulling any ads from the air during the showing of the movie, to prevent any viewer association between pet food and bird flu.

Summary of the Bird Flu Example

So, what did we demonstrate from our Mining the Future analysis of the bird flu story? First of all, we showed that we could track the evolution of the story both in terms of topics as they evolved over time and in terms of movement across countries. Next, we showed that we could detect specific aspects of the story that were not well known to the organization, where a small change in corporate behavior might help to mitigate the risks of negative association between a news event and the company. Finally, we understand the overall landscape of what is happening with this story so we can make intelligent predictions about the likelihood of it continuing to be a growing and relevant issue to our company in the future.

The advantage of the *Mining the Talk* approach is that it gives us the fullest possible picture of an external event in its entirety, so that the business can make informed decisions regarding the actions that need to be taken to deal with the event.

Mapping the Worry Space

Being aware of outside events that may affect your company is one important application of *Mining the Talk* to see the future. But there are many more ways to use information available on the Web to anticipate where markets are moving and potentially get the jump on your competition. To see how this works, we take an example from the banking industry. In this example, we are interested in mapping out the "worry" space. The point is to see what potential customers are most worried about and then to try to spot interesting trends that could lead to new product ideas—products a financial institution might be able to offer that would address the subject of these worries. This is very similar to the new product introduction study we saw in Mining for Innovation. The difference here is that we didn't have any particular product in mind, but were instead trying to use Future Mining techniques to generate entirely new product ideas based on web data trends alone.

It all begins with a query. In many cases, getting the query right is the difference between analyzing interesting and relevant data that leads to insight and reading a lot of junk. The word "worry" by itself is a little too general, and so likely to bring in too much noise along with the signal. Our first attempt to narrow the field was the query "worry and protection." When we gathered blogs that matched this query, they generated the taxonomy shown in Figure 6-6.

	Class Name	Size	Cohesion	Distinctness
1	religious	542 (10.89%)	32.57%	74.20%
2	disease protection	124 (2.49%)	30.32%	61.68%
3	mysticism	157 (3.16%)	33.43%	75.96%
4	reproductive health	398 (8.00%)	27.01%	61.68%
5	environment	140 (2.81%)	28.11%	77.91%
6	legal cases and physical cas...	154 (3.09%)	24.88%	73.15%
7	protection from harm	219 (4.40%)	23.94%	63.44%
8	global politics	194 (3.90%)	25.12%	71.02%
9	government and laws	188 (3.78%)	25.11%	68.52%
10	protection plans	514 (10.33%)	24.05%	68.43%
11	questions and answers	205 (4.12%)	22.41%	69.39%
12	children	253 (5.08%)	20.99%	66.64%
13	investment	334 (6.71%)	21.62%	68.31%
14	Miscellaneous	1554 (31.23%)	10.58%	65.47%
	TOTAL / AVERAGE	4976	21.29%	67.90%

Figure 6-6 Taxonomy of "worry and protection"

This is not quite what we are looking for—too much emphasis on religion, reproductive health, and politics, and not enough on issues related to finance. The next attempt is the query "worry and family" based on the idea that we want to address not just general financial worries, but those related to family finance. This is a taxonomy generated by snippets over the word "worry" using web pages that matched the query "worry and family" (see Figure 6-7).

| Context | 1. Query Refinement | 2. Query | 3. Feature Space | 4. Explore | 5. Analysis | 6. Done |

| Dictionary Tool | View Selected Class | Subclass | Merge Classes |

Taxonomy Level: Root

	Class Name	Size /	Trend
70	Miscellaneous	11444 (19.21%)	9/10/02
56	children	5413 (9.09%)	8/29/02
58	worry about friends	4200 (7.05%)	10/19/02
28	worry about other people	3659 (6.14%)	8/28/02
55	house/home	3402 (5.71%)	12/20/02
21	work	3076 (5.16%)	8/21/02
1	legal expenses	1809 (3.04%)	11/24/01
11	Genralized Anxiety Disorder	1646 (2.76%)	12/10/02
57	worried about parents	1615 (2.71%)	8/19/02
22	health	1531 (2.57%)	8/5/02
18	worried about telling somebody something	1297 (2.18%)	7/23/02
53	don't worry be happy	1188 (1.99%)	10/21/02
16	fear	990 (1.66%)	8/11/02
42	nothing to worry about	929 (1.56%)	9/6/02
60	money	898 (1.51%)	10/13/02
49	financial planning	871 (1.46%)	1/2/03
25	cancer	831 (1.40%)	8/15/02
34	providing for family	821 (1.38%)	9/16/02
41	service offerings	789 (1.32%)	12/7/02
6	worry disorder	647 (1.09%)	10/6/02
46	war families wait for news	612 (1.03%)	11/3/02
13	travel,vacation	593 (1.00%)	2/15/03
24	future	573 (0.96%)	9/10/02
23	school	513 (0.86%)	9/27/02
61	medical	495 (0.83%)	8/4/02
37	loss of information	416 (0.70%)	11/6/02
63	spouse	377 (0.63%)	8/3/02
48	books	373 (0.63%)	8/2/02
27	sleeplessness	365 (0.61%)	9/2/02
51	survey results	362 (0.61%)	8/30/02
17	change	347 (0.58%)	9/2/02
2	moving (relocating)	343 (0.58%)	10/6/02
54	god	314 (0.53%)	9/25/02
19	dealing with other people	305 (0.51%)	8/8/02
30	death	274 (0.46%)	11/11/02
32	water concerns	273 (0.46%)	7/26/02
15	disease	268 (0.45%)	12/1/02

| Visualization | Class View | Class Table | Class Tree |

| Trend | Compare Taxonomies | Keyword Taxonomies | Read Taxonomies | Read Template | Save |

Figure 6-7 Taxonomy of "worry and family"

This appears to be far more interesting. It gives us a nice breakdown of the worry space into its constituent components. Now we want to focus on those particular worries that are increasing lately. Sorting categories by recency of occurrence leads to the list shown in Figure 6-8.

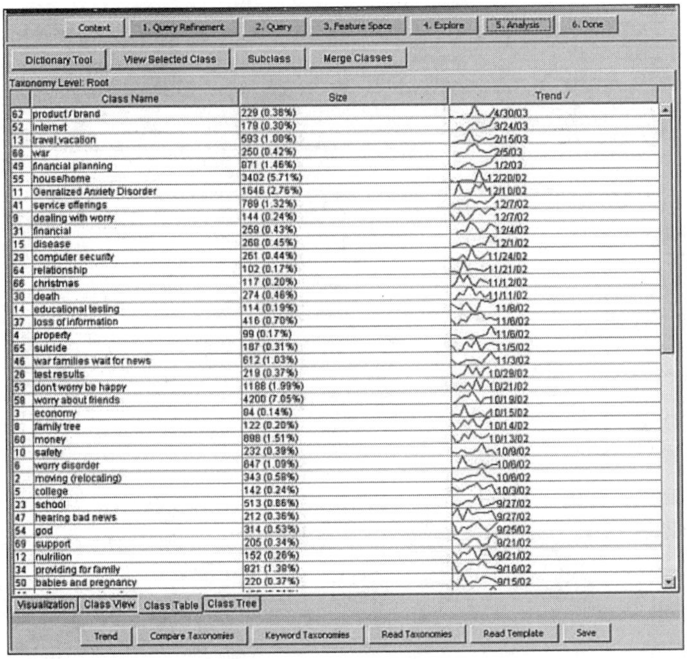

Figure 6-8   Taxonomy sorted by recency

Several categories leap out as being interesting and recently increasing with time.

House/Home

"Your dream suggests some sort of emotional turmoil occurring in your home life. I get many dreams from people who dreamt about a flood hitting their home, and they worry about family members coming out of it okay."

"Again, as many families learn, acquiring a home is really only the beginning of the financial challenge. A constant worry that haunts many homeowners is falling behind on a mortgage...."

Financial Planning

"Illness and the unforeseen loss of a loved one can be a huge financial burden. [Company name] provides exclusive and affordable coverage so that you won't have to worry about financial matters during these trying times."

"You know, there are all sorts of worries—if they find out they have a genetic disease, will they be discriminated against for health insurance, life insurance, or in their employment or their social activities. On the other hand, other families want to know because they want to do financial planning, family planning, or they just worry about it all the time and their anxiety level is very high, or they'd like a resolution to this life-long anxiety. So there are reasons to do and not to do testing."

"Life insurance ensures that the surviving spouse is not suddenly faced with two people's financial liabilities and only one person's income, or sometimes no income. In addition, planning a funeral for a loved one is painful enough without having to worry about where you will get the money to pay for it."

Travel/Vacation

"That way you could at least take a good vacation and not worry about being stranded someplace."

"We will plan your trip, contact the airlines, and make reservations at the hotel. We take the worry out of your vacation."

"Your Vacation Nanny is highly trained and is on hand to take the worry out of your holiday. Warm, attentive, and friendly, she also respects your privacy and will be there only when needed"

Loss of Information

"Because the messages in your mail account are stored securely at a central location, you don't have to worry about losing important information if something happens to your computer."

"There is one potential downside: Privacy advocates worry that too much personal information about your family is being compiled and given to advertisers."

Computer Security

"You will not worry anymore about someone discovering what is on your computer."

"AMAZING, what a program! Protected hides files, denies access to my important files, gives me information on all the users that use my computer. JUST GREAT. Finally I'm the boss of this computer and can let all my family use the computer without worry for the consequences. Thanks guys. YOU ARE THE BEST."

"Oooh, wow, this is so exciting, customizing my desktop, having my own links without worrying about privacy...I'm likin' this computer."

Product/Brand

"We have a variety of products by a brand-name manufacturer so that you have peace of mind. Let us worry about your security while you and your family just live."

"There has never been a product like the Miracle Soaps before! You won't have to worry about locking up poisons or toxins—there are NONE in our products."

These examples helped generate several interesting ideas for financial services products that might do well in the near future, as follows:

1. Mortgages that provide long grace periods under certain circumstances (for a higher fee, of course).
2. Financial planning specifically for those who have lost a spouse.
3. Travel insurance that reimburses you not only for canceling a trip, but for other types of travel-related misfortunes as well.
4. Data "security bank" that lets you store your data in a secure way just as you do your financial assets.
5. Providing financial services customers the same level of security protection on their home computers that financial institutions have on their own.
6. Providing advice on brands whose products are "good investments," much the same as providing advice on companies that are good financial investments.

Mining the Talk is a powerful approach to brainstorming ideas about future product offerings, because it focuses attention precisely on those issues currently faced by real customers in the marketplace. Some of the ideas generated in this way may seem pretty obvious in hindsight, but a surprising number of times, obvious ideas are totally off the radar screen of companies because they don't see the trend of customer thinking until it hits them in face (or on the balance sheet).

Modeling the Future of Nanotechnology Based on Historical Patterns of Microfibers[3]–By Larry Proctor

In order to use *Mining the Talk* techniques to generate models that can predict the future, one must start with a historically accurate model of previous events. This doesn't seem so hard, unless there are no "historically accurate" models of the past. In this engagement, the challenge we faced was to model future uses of nanotechnology in order to evaluate the impacts on the environment over a 10–30 year horizon. This request presented some unusual challenges:

- There is very little historical information for nanotechnology, since it is an emerging field of study.

- There is a lot of hype about nanotechnology, and it is difficult to separate fact from fiction. Nano is becoming a generic term, commonly defined as anything that is less than 100 of a nanometer (1 millionth of a meter); it is also used as a generic measure such as nano-scale, nano-sec, and nano-size.

- Nano encompasses a wide range of technologies, from nanofibers to carbon nanotubes, and is used in a number of products, from fuel cells to medical instruments.

With the Mining the Future approach as the basis, here is the specific method used to build historical models to predict future events:

1. Identify a technology that has similar characteristics to nanotechnology and has been in the marketplace long enough to have an impact on industrial or consumer products. We refer to this as a Retro Model.
2. Identify content that has consistent historical accuracy and comes from an authoritative source.
3. Using the *Mining the Talk* method, model the technology lifecycle from "science to market" for a long-enough timeframe to identify patterns that can be used as a template of how nanotechnology may evolve in the marketplace.
4. Apply the retro models to nanotechnology projecting near and long-term trends.
5. Develop future models (10 years) with signposts.

Identify Similar Technology

One of the key criteria of a retro model is the maturity of the technology. A powerful measure of technology maturity is the ratio of patent granted vs. patent applications within a time frame (see Figure 6-9).

Technology	Number of Patents	Time Frame	Applications / Granted
Microfiber	1037	1976 - 2006	23% / 76%
Nano (fibers)	601	2001 - 2006	74% / 26%
Nano	6405	1998 - 2006	81% / 18%
Carbon Nanotubes	7904	2000 - 2006	72% / 28%

Figure 6-9 Ratio of applications vs. granted patents

Of all of the potential technologies evaluated, only microfibers had maturity and longevity to ensure the quality of a retro model. To confirm that microfiber was a good retro model for nanotechnology, a detailed comparison of how the two technologies were being used was performed. Figure 6-10 shows a result of this comparison.

Use of Technology								
Microfiber	**Medical -** Bioengineered tissue substitutes	**Textile -** Multilayered, breathable textile fabric	**Filters -** oil-in-water emulsion contaminated	**Cleaning -** microfiber cover for cleaning tool	**Industrial -** high performance vacuum-sealed insulations			
Nanotechnology	**Medical -** delivery of drugs, therapeutic peptides	**Textile -** Wearable composite material products	**Filters -** Nano-Scale Filler in Downhole Applications	**Cleaning -** cleaning metal from a substrate or coating metal	**Industrial -** flame retardant and as a fire-proof seal	**Semiconductors -** Dual-gate device and method	**Fuel Cell -** Catalyst composition for cell, gas diffusion layer	**Display Devices -** portable multifunction display panel

Figure 6-10 Technology usage comparison of microfibers and nanotechnology

In a number of key areas, both microfibers and nanotechnology had similar technology uses, although nanotechnology also had extensive use in the electronics industry. This required additional models of nanotechnology to ensure these additional uses are considered in the retro models.

Identify Content Sources

The next major hurtle was identifying content sources, since historically accurate retro models require consistent quality over time, trusted sources, and similar lexicons. The United States Patent and Trademark Office content, covering 1976 to 2006, was chosen. The advantage of patent content over other authoritative sources is that it comes from a trusted source and has a consistent format for reporting.

Model the Technology Lifecycle

Most "material" technologies like microfibers and nanotechnology follow a similar adoption curve. Understanding this curve proved to be helpful when making assumptions on the shape of retro models. Using Geoffrey Moore's[4] technology adoption model, microfiber patent categories were developed using the *Mining the Talk* method and then overlaid on technology adoptions model (see Figure 6-11).

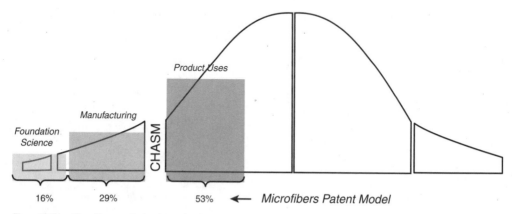

Figure 6-11   Microfibers on technology adoption curve

- *Foundation Science*—Patent classes that are oriented to basic science in the technology.

- *Manufacturing*—Patent classes that address the technology of transforming the science into raw material.

- *Product Uses*—A summary of the following three patent classes:

  Industrial Uses—Patent classes used to produce raw materials or products that are for industrial uses.

  Consumer Uses—Patent classes that reference specific end-user products.

  Medical Uses—Patent classes that reference medical delivery systems or devices.

Preliminary text analysis on microfiber patents indicates a technology that is in a mature state (53% of patents in product uses), with steady growth in foundation sciences patents (16% of all patents, with 54% of them being applied for the last five years). Additionally, having reviewed much of the textile literature, a number of the references to nano are in fact microfibers.

Building the Microfiber Retro Model

Since the objective of the project was to understand the future nanotechnology capabilities 10 to 30 years in the future, it was decided to group the 30 years of patent history into four categories, ranging from 5 to 10 years. For each of the categories, all of the relevant patents were extracted from the USPTO and were classified into taxonomies using *Mining the Talk* methods. The following table is an extract of two patent taxonomies (see Figure 6-12).

Percentages of patents in a category are more important than the actual number of patents; this provided capability to normalize the categories across all the time periods.

1976 - 1983		1984 - 1995	
Foundation Science	52%	Foundation Science	17%
Building Polymeric Microfibers	32%	Textile Fibers	14%
Create Microfiber Webs	20%	Microfiber Membranes	3%
Methods for Manufacturing	21%	Methods for Manufacturing	29%
Production Process	5%	Method for Creating Woven / Non-Woven Material	24%
Building Microfibers	16%	Manufacturing Microfibers Polymers	6%
Industrial Uses	27%	Industrial Uses	34%
Microfiber Insulation	19%	Create Layers for Absorbent Material	11%
Filters	8%	Microfibers Containers for Hazardous Liquids	4%
		Industrial Filters	9%
		Industrial Use of Microfiber Glass	8%
		Heat Resistant Microfibers	2%
		Consumer Uses	6%
		Microwave Packaging	2%
		Liquid-Sorbent Microfibers	4%

Figure 6-12 Retro models for two time periods of microfibers

Next, the patents were categorized using *Mining the Talk* methods at the detail level (for example, microwave packing, industrial filters). To allow these models to be used as forecasting models, the decision was made to roll up the classes into five levels (Foundation Science, Manufacturing, Industrial Uses, Consumer Uses, and Medical Uses). Figure 6-13 represents the evolution of microfibers over a 30-year period.

This model has two views: the left hand scale shows the percentages of each category grouping over time, and the right hand scale shows the number of patents per year. This retro model reveals a lot about the microfiber technology maturity and adoption.

Technology to Market—Microfibers have gone through an atypical "technology to market" cycle for the past 30 years. During this cycle, the average number of patents were 14 per year, and the number of products for industrial use increased by 22%, with significant growth in microfiber for absorbent material, containers for hazardous liquids, heat-resistant materials, and industry filters.

Technology Shifts—The last five years have shown significant changes in the Foundation Science trends:

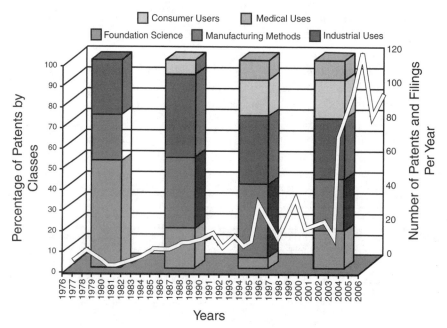

Figure 6-13 Retro model of microfiber by patent type

- The growth in number of patents has gone from an average of 14 per year to an average of 64 per year for the last 12 years.

- The number of "Foundation Science" patents has increased eight-fold (from 10 to 85 patents in the last 4 years), with all of the new patents being related to creation of nanofibers, carbon fibers, or carbon nanotubes.

Growth of Products—The growth in consumer and medical products have been significant for the last 12 years:

- Consumer products represent 45% of all microfiber granted patents. Consumer patents fall in two categories: products that are made from microfiber materials, and microfiber spun into textiles.

- Medical uses of microfibers are relatively new in the last five years, which is similar to the growth pattern of consumer products.

Apply the Retro Models to Nanotechnology Projecting Near and Long-Term Trends

What does the growth curve look like for nanotechnology for the next 30 years? Our approach to address this perspective was to develop a limited number of scenarios that were modeled. Figure 6-14 represents the results of these scenarios.

- *Emerging Scenario*—This predicts that nanotechnology will follow the pattern similar to the recent history of nano.

- *Mature Scenario*—This predicts that nanotechnology will follow a pattern of a mature technology, similar to microfibers.

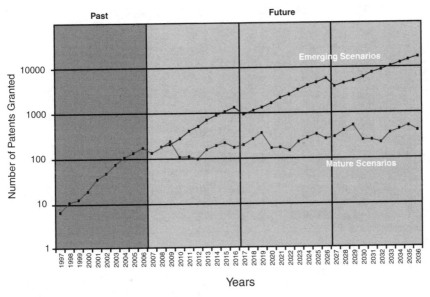

Figure 6-14 Scenario base nanotechnology projections

The variability on both emerging and mature curves is based on the repeating patterns from the retro models. The major objectives of these models are to show boundary limits for each scenario. Since this is a logarithmic scale, the difference between the mature and emerging scenario can be significant (for example, 2005 Mature Scenario is 234 and Emerging Scenarios is 14,345 patents, respectively).

The trajectory between emerging and maturing scenarios is significant, and this could result in dramatically different results on the environment. If nanotechnology is in an early emerging cycle, the impact of this technology could be as pervasive as the semiconductor. If nanotechnology is in a mature cycle, the impact would be limited to industrial and consumer products.

In summary, with the current maturity ratio running 70% applications/30% grants, nanotechnology appears to be in the early stages of it maturity cycle. Viewing nanotechnology from a technology to market perspective for the next ten years can help to clarify its future.

The model represented in Figure 6-15 is built on the hypothesis that nanotechnology will continue to grow at a similar rate it has for the last five years, and the type of granted patents will have similar characteristics to the microfiber retro model in its emerging/maturing phase.

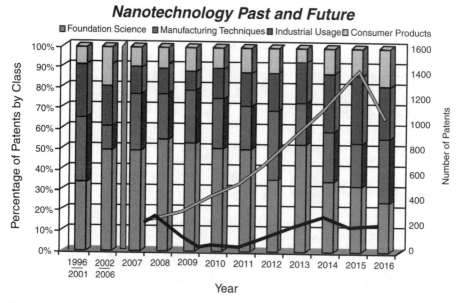

Figure 6-15 Ten-year forecast of nanotechnology

What does the model reveal about the technology to market cycle for the next ten years?

- *Technology curve*—The model indicates that for the next seven years, "Foundation Science" will be the preponderance of granted patents, with 36% of all patents granted.

- *Industrial use*—The model indicates that in the last four years of this cycle, 26% of all granted patents will be in the "Industrial Use" category, where in the previous six years, it was only 13%.

■ *Consumer use*—This category will have the smallest increase, as only 13% of the granted patents will be for "Consumers Use." Note: This may be misleading since consumer patents may not have nano referenced in the patents.

Using Future Models and Signposts to Monitor the Future

The future model lays out the roadmap for how nanotechnology may evolve. To know if this is the right roadmap, directional measures need to be put into place—they are called *signposts*. Some examples of signposts for the nanotechnology model may include the following:

■ *Maturity signpost*—The current ratio of patent to grants is running about 70% application/30% grants. When this starts to invert, nano will move from emerging to maturing.

■ *Uses signpost*—Currently, the % of "Foundation Science" patents are the most prevalent of all patents; as the number of "Foundations Science" patents decrease as a percentage, more patents will emerge in the "Industrial Use" category, and then in the "Consumer Use" category. According to the models, this should occur in seven to eight years.

■ *Market signpost*—New products coming in the market will be imbedded into industrial product such as MEMS, Filters, and Optical devices. The number of categories of industrial use products will increase four times over the ten-year cycle.

Ideas and Signposts in Patent Data—By Ray Strong

A good representation of the future commercial world can be found in issued patents and applications for patent, if we know how to read it. The source data are found in public documents that are available as soon as 18 months after a patent application is filed in the U.S. From this public data, we build what are called technology landscapes. We analyze whole documents rather than snippets to build our technology landscapes, and sometimes the most important information we glean is not statistical but rather the existence (or nonexistence) of patent activity in a particular narrow area.

Technology Landscapes

A *technology landscape* is a multidimensional visual representation of current and past activity in a specified area of technology. Before we can analyze trends, we have to select the set of patent documents to be studied. Then we build a taxonomy over the selection. Finally, we analyze trends and investigate anomalies within the taxonomy selected.

We often start with a set of key words plus a set of patent documents that are already of interest. Here we can take advantage of a wealth of structured data including the official USPTO taxonomy of patent documents. For example, we can expand a small set of patent documents to include all those patent documents that share one or more official classification numbers with the original set. Since the official classification is a hierarchy, we can expand or contract the size of our domain of interest by moving up or down the hierarchy. We also expand the original key words with synonyms and with high-frequency terms that occur in the result set of expanding via the official classification. Finally, we can unite documents obtained from both key word and patent classification searches.

We have three basic choices of taxonomic classification:

1. We can use the primary official USPTO classification or the set of classifications associated with each document to provide a ready-made taxonomy.
2. We can analyze with respect to primary academic and research discipline, using descriptions of each selected discipline as keywords or as seed documents in a k-means classification.
3. We can analyze with respect to primary application or purpose of the patent, using descriptions of chosen applications as seed documents in a k-means classification.

Note that each of these taxonomies has significant overlap and ambiguity. Often, the most interesting inventions are found as unusual combinations of several disciplines, applications, or official technology classes. Moreover, we can do a random seed k-means classification and produce what is likely to be a mix rather than a pure technology, academic discipline, or application area-based taxonomy. In practice, we try several different taxonomies to see what insights each may provide. Also, our choices are often guided by subject matter experts and experts in the study of the future who may give us a set of alternative technologies envisioned as possible means to a challenging application. For example, we might study alternatives to the use of fossil fuels for the production of electrical power. The taxonomy could be based on energy sources or more completely on the application areas of conversion of different energy sources into electrical energy. This would be an application-based taxonomy rather than one based on academic discipline (see Figure 6-16).

Having developed taxonomies, we perform a trend analysis similar to those we did earlier in this chapter on snippets of web data. We assume that the patent data provides a proxy for data on research investment, and we expect a good correlation between the pattern of patent activity in a given area and pattern of investment in the same area. But what does it mean when an area that was hot suddenly cools off or vice versa? To make predictions based on sudden changes in the pattern of patent activity, we need to look closely at individual patents and also search the Web for talk about the area of the patent around the time of the significant trend change. But as a very rough working hypothesis, we assume that a sudden spurt of activity in a research discipline arises from an announced initial breakthrough and corresponds to a significant increase in research investment. A dual hypothesis suggests that a sudden decrease in patent activity around an application area indicates that a significant application challenge has been solved, with consequent diminution of research investment in this area. We don't predict the future based on these hypotheses. They just tell us what to look for. Figure 6-17 represents how image technology is a rising trend in sensor applications.

Taxonomy Level: Root			
Class Name	Size	Cohesion	Distinctness
1 gas & fuel	85 (1.70%)	49.18%	40.05%
2 position & location	9 (0.18%)	48.79%	40.91%
3 voltage & current	72 (1.44%)	47.64%	28.24%
4 thermal	212 (4.24%)	43.53%	42.34%
5 radar	43 (0.86%)	41.14%	25.12%
6 magnetic	102 (2.04%)	39.51%	37.07%
7 image	291 (5.82%)	39.25%	34.34%
8 speed & motion	102 (2.04%)	38.57%	30.81%
9 optical	223 (4.46%)	38.06%	12.55%
10 fluid & flow	114 (2.28%)	36.45%	28.36%
11 vibration, pressure & weight	467 (9.34%)	33.90%	23.75%
12 acoustic & sonar	129 (2.58%)	31.38%	13.94%
13 Miscellaneous	3149 (63.01%)	26.88%	12.55%
TOTAL / AVERAGE	4998	31.13%	18.25%

Figure 6-16 An application-based taxonomy of types of sensors over patent data

○ Feature Refinement ○ Category Refinement ● Text Trends		
Dictionary Tool View Selected Class Subclass Merge Classes		
Taxonomy Level: Root		
Class Name	Size	Trend
7 image	291 (5.82%)	3/19/98
3 voltage & current	72 (1.44%)	4/25/97
4 thermal	212 (4.24%)	9/20/96
8 speed & motion	102 (2.04%)	7/3/96
5 radar	43 (0.86%)	2/13/96
1 gas & fuel	85 (1.70%)	2/10/96
11 vibration, pressure & weight	467 (9.34%)	11/27/95
12 acoustic & sonar	129 (2.58%)	11/9/95
9 optical	223 (4.46%)	6/3/95
6 magnetic	102 (2.04%)	2/4/95
13 Miscellaneous	3149 (63.01%)	12/22/94
10 fluid & flow	114 (2.28%)	9/3/94
2 position & location	9 (0.18%)	8/20/94
TOTAL / AVERAGE	4998	

Figure 6-17 Trend analysis of patent activity by sensor application

In addition to the trending, we attempt to assess the technological maturity of an area by studying typical patents and ascertaining whether any commercial applications have emerged. We also attempt to extrapolate from the trend of particular improvements in apparently well-funded disciplines in order to predict near future advances and their relevance to various industries and enterprises. We can look at combinations of categories and find opportunities that may have been overlooked as well as quiet areas where we can try to analyze what kind of breakthrough would be needed for revitalization. It is always interesting to try to understand the role of the ubiquitous miscellaneous category, especially in cases where its trend is dramatically decreasing. Perhaps this decrease means that the technology is maturing enough that it is beginning to stabilize into definite sub-categories, and fewer and fewer patents fall outside of the main line research.

Using Future Models and Signposts to Monitor the Future

In order to track models over time, the following signposts can be set up to continuously monitor patent activity in this area:

- *Maturity signpost*—Look for decreases in the number of unclassified patents with corresponding growth in the number of patents by sub-categories.
- *Research investment*—Research investment lags in the number of patent application files, by three years. Determine the amount of research investment by tracking number of applications for each category.

Summary

To see the future, *Mining the Talk* relies on time-stamped comments drawn from many different sources having varying degrees of reliability. It then applies taxonomy generation to generate meaningful categories followed by an analysis phase that compares categories across time, generally looking for a tell-tale spike or wave pattern that has either just started, is in process, or nearing completion. By observing what point the pattern appears to be in, the analyst can provide a company with early warning information on changing market conditions, or provide insights into future customer needs.

What the reader should take away from this chapter is the knowledge of the possibility of using unstructured information sources to gain critical knowledge of what the future business environment may look like. Such knowledge is becoming more and more critical to have if businesses are to successfully compete in an ever-changing marketplace.

Endnotes

1. Pre-grants, also known as patent applications, are the invention filings that are published before the patent is issued. Not every pre-grant actually becomes a patent. That depends on the judgment of the patent office. It often takes several years before a published patent application actually becomes a granted patent.

2. SAPA—AFP. March 2, 2006.

3. The authors wish to acknowledge Angela Coulton, Head of SCP Evidence Based Development for Department of Environmental Food and Rural Affairs (DEFRA), as the source of the idea to compare the evolution of nanofiber technology with the earlier evolution of microfiber technology.

4. Moore, Geoffrey A., "Crossing the Chasm: Marketing and Selling High-Tech Products to Mainstream Customers." *HarperBusiness*, Rev. edition (July 1999).

7

Future Applications

This chapter is a little different from those that came before. Everything we have described up until now is real technology that exists today and that has been used repeatedly, both internally at IBM and on customer engagements. In this chapter, nothing we discuss exists yet, except in my head. As I've exposed this technology to more and more people and shown them the breadth of applications that the method can successfully handle, frequently I am asked the question, "Can it do X?," where X is something totally off the wall that I never considered to be within the realm of possibility when the method was conceived. And so I tell them, regrettably, that X is not possible, or feasible, or practical, or wise. And then I wake up in the early morning and I'm taking a shower and suddenly I think to myself, "Hmm...I wonder if that might work after all." Those are the kinds of ideas that this chapter is about. I make no claims that anything in this chapter is remotely possible, but neither can I say for certain that anything in here is impossible. Think of these as advanced exercises for the reader.

Evaluating the Effectiveness of Talk on the Reader

An IBM Global Services employee in Europe, Kees Klokman, whose job it was to put together proposals for big services engagements, asked me the following question: "Is there any way to use text mining to evaluate the "communication style" of a proposal?" His reason for asking was to better understand and evaluate proposals we submitted to customers based on how well the proposal expressed the solution in terms the customer would find compelling. IBM, he explained, is a very "analytical" company, and thus our proposals tend to reflect this bias by being very technically detailed, but weaker in other areas. Other companies that are not as technically oriented might be won over by proposals that are more "amiable" or "expressive." Figure 7-1 shows a summary of the different styles and what they mean.[1]

Styles/Characteristics	Driver	Amiable	Expressive	Analytic
Needs	To win	To avoid pain	To be adored	To be right
Wants	Control	Approval	Recognition	Respect
Questions	What	Why	Who	How
Strength	Decisive	Listens	Enthusiastic	Thorough
Weakness	Insensitive	Won't fight	Impulsive	Can't improvise
Effort	Efficient	Cooperative	Interesting	Accurate
Provide	Results	Safety	Fun	Details
Saves	Time	Relationships	Effort	Face
Emphasizes	Options	Assurances	Incentives	Evidence
Avoids being	Defensive	Pushy	Rigid	Vague
Decisions	Quick	Careful	Fast	Unhurried
Remembers	Goals	People	Future	Process

Figure 7-1 Communication styles

What an interesting idea. Certainly it would make sense that a mismatch of communication styles could well be responsible for a failure to win a sales engagement. Further, it ought to be possible to define the types of words that are associated with each style. In fact, if we had sufficient text examples representing each communication style, we could create a centroid (or other text classifier) for each one and then rate any given document according to how well that document (or any part of that document) matched one of the four styles.

Then of course, we could analyze publicly available data including the request for proposal from the company we are bidding to work with, and try to match our proposal's style to that style. *Mining the Talk* tools could even critique the proposal writer's work as the document was being put together, pointing out paragraphs, and even individual sentences, written in the wrong style—almost like a spell checker for style.

This line of reasoning started me thinking in even grander terms. Why not collect a set of winning proposals and set of losing proposals and put these together into a taxonomy of two categories: wins and losses. Then look for feature correlations using a feature co-occurrence table to discover those words and phrases that are correlated with wins and those correlated with losses. Then use these lists to develop a proposal checker that would evaluate the language of a proposal for overall "likelihood" of success.

All of this seems pretty doable from a *Mining the Talk* perspective—the only question is, would it work? Would it actually improve IBM's win rate to evaluate proposals in this way and modify them based on the results? Many in IBM have expressed serious doubts. So much goes into a decision to accept or reject a proposal that has nothing to do with what gets printed on the page (or so the reasoning goes) that it is a waste of time to spend significant effort fussing with the proposal "wording." Maybe so. But I continue to be intrigued by this idea. After all, human decision making is not entirely a rational process. Could we somehow tap into the unconscious biases of readers and subtly influence their decisions with careful word choices? Why not? Isn't this just what advertisers, politicians, and propagandists have been doing for decades?

You might well ask: "If I'm so intrigued by the idea, why don't I just try it and find out?" Well, it's not as easy as that. First of all, a significant population of past winning and losing proposals is very hard to come by. To date, my best efforts have only collected 25 of each (wins and losses). So far, the results on this very small set look promising, but it's still far too small a collection. And then if I do create such a model, I have to show beyond a doubt that it's effective before a skeptical proposal-writing community is likely to adopt any recommendations. Getting reliable data for communication styles is equally difficult. Still, this is one of those ideas I feel confident I'll get back to someday. It's just too powerful to ignore. Evaluating the effect of text on the reader is a completely new area for *Mining the Talk*, and if it works, it could open the way for a myriad of new business applications.

You Are What You Read

A conversation that I had with my Director, Jim Spohrer, over lunch prompted this idea. Suppose we kept a record on each of our hard drives of the text of every web page we looked at day after day. The corpus of talk we would then collect would be a compendium of every subject we found interesting enough to read about on the Web.

Assuming the Web was our primary source of news and information, this cache would be a pretty fair representation of what interested us, what kinds of things we cared about, and the areas where our knowledge was strongest.

Now imagine we used *Mining the Talk* techniques to build a taxonomy over this information. The centroids for the categories in this taxonomy would represent miniature models of our interests. Now what if two people who don't know each other sit down to have a conversation. If each of them has a taxonomy object like the one described previously, they could put the two objects together and let them interact. The result would be a list of potential topics the two individuals have in common (i.e., look for centroids in different taxonomies that have minimal cosine distance).

This may seem like nothing more than a cute parlor trick, until one thinks about what the world would be like if most people had these taxonomies and if they were stored on compatible devices that could communicate across distance. It sounds almost like science fiction—computers using mental telepathy to bring people together who don't even know each other without the benefit of speech. And yet, there doesn't seem to be any significant technology lacking to make this application a reality, TODAY! Again the primary inhibitor seems to be that the corpuses don't yet exist with which to try out the experiment. Without data, there are no taxonomies, and without taxonomies, there is no way to connect two people. So we are left to wonder…would it really work? How would people use the capability? What are the privacy issues involved? I suspect we will soon all be learning the answers to all these questions.

Taxonomies as Knowledge Repositories

One of the key by-products of performing an edit of a taxonomy generated via clustering in some domain is that it captures something fundamental about how the analysts thinks about that domain. For example, the act of putting all the different password, security lockout, and login problems into a single category called "reset password" captures something the analyst knows about the computer helpdesk domain that goes beyond what the data says all by itself. Once that knowledge is instantiated in a taxonomy category, it seems a shame to do it all over again the next time a different helpdesk has a password problem. There should be a central repository where these objects are collected, saved, and somehow retrieved at the appropriate time to be reused and leveraged again whenever they could be useful. This could make the *Mining the Talk* process much more scalable and practical for application with far less need for expert analyst involvement in each new domain. Moreover, taxonomies could be higher quality because they would take advantage of the expertise leveraged from multiple analysts' experience. I have had some experience applying centroids from one taxonomy into another taxonomy built in a related area, by mapping feature spaces one to the other, and I've been mostly content that the results are reliable and the method effective.

The difficulty I've had with implementing this approach is that the knowledge contained in a taxonomy is a mixture of explicit knowledge and tacit knowledge. The explicit part is the centroid model of the category and the category name. The tacit part is the underlying motivation and reasoning for the category in the first place. In the case of the password category, this is pretty clear, but in general, this is not always the case. Without the "backstory" behind the categories in a taxonomy, it is really difficult to reuse them on a different set of data. Up to this point, I have not figured out a painless way to make this tacit knowledge explicit, and therefore the idea of capturing knowledge via taxonomies has gone largely unrealized.

Some Musings on a New Discipline in *Mining the Talk*

The approach to mining unstructured information that we have outlined in this book is unique. It basically takes unstructured mining out of the lab, where it's all about the data, and brings it into the real world, where business objectives inform every stage of the information analysis process. In some ways, this is similar to the way Knowledge Engineering took Artificial Intelligence principles from the lab and made them applicable to achieving the specific business objective of capturing expertise.

We think the approach we have described for *Mining the Talk* has the potential to become just such a discipline. In the not-too-distant future, we can envision the job description of Unstructured Information Engineer becoming commonplace among sought-after skill sets by forward-thinking companies.

Job Description

Title: Unstructured Information Engineer
Pay Range: Band 8
Report to: Engineering Manager
Job Summary: Create Business Value from Unstructured Information.
Duties and Responsibilities:

- Interview stakeholders to understand business objectives.
- Identify sources of unstructured information that relate to these objectives.
- Explore repositories to select most relevant documents.
- Understand unstructured information by creating taxonomies that capture business objectives.
- Analyze taxonomies against each other and against structured information to identify interesting correlations that lead to business insights.
- Perform other related duties as required.

Knowledge, Skills, and Abilities:

- Deep knowledge of unstructured mining algorithms and their application
- Software engineering/programming skills
- Statistics
- Database principles
- Ability to become quickly familiar with new domains and terminology, create consistently reliable analysis results, and communicate those results to stakeholders
- Ability to invent new approaches to solving problems as the need arises

Credentials and Experience:

- Bachelor's degree in Math or Computer Science with Statistics
- Master's degree in Computer Science or equivalent experience preferred

Special Requirements:

- A love of reading. A passion for discovery.

We can highly recommend this job from personal experience. For us, it has provided a never-ending stream of interesting problems and exposure to many different areas of IBM's business. We trust that our love for this work has come through the pages of this book.

Summary

We hope the ideas presented in this chapter have stimulated the reader's imagination with regard to the variety of ways that *Mining the Talk* techniques could be applied in the future. Part of our motivation for writing this book is to let innovative people know just what this technology is capable of, so that they can find new and unique applications. Ultimately we feel confident these new ways of thinking about how we leverage the vast amount of unstructured information available to us will lead to amazing new applications in this space. Let's get to work and realize the full potential of this exciting new technology.

Final Words

So by now the reader should have a healthy respect for the process of *Mining the Talk*, both in terms of the marvelous ends it can achieve and from the perspective of what it takes to achieve those marvelous ends. Neither of these attributes should really be surprising. After all, we knew the data had something to tell us; otherwise, why mine it in the first place? But we shouldn't expect that a computer could tell us something relevant to us about that data, unless we first define what "relevant" is. And that requires a careful alignment of our knowledge of domain-specific concepts to the precise elements and characteristics of the data that map to those concepts. The *Mining the Talk* method may not be the only way to achieve this alignment. But we would be very skeptical of any claims that this can be done effectively with little or no effort on the part of a data analyst and without capturing domain expertise. Capturing business objectives and domain knowledge is critical to getting an effective result at the end. Skipping this step is a shortcut that will most likely lead to an analysis that is less meaningful than it could be. And in the end, that may cause far more loss of corporate blood (man hours) and treasure (dollars spent or revenue lost) than would have been spent on *Mining the Talk* the right way in the first place.

In any event, we trust this book has helped you find an approach that works for your data and business problem. If so, we also hope you'll share your experiences with us (both good and bad) so together we can continue to grow in our ability to shed light on the vast areas of unexplored text repositories.

Endnote

1. Adapted from Bolton, Robert and Bolton, Dorothy. *People Styles at Work: Making Bad Relationships Good and Good Relationships Better*. New York: Ridge Associates Inc., 1996. http://www.amazon.com/People-Styles-Work-Relationships-Better/dp/0814477232.

A

The IBM Unstructured Information Modeler Users Manual

It did not seem right to describe a methodology without providing the tools you need to implement it. Therefore, this appendix describes a specific tool that implements the *Mining the Talk* method. A demo version of this software, which is called the IBM Unstructured Information Modeler, is available free from IBM Alphaworks (http://www.ibm.com/alphaworks/tech/uimodeler). This software was used to win the "contest" that was described in the opening chapter of this book.

A note on terminology: In most of this book, I refer to the components of a taxonomy as "categories." In the IBM Unstructured Information Modeler software and in this user manual, categories are mostly referred to as "classes." This is mostly due to the fact that the original codename for the software was "eClassifier."

Introduction

The IBM Unstructured Information Modeler toolkit is designed for data analysts for use on unstructured data sets. An example of such a data set would be problem ticket logs from a computer helpdesk. The data analyst's task is to find out what are the commonly occurring problems and to write or find solutions that will solve these problems in an automated way. IBM Unstructured Information Modeler helps the data analyst perform this task by automatically classifying the unstructured data set and providing insight into the categories. IBM Unstructured Information Modeler further allows the user to modify the automatically created categorization to incorporate any domain knowledge that the user may have to make the categorization more sensible. Once the classification has been completed, IBM Unstructured Information Modeler can generate reports and create a classification engine for categorizing new problem tickets. In addition, IBM Unstructured Information Modeler can do trend analysis by day, week, or month and correlation analysis against a user-supplied categorical feature.

This Alphaworks version of IBM Unstructured Information Modeler is only applicable to data sets containing between 1,000 and 10,000 examples, where each example is made up of between 1 and 20 sentences of unstructured text. Optionally, each example may be provided with a creation date and one or more categorical values (e.g., machine type). IBM Unstructured Information Modeler is 100% pure Java, so it can run on many different computer platforms. For the sake of simplicity, this manual assumes a Microsoft Windows platform. IBM Unstructured Information Modeler is enabled by the Java 1.4 runtime.

IBM Unstructured Information Modeler Specifications

- **Architecture:** Pure Java application.
- **Operating systems:** Runs on AIX, Linux, and WinTel platforms.
- **Data formats:** ASCII text, in a format that is easily exported from most databases.
- **Scalability:** The full version of IBM Unstructured Information Modeler can be executed on over one million problem ticket examples using ordinary PC hardware in a few hours time. This Alphaworks version is limited to 10,000 examples at a time.
- **Installation:** Can be downloaded from the Alphaworks website and installed on the user's machine in minutes.
- **Applications:** A generic application that can be applied, not just to helpdesk logs, but to almost any form of electronic text data.

Installation

Install Java

IBM Unstructured Information Modeler requires Java version 1.4 or higher be installed for it to run. Most computers already have this, but if you need a copy, you can find it on the Web using a standard search engine.

NOTE: If you have Java 1.3 (or older) installed, it will remain in the Add/Remove Programs until you do an Uninstall. It is strongly suggested that users remove the older installation before installing this version.

Once Java is installed, you are ready to install IBM Unstructured Information Modeler. Visit the IBM Alphaworks website to obtain the download package at http://www.alpahworks.ibm.com.

Input Data Format

IBM Unstructured Information Modeler takes as its primary input a single text file containing one text example per line. Line returns are not allowed within an example. The file should be in ASCII format and should not contain blank lines. This file should be named "text.dat." An example data set in this format should be included with the installation software.

Creation dates for each example may be provided in a separate file. There should be one date on each line of this file in the format "MM/DD/YYYY." (Please note: If you use a European date style in your computer's Regional Settings, then the format should be "DD/MM/YYYY.") There should be exactly the same number of lines in this file as there are in "text.dat." The name of this file should be "dates.dat."

Categorical information may be provided in (an) additional separate file or files. There should be one category name on each line of this file, and there should be exactly the same number of lines in this file as there are in "text.dat." The name of this file should end in ".class" or ".cat."

The user is strongly advised to create one directory for each data set to be analyzed and put a "text.dat" in this directory along with all associated files. These data set directories should be different from the directory where you installed IBM Unstructured Information Modeler.

When exporting data from a database or spreadsheet, use the following procedure:

1. Export enough records to be useful—probably at least 1000.
2. Export in ASCII, comma separated value format, or tab delimited format.

3. Export all test fields of interest, including problem description, problem resolution, abstract, date, model, and so on. Do not limit the number of characters per field.
4. Each example should be contained on exactly one line of the file.
5. No line returns should be embedded in an example.
6. The unstructured information should be separated and put into a "text.dat" file. The creation date should be put into a "dates.dat" file.
7. Other structured information can be put into separate files, one file per column. Each of these files can be named with the column label and end with a ".class" extension.

If the unstructured information in the spreadsheet contains embedded line returns, or if you are not sure if it does or not, use the following procedure to create the "text.dat" file:

1. Create a temporary spreadsheet and copy all the text columns from the original spreadsheet to this new one.
2. Insert a new empty column "A" at the left-hand side.
3. Fill the column with the character sequence "#@#" in every cell. (You can use the "drag mouse" feature to fill a column from a single cell in MS Excel.)
4. Save the file out as "text.csv" in comma separated value format in the directory where you are going to run IBM Unstructured Information Modeler.
5. Exit Excel.
6. Go to the directory where you put "text.csv" and make sure that the files "text.dat" and "sft.hash" do not exist there. If they do, delete them.
7. Execute "run.bat."
8. Click on the "OK" button in the initial screen.
9. The system will ask you for the location of the input file. Select "text.csv."
10. The system will ask for the line delimiter. Enter "#@#."
11. From here on, run IBM Unstructured Information Modeler as normal.

Starting IBM Unstructured Information Modeler

IBM Unstructured Information Modeler can be executed in one of two modes: "run" and "saved." In the installation directory sample, "run.bat" and "saved.bat" files are provided.

For demo purposes, you may start IBM Unstructured Information Modeler by clicking on "run.bat" or "saved.bat." Clicking on run.bat will start IBM Unstructured

Information Modeler from scratch on the example data set, causing it to build a new dictionary and classification. If you select "saved.bat," IBM Unstructured Information Modeler will ask you to select a previously saved classification. Select "saved.obj" and click on OK.

When you are ready to work with your own data set, create a new directory and make a copy of "saved.bat" and "run.bat" to put into it. Add a "text.dat" file in the format described previously and you should be ready to run. The first time, use "run.bat" to start IBM Unstructured Information Modeler on this data set. From then on, use "saved.bat" to load in previously saved sessions.

The IBM Unstructured Information Modeler Classification Process

The process of creating a meaningful and useful classification with IBM Unstructured Information Modeler is described in this section.

Run

The first step is to execute the "run" command on the directory where your "text.dat" file containing the free-form text is located. In addition, this directory may contain optional files that help IBM Unstructured Information Modeler to create a dictionary of terms for use in analyzing the text (see the "Dictionary Files" section).

An initial run setup dialog will come up. This dialog allows you to specify the number of classes and the size of the dictionary. The more dictionary words and classes you create, the more memory (RAM) will be used up on your machine and the slower the process will run. The default values are usually acceptable for most data sets.

You are given a choice as to how you may generate classes in IBM Unstructured Information Modeler. The default method is to let the system generate classes for you, using the *k*-means clustering algorithm. The other method uses the Intuitive or "Keyword" clustering algorithm. This takes longer but usually provides better results.

A checkbox allows you to specify whether or not you want to adjust the number of classes after the initial clustering. In general, this is a good idea, but it may result in fewer classes being displayed at the end than you asked for originally (since some of the classes may be merged together).

Another checkbox allows you to indicate whether or not phrases should be generated in the dictionary. In general, this is a good idea, but for data sets containing unusually large vocabularies, it may make more sense to use only single word features. The "Number of Sentences to Analyze in Each Example" feature allows the user to limit how far IBM Unstructured Information Modeler will read in each example during processing. This assumes that most useful information, for purposes of classification, is contained in the first few sentences of each example. If you know this to be the case for your data set, then selecting this feature will lead to a better classification in a shorter period of time.

The input "text.dat" file may be checked by selecting the "Check File" button. This will determine if there are any "partial" line return characters embedded in the file that might cause the system to misread where one example ends and the next one begins. The system can correct this type of problem automatically if you wish.

The "Filter" button allows you to specify a specific subset of the data to be used for processing while ignoring the remaining data in the text.dat file. This is done by means of a corresponding filter file that specifies the kind of each example in the "text.dat" file. Such a filter file should have the same number of lines as "text.dat" and each line should contain a character string that identifies the kind of each example.

The "Load Previous" button allows you to select a previously saved session to load in rather than running from scratch (see Figure A-1).

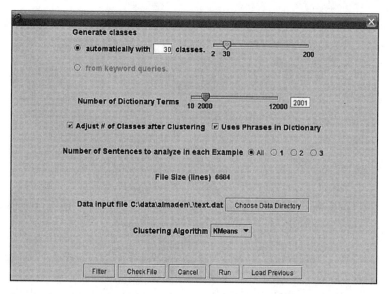

Figure A-1   Initial start screen

Once you select "Run," IBM Unstructured Information Modeler will analyze the data for a few minutes. Basically, IBM Unstructured Information Modeler makes three passes through the data set. The first pass finds all frequently occurring words, while the second pass finds all frequently occurring phrases. This allows IBM Unstructured Information Modeler to create a dictionary of terms. The third pass then discovers for each example, how many times each word and phrase in the dictionary occurs.

After the third pass, IBM Unstructured Information Modeler runs a "clustering" algorithm on the data set to create an initial classification. The result is an initial classification displayed in the Class Table view. An example of such an initial classification is shown in Figure A-2.

eClassifier: C:\data\almaden\./text.dat

File   Edit   Execute   View   Subclass   Help

| Dictionary Tool | View Selected Class | Subclass | Merge Classes |

Taxonomy Level: Root

	Class Name	Size	Cohesion	Distinctness
1	password	225 (3.37%)	66.43%	70.74%
2	id	120 (1.80%)	60.19%	48.43%
3	adsm	136 (2.03%)	57.35%	77.56%
4	print	1179 (17.64%)	56.81%	36.76%
5	install	506 (7.57%)	55.72%	55.74%
6	address	230 (3.44%)	55.09%	69.72%
7	calendar	132 (1.97%)	54.86%	64.94%
8	quick_fix	330 (4.94%)	53.94%	77.46%
9	email	404 (6.04%)	51.02%	54.57%
10	network	242 (3.62%)	49.73%	73.77%
11	page,refresh	97 (1.45%)	48.05%	90.94%
12	file	314 (4.70%)	47.64%	77.36%
13	afs	233 (3.49%)	47.60%	70.74%
14	server	213 (3.19%)	47.34%	70.72%
15	database	202 (3.02%)	47.32%	54.57%
16	drive	155 (2.32%)	46.74%	75.48%
17	vm	153 (2.29%)	45.68%	71.59%
18	note	669 (10.01%)	45.20%	48.43%
19	print,netscape	116 (1.74%)	43.41%	36.76%
20	problem	166 (2.48%)	40.03%	74.51%
21	system	238 (3.56%)	37.77%	73.27%
22	change	132 (1.97%)	37.24%	74.32%
23	aix,wants,info	169 (2.53%)	36.57%	55.74%
24	named,add,access,bin	113 (1.69%)	32.33%	75.58%
25	work,config,connect,set..	210 (3.14%)	27.93%	73.77%
	TOTAL / AVERAGE	6684	49.61%	60.14%

| Visualization | Class View | Class Table | Class Tree |

Figure A-2   Initial clustering

In the example, IBM Unstructured Information Modeler has created 25 classes of varying size and given each class a name based on the most frequently occurring words in the examples of the class. If a single term occurs in most of the examples in a class, then this becomes the class name. Otherwise, more terms are added to incorporate those examples that are not covered by the first term (words separated by commas). Eventually, if no set of five terms covers most of the examples, then the class is simply called "Miscellaneous."

Before the user goes very far in exploring the classification, it is wise to spend some time editing the dictionary IBM Unstructured Information Modeler used to create it. The dictionary is the list of words or phrases that IBM Unstructured Information Modeler found occurred most often in the text, other than those words that are in the stopwords list. The user may edit this dictionary to remove those terms that are not useful for the purposes of problem categorization. A Dictionary Tool is provided for this purpose. Since work done in the dictionary tool only applies to a single data set analysis, it is recommended that any deletions you make of a more general nature (those you want to apply to other data sets you work with in the future) be reflected in the stopwords list. The system will ask you if you want to add to this list whenever you make a word deletion.

Dictionary Editing

Before we waste any time with this initial classification, it would be wise to validate the dictionary that IBM Unstructured Information Modeler used to create it. To do this, we use the Edit -> Dictionary Tool command from the menu bar. The result is a pop-up window that looks like Figure A-3.

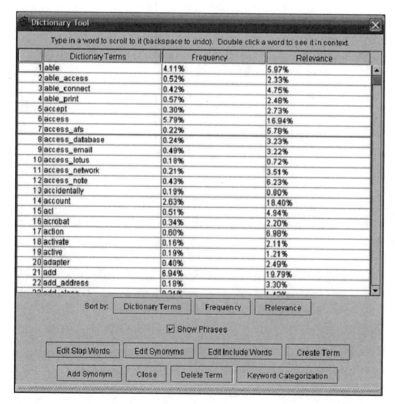

Figure A-3 Dictionary Tool

The primary purpose of this tool is to edit the dictionary so as to remove those terms that have no classification value. Doing this early on will make the classification process much easier, because it will make IBM Unstructured Information Modeler more effective in creating automatic classifications based on word occurrence. Select one or more terms in the table using "Ctrl-Click" and then select the "Delete Term" button to remove them. You may be prompted about removing phrases containing the word(s) you selected. The terms you should delete are those that do not contribute useful information about the problem ticket. An example would be the proper names of persons who work at the helpdesk. Names like "John" and "Mary" should be removed from the dictionary because they don't help us to classify the problem tickets based on their underlying symptoms and resolutions.

Rather than searching tediously through the whole dictionary to find all proper names, IBM Unstructured Information Modeler provides a facility for finding these based on word capitalization. To use this facility, click on the "Proper Name Occurrence" button. The system will search the text to find the number of times each dictionary word is capitalized. It will then add a new column to the table showing this percentage. If we sort by this column (by clicking on the header), we see something like Figure A-4.

	Dictionary Terms	Frequency	Relevance	Proper Name Occ...
81	ann	0.27%	1.25%	100.00%
101	arcprt01	0.57%	2.65%	100.00%
142	barbara	0.13%	1.38%	100.00%
145	bev	0.10%	4.02%	100.00%
146	bill	0.16%	0.87%	100.00%
153	bob	0.18%	1.01%	100.00%
176	bruce	0.24%	0.65%	100.00%
180	butler	0.49%	1.98%	100.00%
182	byron	0.16%	1.61%	100.00%
205	carbajal	0.12%	0.87%	100.00%
221	center	0.60%	8.68%	100.00%
235	chapdelaine	0.16%	10.14%	100.00%
248	clementina	0.51%	5.71%	100.00%
324	contr	0.25%	3.91%	100.00%
339	corel	0.21%	1.38%	100.00%
355	crash	0.76%	2.85%	100.00%
388	dan	0.33%	1.73%	100.00%
404	day	0.49%	1.78%	100.00%
447	direct	0.79%	4.53%	100.00%
484	draw	0.19%	1.40%	100.00%
547	epson	0.12%	0.56%	100.00%
548	eric	0.64%	2.82%	100.00%
592	figaro	0.36%	1.51%	100.00%
670	gary	0.10%	1.67%	100.00%
673	geiger	0.06%	3.03%	100.00%

Figure A-4   Proper name occurrence

This should bring the proper names in the text to the top of the list. Now it's easy to select and delete these non-meaningful terms.

After we have finished deleting terms, we should run the clustering algorithm again to be sure we have the best possible classification to start with. To do this, select Execute->Generate New Classification from the menu bar. Note that if you start IBM Unstructured Information Modeler over again using "run.bat," you will lose any changes you have made to the dictionary through the Dictionary Tool. Only changes made to the stopword list of the stock phrases list will be remembered (see the next section).

Dictionary Files

The user may, if desired, provide IBM Unstructured Information Modeler some up-front information about the domain by supplying dictionary files. These files help IBM Unstructured Information Modeler to create a better dictionary than it would otherwise be able to. These files may be modified by selecting the appropriate Edit button in the Dictionary Tool.

Stopwords

The information provided in the "stopWords.txt" file tells IBM Unstructured Information Modeler which words NOT to include in the dictionary. This is typically a list of non-informative adjuncts, prepositions, and so on. A default stopword list is provided with IBM Unstructured Information Modeler and is embedded in the IBM Unstructured Information Modeler.jar file. Any stopwords the user adds to the external stopWords.txt file (the one in the directory where text.dat is located) will be in addition to those that are named in the embedded stopWords.txt file.

IncludeWords

The information provided in the "includeWords.txt" file tells IBM Unstructured Information Modeler which words MUST be included in the dictionary, no matter how frequently or infrequently they occur. The includeWords file format is one word per line, with synonyms separated by a "|". This allows "spaces" to occur inside words.

IncludeWords are actually very powerful. Each line is actually a "regular expression." The rules for forming regular expressions in IBM Unstructured Information Modeler are defined by the Java 1.4 specification (http://java.sun.com/j2se/1.4.2/docs/api/java/util/regex/Pattern.html).

An example of some regular expressions are shown here:

```
DateString|\d/\d\d/\d\d
PriceString|\$\d+\.\d\d
PlanetString|Mercury|Veunus|Earth|Mars|Jupiter|Saturn|Uranus|Neptune
IBM|IBM|International Business Machines|big blue
```

The first line creates a feature called DateString whenever it sees something like 9/27/06 anywhere in the text of an example. The second line creates the term PriceString whenever it sees something like $23.05. The third line creates the term PlanetString whenever one of the names of the planets appears in the text. And the last line creates the term IBM whenever any of the identified names for the company are used. Note that when more than one pattern is given on a line with "|" separating the patterns, then the first pattern is taken to be the term name and is not used for matching purposes.

Synonyms

The information in the "synonyms.txt" file tells IBM Unstructured Information Modeler which words are to be considered synonymous for the purposes of classification. Often, words that have the same basic root (such as print, printing, printer) should be considered synonyms. A default synonym list is provided with IBM Unstructured Information Modeler. The user may modify this list and copy it to the directory where "text.dat" resides in order to employ it.

A new synonym list may be generated by selecting the Generate button when editing synonyms.

Stock Phrases

Some data sets may contain "boilerplate" text that interferes with IBM Unstructured Information Modeler's ability to classify by word similarity. Examples would be fill-in-the-blank forms containing text such as "Area Code" and "Social Security Number." The dictionary file, "stock-phrases.txt," is used to deal with this problem. Each line of the file contains a phrase that is to be excluded by IBM Unstructured Information Modeler from consideration in building the dictionary. The phrase should occur with the same capitalization and punctuation as it occurs in the text of the documents. Note that individual words that should always be ignored should not be put in this file, but in the stopWords.txt file instead.

IBM Unstructured Information Modeler also has a tool for generating potential stock phrases. This tool can be employed by selecting the Generate button when editing stock phrases.

After you have finished editing stock-phrases.txt, it is best to start IBM Unstructured Information Modeler over again to completely redo the dictionary and the classification.

Merging Similar Classes

After you have created a good dictionary, the next step is to find classes that IBM Unstructured Information Modeler has differentiated that are not different enough to warrant such separation. In other words, we want to merge similar classes. We can easily find candidates for merging by selecting View->Sort by->Class Distinctness from the menu bar.

Classes with a low distinctness score are now listed at the top. At this point, we could have IBM Unstructured Information Modeler automatically merge classes that it thinks are similar using the Execute->Merge Similar Classes command. Or we can make the decision about which classes to merge ourselves after investigating classes more carefully in the Class View.

Naming Classes

After merging similar classes, the next step is to systematically go through the classes that remain and make sense out of them. The name that IBM Unstructured Information Modeler assigns to each class is usually not sufficiently descriptive to communicate all that the class is about. The user should explore each class using the Class View and then give the class an appropriate name.

The order in which you explore the classes is important. By default, the classes are sorted in order of cohesion (highest to lowest). Now in Class View, you can easily work your way through the classes, starting with the most cohesive first. These classes are usually more easily understood than less cohesive ones.

To understand a class in Class View, first look at the Word Frequency double bar chart in the lower-left corner of the screen. This chart will quickly tell you which words or phrases occur in the class with highest frequency. In some cases, you may immediately grasp what the class is about from this chart alone.

Next, look at the example text displayed in the right-hand side. Begin by looking at the Most Typical examples (using the Sort by: Most Typical menu option). This will bring to the top the examples that best typify the class. Generally, you should not need to look beyond the first three or four examples to get an initial feel for the class.

To give the class a new name, simply click with your mouse in the menu box at the upper-left corner of the Class View and edit the name displayed in the box. Hit the enter key when you are done.

Splitting Classes

As you go through the naming process, you will probably find that some classes are harder to name than others. Especially as you get toward the bottom of the list, the less-cohesive classes tend to have many disparate examples that seem to have no common thread. You may wind up calling these classes "miscellaneous." These are the classes that need further work.

Classes that have a mixture of unconnected examples may be modified in some way that makes the result more coherent. IBM Unstructured Information Modeler provides several methods for dealing with poorly defined classes.

Deleting a Class

A bad class may simply be deleted from the classification. This can be done via the Execute-> Delete Classes menu bar command. The dialog that pops up allows you to select one or more classes for deletion. When you delete a class, the examples of that class will move over to the next nearest class.

The danger of deleting a class and letting its examples go elsewhere, is that this may mess up some other class in the classification. To check this before doing a delete, click on the View Secondary Classes button in the Class View.

This action presents a pie chart indicating where the class examples would go if the current class were deleted. You can even click on a slice of the pie to see the text of the examples that it represents (see Figure A-5).

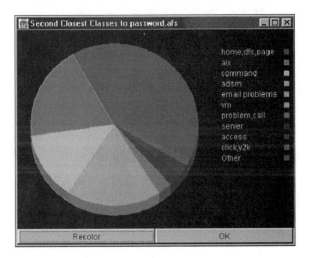

Figure A-5   Secondary classes

Keyword Search

You can find all examples in a class that contain a given keyword and create a separate class containing these examples, removing them from the current class. This is done through the Edit->Keyword Search menu bar command (see Figure A-6).

Simply type in the keyword and select the checkbox to indicate you want only examples in the current class. You can click on the "Show Examples" button to be sure these are the examples you want, and if so, click on "Create Class" to create a new class with these examples.

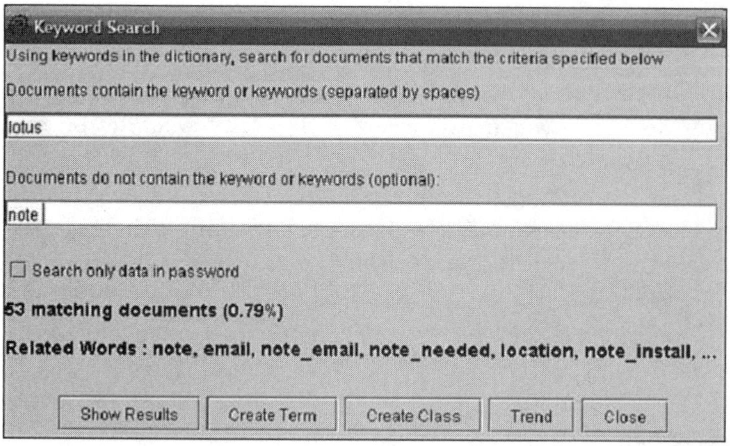

Figure A-6   Keyword search

Note that you can only search for words that occur in the IBM Unstructured Information Modeler dictionary. If you search for a word and it does not occur, even though you know it exists somewhere in the text, this is an indication that the word did not get included in the dictionary. Use the Create Term button to create this term automatically in the dictionary.

The negated word box allows you to search for examples that do not contain certain words. For instance, in Figure A-6, we are searching for examples that have the word "lotus," but not the word "note." The "Related Words" display lists those dictionary terms that are most correlated in their example occurrence with the word you entered in the first box.

Delete/Move Examples

You can manually select individual examples to move or delete from a class via the Delete/Move Examples button in Class View. Before you select this button, you should have identified the example numbers of the examples you wish to remove in the example viewer. The examples you select may be deleted entirely, moved to a new class that you create, or moved to an already existing class.

Subclass

You can subclass a poor class in the hopes of making it better by a divide and conquer approach. Select the row of the class you wish to subclass and then click on the Subclass button. Analyze the subclasses that are then displayed and give names to the ones that are coherent. You can then move these back up the hierarchy by dragging and dropping them in the Class Tree View. When done, you can eliminate the remaining subclasses by using the Subclass->Remove Current Subclassification command in the menu bar.

Know Your Limitations

In the end, all these methods may fail to produce completely pure classes. Some miscellaneous classes are to be expected in most real-world data sets. It is usually best to focus your efforts on the 80% of the data that is easily amenable to classification and not waste too much time on the remaining 20%.

Fine Tuning

After your classification has begun to stabilize, you should go back through each of the classes one more time to find the outliers (i.e., those examples that don't quite fit into the class they belong to). This can be done in Class View by selecting Sort by: Least Typical. The result will be a display of those examples that fit least well into the class they are assigned to. You can then decide whether to leave these examples where they are, move them somewhere else, or delete them.

Save Your Work

Before you exit from IBM Unstructured Information Modeler, use the File->Save command to save the state of the software into a ".obj" file. This can then be read back in at any time using the File->Read command or by starting IBM Unstructured Information Modeler with "saved."

Interpreting IBM Unstructured Information Modeler Views

In the main window of IBM Unstructured Information Modeler at the bottom of the screen, there are four tabs indicating the four views of the data that IBM Unstructured Information Modeler provides. Each of these views shows the input data set from a different perspective. The meaning and purpose of each view is as described next.

Class Tree

IBM Unstructured Information Modeler allows the user to create a classification hierarchy, where each class may be further subdivided into many subclasses. The Class Tree allows the user to navigate and modify this hierarchy. Individual classes can be merged and moved in this view. This is the highest-level view of the classification (see Figure A-7).

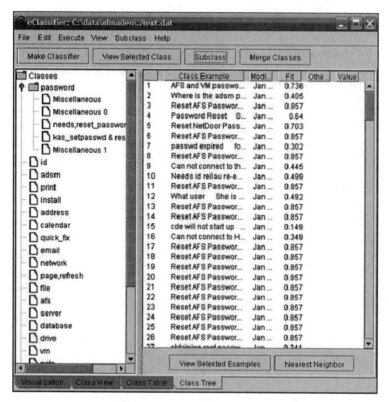

Figure A-7 Class Tree view

To select one node in this view, simply click on the name or the icon for that node on the left side. This will display that node's examples in a table on the right-hand side. To select more than one node, hold down the Control key while selecting. Once a node is selected, you can right click to bring up a menu of operations that can be performed. Or, use the Merge or Delete buttons in the toolbar.

You can use the Class Tree to navigate by selecting a node and then selecting the View Selected Class button (above). If a folder was selected, this will cause the classification to be displayed in the Class Table. If a leaf node was selected, this will cause the leaf node to be displayed in the Class View.

You can use the Class Tree to move nodes in the hierarchy by selecting the node to be moved and dragging it to the folder where you want it to reside. You can only drag leaf nodes in this way, not folders.

You can use the Class Tree to merge multiple classes into a single class or folder by selecting the classes to be merged and then right clicking. From the pop-up menu, select "Merge" or "Merge as Subclass" to create a new leaf node or new folder, respectively.

Clicking on the "View Selected Examples" button shows a display of the text of the selected examples.

Clicking on the "Visualize Examples" button takes you to the Visualization Screen where you can see the selected examples circled (see Figure A-8).

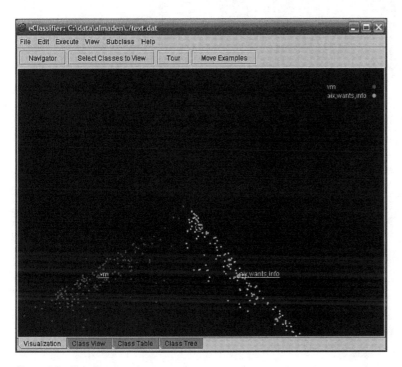

Figure A-8   Visualize examples

Class Table

This is the default view. This view displays only one level of the Class Tree at a time. The level displayed is labeled at the top of this view. The Class Table provides numerical statistics about each class in comparison to the other classes. It acts much like a spreadsheet where the data can be sorted along any dimension (see Figure A-9).

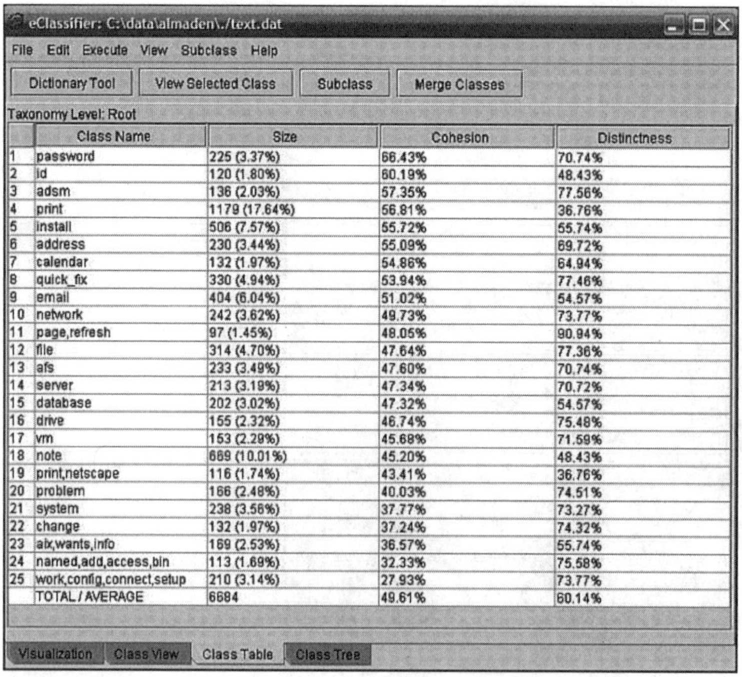

	Class Name	Size	Cohesion	Distinctness
1	password	225 (3.37%)	66.43%	70.74%
2	id	120 (1.80%)	60.19%	48.43%
3	adsm	136 (2.03%)	57.35%	77.56%
4	print	1179 (17.64%)	56.81%	36.76%
5	install	506 (7.57%)	55.72%	55.74%
6	address	230 (3.44%)	55.09%	69.72%
7	calendar	132 (1.97%)	54.86%	64.94%
8	quick_fix	330 (4.94%)	53.94%	77.46%
9	email	404 (6.04%)	51.02%	54.57%
10	network	242 (3.62%)	49.73%	73.77%
11	page,refresh	97 (1.45%)	48.05%	90.94%
12	file	314 (4.70%)	47.64%	77.36%
13	afs	233 (3.49%)	47.60%	70.74%
14	server	213 (3.19%)	47.34%	70.72%
15	database	202 (3.02%)	47.32%	54.57%
16	drive	155 (2.32%)	46.74%	75.48%
17	vm	153 (2.29%)	45.68%	71.59%
18	note	669 (10.01%)	45.20%	48.43%
19	print,netscape	116 (1.74%)	43.41%	36.76%
20	problem	166 (2.48%)	40.03%	74.51%
21	system	238 (3.56%)	37.77%	73.27%
22	change	132 (1.97%)	37.24%	74.32%
23	aix,wants,info	169 (2.53%)	36.57%	55.74%
24	named,add,access,bin	113 (1.69%)	32.33%	75.58%
25	work,config,connect,setup	210 (3.14%)	27.93%	73.77%
	TOTAL / AVERAGE	6684	49.61%	60.14%

Figure A-9 Class Table

The meaning of each of the columns is as follows:

Class Name

Each class in IBM Unstructured Information Modeler is given a unique name by the system. The user has the option of changing this name at any time. Clicking on the Header for this column causes the classes to be sorted in alphabetical order.

Size

The number of examples contained in each class. The value in the last row indicates how many examples are in the entire classification in total. Clicking on the Header for this column causes the classes to be sorted by size. Each example belongs to exactly one class.

Cohesion

A measure of how similar the examples in a class are to the mean (average value) of the class. This is the inverse of the class error. High cohesion is desirable. The average cohesion is shown in the last row for this column. If a class has 100% cohesion, this means that every example in the class uses exactly the same dictionary terms as every other example in the class. If a class has 0% cohesion, this means that every example in the class uses completely different dictionary terms than every other example. Most classes will fall somewhere in between these two extremes.

Distinctness

A measure of how different each class is from its nearest neighbor. This is a measure of class uniqueness. The two classes with the lowest score in this column are the two most similar classes in the classification. Classes with low distinctness are candidates to be merged together. High distinctness is desirable. If a class has 100% distinctness this means that the words used in this class are completely different than the words used in every other class. If a class has 0% distinctness, this means that there is at least one other class somewhere in the classification that uses exactly the same dictionary words as this class. Most classes will fall somewhere in between these two extremes. Note that there will always be at least two classes having the lowest distinctness value in the classification. This is because we measure distinctness by looking at the nearest neighboring class and these two classes are nearest to each other.

Keyword Match

After an Edit->Keyword Search command is completed, a column will be added to the Class Table indicating the frequency of the keyword occurrence in each of the classes. This is given as the percentage of examples within each class that match the given keyword.

Double clicking on any table row should bring up that class in the Class View panel.

Class View

This is a more detailed view of the classification. It looks at only one class at a time and allows the user to see the text of the individual examples that make up the class. It also shows important statistics about frequently occurring words and phrases. This view is critical for understanding what a class is about (see Figure A-10).

In the upper-left corner is a menu for selecting the Class you wish to view. You can also edit the name of the class by clicking inside this menu box and typing in a new name and hitting the Enter key or by selecting the Rename button.

Just below this is the Class Components view. This diagram indicates the major components of the current class, identified by {+/-} dictionary term. For example, in Figure A-10, we see that for the "password" class, 99.11% of the examples have the term "password," but 40.05% of all examples that have the term "password" do not belong to this class. Clicking on any button in this display will cause the system to display the examples corresponding to that button. A new class can then be created from these examples if desired.

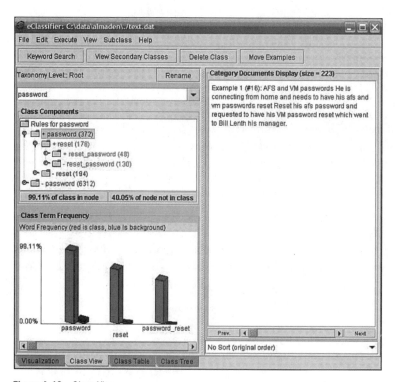

Figure A-10 Class View

In the lower-left corner is a Class Term Frequency bar graph. The graph is scrollable to show the entire dictionary. The terms in the graph are sorted by how much more frequently they occur in the current class than in the parent class (or the data set as a whole). Putting the mouse over any bar in the graph will show that bar's value. Clicking on a bar will display the examples that the bar corresponds to. This graph is a very powerful tool in understanding what a class is all about.

On the right-hand side is a display of the text of the examples contained in the class. The examples are displayed one at a time in the text window. The scrollbar at the bottom controls which example is displayed. The order in which the examples appear is controlled by the Sorting menu below the text window. You can sort by typicality, keyword, or solution authoring usefulness (see "Sort Menu").

Visualization

This view is a graphical representation of the examples contained in the current class (the class displayed in the Class View), along with the examples of some of the most closely related classes. This view is most useful in gaining an understanding of the relationships between and among a small number of different classes (see Figure A-11).

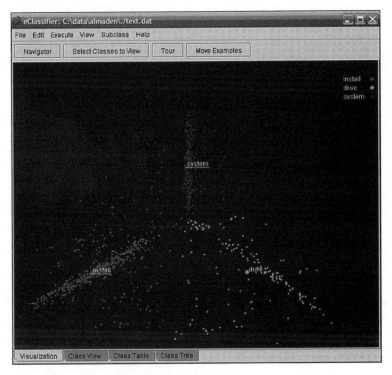

Figure A-11   Visualization scatter plot

This scatter plot should be interpreted as follows:

1. The small dots represent examples in the data set.
2. The icons represent class centroids. The centroid is the mean of a class.
3. Circular icons represent the primary centroids upon which the scatter plot is based. The axes are drawn through the primary class centroids.
4. Square icons represent the other centroids.

Since the example points each have as many components (dimensions) as there are dictionary terms, this plot can only show us a partial view of the true document space. Some information is lost. What is not lost is how the document points relate to the primary centroid. This is represented accurately in the scatter plot. Therefore, the user should focus their attention on the primary centroids (circular icons) and the example points that belong to them when they study the plot. The user can change which centroids are primary by "touring" (see "Tour").

You can click on any of the centroid names having a line underneath to make it the current class. Thus, by successively clicking on these class names, you can "navigate" around the classes. You can also left click on any example point or points in the graph to see these examples displayed. To change the selection of primary centroids, choose "Tour" from the right-click menu.

The "Navigator Off/On" button in the toolbar lets you select the visualization mode. Navigator On is the default that allows you to manually navigate around the space. Navigator Off mode simply displays all the classes and the examples at once. This is not recommended for data sets of significant size.

Visualization is a good way to verify the consistency of a small number of classes. If you see a mish-mash of examples between and amongst the primary classes, so that each does not occupy a distinct area of space, this is an indication that the classification may be inconsistent and need some modification. Clicking on the areas of inconsistency will show you which examples are causing the confusion. These examples may need to be moved from one class to another.

IBM Unstructured Information Modeler Menus, Buttons, and Other Commands

This section provides a complete list of all controls available in the IBM Unstructured Information Modeler GUI, along with their function. If you are new to IBM Unstructured Information Modeler, it is recommended that you first read the section entitled "The IBM Unstructured Information Modeler Process."

Note that a toolbar is provided at the top of IBM Unstructured Information Modeler, which provides different buttons depending on which view you are currently looking at. These buttons are meant to be shortcuts to the most commonly used operations in the corresponding view. Most of these shortcut operations are also available via the pulldown menus. For simplicity, they are described only once, as menu operations.

File Menu

The File pulldown menu in the upper-left corner is described here. It contains operations that have to do with input/output files.

Read Classification

Used for reading in a ".class" file. This is a structured field that you want to use instead of IBM Unstructured Information Modeler clustering to provide a classification of the data. The format is standard ASCII text, one class name per line with the same number of lines in this file as there are in "text.dat." When this operation is completed, the old classification scheme will be completely replaced by the classification in the given input file.

Read

Read in a previous classification ".obj" file. Objects can be read that pertain to the same data set or to a different data set. If you choose the object from a different directory than the current one, the system will ask you whether to keep the same examples you are currently viewing, or to load in the examples that are in the new object's directory. If you choose to keep the same examples, the system will classify the examples into the most similar class of the new object.

Save

Save out a classification ".obj" file. You should do this fairly frequently as you make changes, giving different file names to each result so that you can back up easily at any point in the process if things go amiss.

The classification object file contains all the information IBM Unstructured Information Modeler needs to bring up the classification where you left off. The only thing not retained is the contents of "text.dat," "dates.dat," and so on. You should therefore save your object in the same directory as these files in order to be sure you can read it in successfully next time.

Make Classifier

Create a classifier that can take future data and accurately determine which category in the classification it falls into (see Figure A-12).

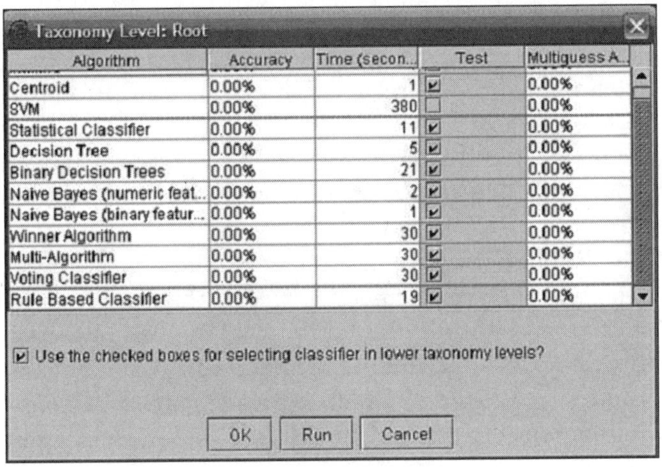

Taxonomy Level: Root

Algorithm	Accuracy	Time (secon..	Test	Multiguess A..
Centroid	0.00%	1	☑	0.00%
SVM	0.00%	380	☐	0.00%
Statistical Classifier	0.00%	11	☑	0.00%
Decision Tree	0.00%	5	☑	0.00%
Binary Decision Trees	0.00%	21	☑	0.00%
Naïve Bayes (numeric feat..	0.00%	2	☑	0.00%
Naïve Bayes (binary featur...	0.00%	1	☑	0.00%
Winner Algorithm	0.00%	30	☑	0.00%
Multi-Algorithm	0.00%	30	☑	0.00%
Voting Classifier	0.00%	30	☑	0.00%
Rule Based Classifier	0.00%	19	☑	0.00%

☑ Use the checked boxes for selecting classifier in lower taxonomy levels?

[OK] [Run] [Cancel]

Figure A-12 Make Classifier

IBM Unstructured Information Modeler has a number of different modeling algorithms that can be employed. It is suggested that the user try out as many as time permits in order to determine which one is best able to accurately categorize their classification. Selecting the "Run" button will cause the system to evaluate the accuracy of each of the approaches selected in the "Test?" column. After evaluation is complete, selecting OK will cause the most accurate classifier to become the current classifier for the categorization or the user may manually select the algorithm they desire at any time and click on OK for it to become the chosen approach. Once a classifier has been created, the use should save this out to a file by selecting "File->Save." The object that is created will then have the ability to categorize new examples automatically via the IBM Unstructured Information Modeler API, or through the "File->Read Data Set" command.

Read Template

Used for reading in a previous classification from a different data set. This classification would have been generated using IBM Unstructured Information Modeler using the "Save" command. The user will be asked to supply a ".obj" file where a previous IBM Unstructured Information Modeler classification object has been saved. The current data set will then be loaded into this classification and each example placed in the class of the closest centroid. The dictionary will then be changed to the dictionary of the previous classification.

You would use this command to start analyzing a new data set based on a previous classification. This should only be attempted when you suspect some relationship between the two data sets. An example would be when the two data sets come from the same helpdesk at different time periods.

Read Structured Information

Read in a ".class" or ".cat" file containing a categorical variable to be compared with the current classification.

When the Read Structured Information menu item under the File menu is selected, you will be prompted to select a (.class) file. The results are displayed in a co-occurrence table like the one shown in Figure A-13.

Each row represents a class, and each column represents a category found in the structured file. The value in the cell represents the total co-occurrence of the class and the structured field value. The color of each cell indicates the "affinity" of the two values for each other in terms of the expected size of the co-occurrence vs. the actual size. Columns can be sorted by clicking on the header row. Rows and columns can be swapped by clicking on Transpose. Any cell or combination of cells can be selected and the examples viewed or shown in a trend chart.

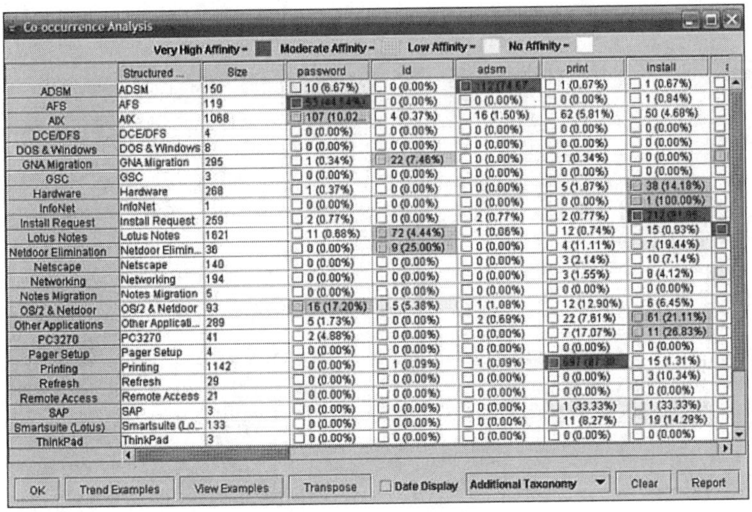

Figure A-13   Co-occurrence table

Save Classification

Save out the current classification as a flat ASCII ".class" file. This is useful for transferring your classification to a database, spreadsheet, or other program.

Generate Report

Generate an HTML report describing the classification and listing 10 interesting examples for each class. All classes at every level of the hierarchy will be included in this report.

Custom Report

Generate a custom HTML report where you tell IBM Unstructured Information Modeler which classes to report on from anywhere in the hierarchy.

Generate Spreadsheet

Generates a comma separated value file describing the class structure and the size of each class. This can be easily loaded into an Excel Spreadsheet program to generate graphical reports.

Exit

Exit the current IBM Unstructured Information Modeler session. Be sure to save your work!

Edit Menu

The Edit Menu provides features that help with the taxonomy editing process.

Cut/Copy/Paste

Cut, Copy, or Paste text from the Example display in Class View. This text can then be copied into another Windows application or vice versa. This will not have any permanent effect on the original text.dat file.

Undo

This undoes the effect of the last operation. Selecting it twice will undo the last two operations and so forth. The undo stack will only be maintained for the length of a session. It starts fresh each time you restart IBM Unstructured Information Modeler. The Undo objects are kept in a separate subdirectory of the directory where your data set resides. The objects are erased between sessions to conserve disk space.

The Undo objects are abbreviated forms of regular saved objects from IBM Unstructured Information Modeler. They usually will not contain the keyword index to the documents in order to save space. Therefore, you cannot always read them into IBM Unstructured Information Modeler from scratch if your system crashes. (So save your work frequently!)

Keyword Search

Finds all examples that match a string of keywords separated by and/or. Words that are not to be included in the search results may also be entered (see Figure A-14).

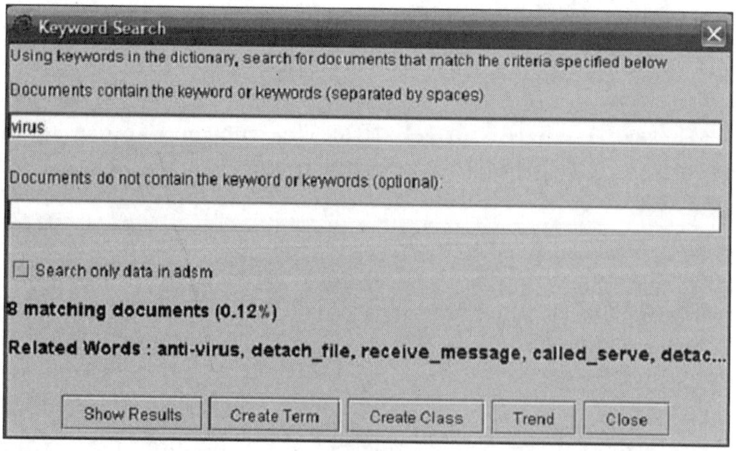

Figure A-14 Keyword search

You can use this command to create your own classes based on a keyword string by selecting "Create Class" from the Keyword Search form.

Note that keyword search only works on words that are in the IBM Unstructured Information Modeler dictionary. Words that occur in the text but are not part of the dictionary will be ignored.

The negated word box allows you to search for examples that do not contain certain words.

The "Create Term" button will allow you to add a new term that does not occur in the dictionary.

Selecting "Show Results" will bring up the display shown in Figure A-15.

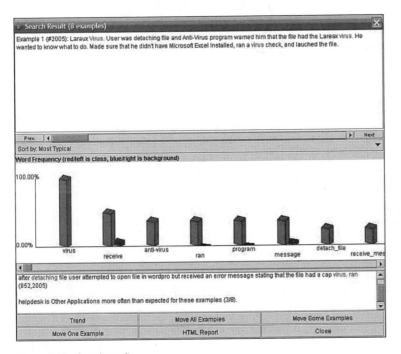

Figure A-15 Search results

From this display, the user can select "Move All Examples" to create a new class based on the examples displayed; "Move One/Some/All Examples" to another class, or "HTML Report" to create an HTML file with the information. The bottom text display is meant to be a short summary of interesting features of the selected examples. The words colored in red are the most "important" (i.e., statistically significant) words in the subset, and the phrase is chosen as a representative example of the use of these words. The numbers listed afterwards refer to the Example numbers of those documents that use all of the listed words in red.

Dictionary Tool

The Dictionary Tool is used to edit the IBM Unstructured Information Modeler dictionary to either add synonyms or to remove unnecessary words or phrases. The Dictionary Tool looks as shown in Figure A-16.

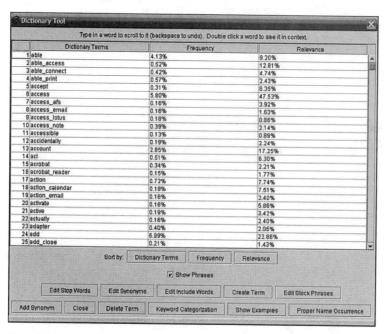

Figure A-16 Dictionary Tool

Frequency indicates in what percentage of the examples the word occurs. Relevancy indicates the maximum frequency the word occurs in any category. Terms with high relevancy should be considered carefully. If these do not convey interesting information, then they should definitely be deleted because they are having an undo effect on the categorization algorithm.

The Proper Name Occurrence button can be used to generate a frequency count of how often each term is capitalized. Many proper names are useful (e.g., Microsoft, Novell), but some are not (e.g., John, Mary). The user should select those that are not useful and use the Delete Term button to remove them.

To add a synonym, select the words that are to be considered synonymous (using Ctrl-Click), and then click on "Add Synonym."

Typing text while viewing this dialog will cause the dialog to scroll to the first occurrence of the typed text. This is a useful way to find a particular word in the dictionary.

You can edit any of the dictionary generation files by selecting one of the four Edit buttons. The system will display an editor like the one shown in Figure A-17 for synonyms.

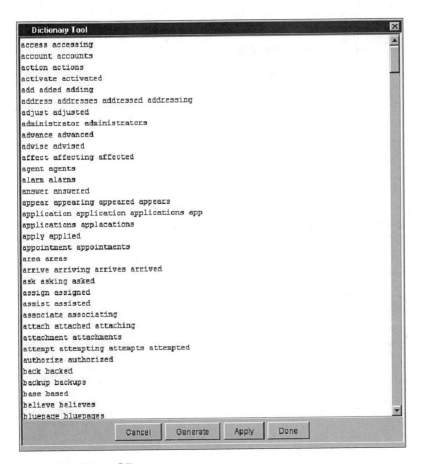

Figure A-17   Synonym Editor

The Generate button (if available) will allow you to generate a new list based on the current text information. The Done button will cause the current changes to be saved, but will not apply the changes to the currently loaded dictionary. The Apply button will save the changes and apply them to the current dictionary.

Execute Menu

The Execute Menu contains functions that perform analytical transformation to the taxonomy.

Generate New Classification

To reclassify is to allow IBM Unstructured Information Modeler to automatically generate a classification of the data set based on word similarity among the examples. The algorithm IBM Unstructured Information Modeler uses to do this is the same as the one used when IBM Unstructured Information Modeler was originally started. From a given starting point, this algorithm finds a classification that minimizes the average error (i.e., the distance between each example and the center of its category). Unfortunately, this is only a local optimum. The solution that IBM Unstructured Information Modeler comes up with will depend greatly on the starting point.

Generate New Classification tells the system to completely ignore the current classification and start over from scratch. The user will be asked how many classes are desired, a random starting point will be generated, and the system will run k-means to completion. All of the classes will be given a new name based on frequently occurring keywords in the class.

Purify Existing Classification

This clustering option tells the system to start from the current classification in generating the new one. The hope is that when this is run, IBM Unstructured Information Modeler will make only minor adjustments to the current classification, making sure that each example is assigned to the nearest classification. Still, the changes may not be insignificant. As examples move around, the meaning of an entire class can become significantly altered, thus causing a ripple effect as all that classes' original examples move to other classes, and they become altered, and so on. Reclassification (even when minor) is a significant operation that may have unintended consequences. Of course, you can always use the "Undo" feature under the Edit menu if you don't like the result you get.

Purify Stepwise

The difference between this option and "Purify Existing Classification" is how many iterations the algorithm is allowed to run. Stepwise will execute only one iteration of k-means before halting. In general, this will cause less unexpected consequences, but may still leave the classification in an "unstable" state. The "Purify Existing Classification" option will run k-means to completion.

Reclassifications are generally good to do whenever you modify the dictionary. This is because dictionary modifications actually change the space in which the clustering algorithm works. Modifying the dictionary will almost certainly cause some change in what the algorithm finds to be the optimum classification.

Classify by Keywords

Allows the user to specify their own classification scheme by entering keyword queries that define each class in the taxonomy. Examples that don't match any query or that match multiple queries will be put in special classes called "Miscellaneous" and "Ambiguous," respectively. The queries can also be read in from a file.

Subclass All Classes

Immediately generates subclasses for all classes at the current level. This will make a shallow Class Tree one level deeper at all nodes. Use this feature to quickly generate detailed classes.

Subclass from Structured Info

Immediately generates subclasses for all classes at the current level. Uses a structured input file containing a designated class name for each example. Use this feature to incorporate a structured classification at a lower level of the class hierarchy.

Delete Classes

This option is used to remove one or more classes from the classification. The examples that belong to this class can either be deleted or moved. If not deleted, each example will go to the next closest class.

Merge Similar Classes

This command automatically merges all classes with similar word content. To be exact, all classes that are dominated by the same term (a term occurring with 90% frequency) will be merged together. Although this is frequently a good thing to do, there may be some cases where two classes are dominated by the same word but really have different meanings.

Refine Miscellaneous

Automatically splits up the Miscellaneous class as many times as necessary to get classes that have meaningful names. The user is asked to provide a class size threshold below which the system will stop splitting. The result should be a classification with no Miscellaneous class, or only a very small Miscellaneous class.

Regenerate Dictionary

This command generates a new dictionary from frequently occurring words and phrases in the text. The classification remains unchanged by this operation. You should regenerate a dictionary after you make manual changes to stopWords.txt, synonyms.txt, or stock-phrases.txt. The alternative is to redo the "run.bat" command.

Generate Class Names

Asks the system to generate class names for all selected classes at the current level. By default, the name is generated based on the *shortest cover name* algorithm. It uses the most frequently occurring word or phrase as the first name, and if that covers most of the examples, then that becomes the class name. Otherwise, those examples that don't contain the name are considered and the word most frequently occurring in these is added to the name, and so on until we run out of examples. This usually generates good names, but the names are not always unique. Numerals will be added after non-unique names.

View Menu

The View Menu contains operations that show different views of the taxonomy.

Class Occurrence vs. Time

Displays a line graph showing one or more classes and how often they occur over time. The time granularity can be set to Monthly, Weekly, Daily, or Hourly. The user may also select to view the data as raw numbers or in percentage terms. The black line on the chart indicates how much of the entire data set occurs at each time interval. The scale for the black line is on the right-hand side of the chart (see Figure A-18).

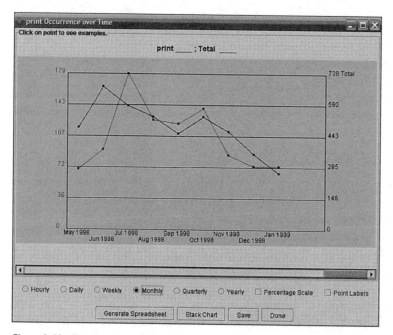

Figure A-18   Trend graph

Point labels may be displayed by clicking on this checkbox. The data in the chart can be output to a spreadsheet by selecting the "Generate Spreadsheet" button. Clicking on any point in the chart will bring up a display of the corresponding examples for that point.

Keyword Occurrence vs. Time

This is the same as "Category Occurrence vs. Time," except that the red bars indicate frequency of keyword occurrence instead of class occurrence. The keywords graphed will be those entered during the last keyword search.

Sort by

Sort the current set of classes via various methods. Unlike the sort that is executed by clicking on the Header row of the Class Table, which has only a local, temporary effect, this sort is global. It affects all the other views, including the Class Tree.

Select Metrics

This feature allows you to select which columns will be displayed in the Class Table view.

Cohesion and Distinctness are the default selections. They were described earlier in this document. The other metrics have the following definitions:

1. Keyword Match indicates what percentage of each class matches a user supplied keyword string.
2. Volume is a measure of the dictionary span of a class (how many different words are used in the class examples).
3. Current Classifier—Indicates how accurately the current classifier can classify the examples of each class.
4. Recency indicates what percentage of each class has a date stamp that falls within the last 10% of the data (chronologically).
5. Term indicates the dictionary term with the highest percentage occurrence in the class.
6. All other metrics are for particular classifiers. They show the predicted accuracy of the selected classifier on unseen documents.

Classifiers are algorithms that define how new examples get classified by a saved IBM Unstructured Information Modeler object.

Dictionary Co-Occurrence

Displays a table of all dictionary terms across different time intervals, with indications for each combination of term and time interval describing how often they occur together, and how unlikely this co-occurrence is (see Figure A-19).

Term	Count	10/16/97	2/11/98	3/12/98	4/13/98	5/21/98	6
able	able	276	15 (1.0)	30 (0.6203...	46 (1.6007...	49 (1.1345...	30 (0.6203...	20
able_access	able_access	35	1 (1.0)	7 (0.04782...	5 (0.39600...	12 (1.5532...	3 (1.0)	4
able_connect	able_conn...	28	1 (1.0)	5 (0.16446...	2 (1.0)	8 (0.00102...	2 (1.0)	2
able_print	able_print	38	1 (1.0)	3 (1.0)	10 (7.6744...	7 (0.08238...	3 (1.0)	2
accept	accept	21	1 (1.0)	3 (0.51132...	3 (0.51132...	5 (0.03449...	3 (0.51132...	4
access	access	388	47 (0.1515...	62 (5.1152...	45 (0.2777...	45 (0.2777...	50 (0.0502...	49
access_afs	access_afs	11	4 (0.00351...	1 (1.0)	0 (1.0)	0 (1.0)	1 (1.0)	0
access_email	access_e...	11	0 (1.0)	2 (0.36483...	0 (1.0)	2 (0.36483...	2 (0.36483...	5
access_lotus	access_lot...	12	2 (0.44047...	1 (1.0)	1 (1.0)	2 (0.44047...	1 (1.0)	2
access_note	access_note	26	2 (1.0)	8 (4.01741...	8 (4.01741...	4 (0.35848...	2 (1.0)	1
accessible	accessible	9	1 (0.91097...	1 (0.91097...	0 (1.0)	1 (1.0)	2 (0.22096...	0
accidentally	accidentally	13	1 (1.0)	1 (1.0)	4 (0.01242...	1 (1.0)	1 (1.0)	1
account	account	177	17 (1.0)	11 (1.0)	25 (0.0633...	15 (1.0)	21 (0.4004...	9
acl	acl	34	2 (1.0)	9 (0.00132...	0 (1.0)	2 (1.0)	7 (0.03892...	3
acrobat	acrobat	23	1 (1.0)	3 (0.62522...	6 (0.00994...	6 (0.00994...	1 (1.0)	1
acrobat_reader	acrobat_re...	106	0 (1.0)	0 (1.0)	2 (0.29106...	5 (2.42916...	0 (1.0)	0
action	action	48	8 (0.12187...	4 (1.0)	9 (0.04236...	4 (1.0)	8 (0.12187...	0
action_calendar	action_cale...	12	1 (1.0)	1 (1.0)	3 (0.08278...	2 (0.44047...	3 (0.08278...	0
action_email	action_email	11	2 (0.36483...	1 (1.0)	1 (1.0)	0 (1.0)	0 (1.0)	1
activate	activate	11	1 (1.0)	0 (1.0)	0 (1.0)	2 (0.36483...	2 (0.36483...	4
active	active	13	2 (0.51654...	0 (1.0)	0 (1.0)	2 (0.51654...	2 (0.51654...	1
actually	actually	11	1 (1.0)	2 (0.36483...	1 (1.0)	2 (0.36483...	2 (0.36483...	1
adapter	adapter	27	1 (1.0)	4 (0.40264...	5 (0.13890...	4 (0.40264...	2 (1.0)	3

Figure A-19 Dictionary co-occurrence table

Selecting a column header will sort based on the values in that column. The color of the cell is an indication of how closely related the term is to the time interval. Darker colors indicate higher affinity.

You can select one or more cells in the chart and then click on the buttons for additional information.

1. **Trend Examples**—Shows when the selected terms occur over time.
2. **View Examples**—Shows all examples that match the selected cells.
3. **Report**—Create an HTML report showing the table and associated examples.
4. **Enlarged View**—Displays a high-level picture of the entire co-occurrence table at different magnifications with a box that you can drag to the location of interest.

Dictionary vs. Categories

This is similar to the Dictionary co-occurrence table, with the difference that instead of comparing the dictionary to time, we compare it to each category in the taxonomy (see Figure A-20).

	Term	Count	print	note	install	quick_fix	email	
able	able	276	41 (1.0)	25 (1.0)	9 (1.0)	4 (1.0)	22 (0.1220...	21
able_access	able_access	35	0 (1.0)	7 (0.04977...	1 (1.0)	2 (1.0)	3 (0.48861...	1
able_connect	able_conn...	28	1 (1.0)	1 (1.0)	0 (1.0)	0 (1.0)	0 (1.0)	0
able_print	able_print	38	37 (2.9898...	0 (1.0)	0 (1.0)	0 (1.0)	0 (1.0)	1
accept	accept	21	0 (1.0)	3 (0.51834...	9 (1.0)	1 (1.0)	1 (1.0)	0
access	access	388	14 (1.0)	56 (0.0031...	9 (1.0)	16 (1.0)	24 (0.7613...	15
access_afs	access_afs	11	0 (1.0)	0 (1.0)	0 (1.0)	0 (1.0)	0 (1.0)	0
access_email	access_e...	11	0 (1.0)	2 (0.36962...	0 (1.0)	0 (1.0)	7 (2.71645...	0
access_lotus	access_lot...	12	0 (1.0)	7 (2.59840...	0 (1.0)	0 (1.0)	1 (0.71169...	0
access_note	access_note	26	0 (1.0)	17 (5.4405...	0 (1.0)	0 (1.0)	0 (1.0)	1
accessible	accessible	9	5 (0.00410...	0 (1.0)	0 (1.0)	0 (1.0)	0 (1.0)	1
accidentally	accidentally	13	0 (1.0)	6 (1.47390...	0 (1.0)	0 (1.0)	2 (0.14145...	1
account	account	177	4 (1.0)	25 (0.0679...	2 (1.0)	4 (1.0)	35 (1.0705...	6
acl	acl	34	0 (1.0)	5 (0.365816)	0 (1.0)	0 (1.0)	4 (0.13917...	1
acrobat	acrobat	23	8 (0.04329...	1 (1.0)	4 (0.09982...	0 (1.0)	0 (1.0)	8
acrobat_reader	acrobat_re...	10	2 (0.90016...	0 (1.0)	1 (0.82197...	0 (1.0)	0 (1.0)	6
action	action	48	0 (1.0)	5 (0.93314...	0 (1.0)	1 (1.0)	17 (1.7076...	1
action_calendar	action_cale...	12	0 (1.0)	0 (1.0)	0 (1.0)	0 (1.0)	2 (0.10910...	0
action_email	action_email	11	0 (1.0)	1 (1.0)	0 (1.0)	0 (1.0)	10 (2.0018...	0
activate	activate	11	0 (1.0)	0 (1.0)	1 (0.90037...	0 (1.0)	2 (0.08038...	0
active	active	13	0 (1.0)	1 (1.0)	0 (1.0)	1 (0.80881...	0 (1.0)	2
actually	actually	11	1 (1.0)	0 (1.0)	0 (1.0)	0 (1.0)	1 (0.64473...	1
adapter	adapter	27	1 (1.0)	3 (0.854755)	8 (3.72583...	1 (1.0)	0 (1.0)	1

Very High Affinity ■ Moderate Affinity ■ Low Affinity ■ No Affinity ■

Trend Examples View Examples Report OK Filter Enlarged View

Figure A-20 Dictionary vs. categories table

Such a table allows you to compare any taxonomy to the underlying dictionary to look for correlations between categories and terms.

Subclass Menu

This menu is only available after you have subclassed at least one category.

Remove Current Subclassification

This completely deletes the current subclassification (the one displayed in the Class Table) and all descendant classes. Use this operation after doing a subclass that you are not happy with.

Rollup

This removes the current subclassification (the one displayed in the Class Table), but retains its classes and puts them at the end of the parent classification. Use this operation when a subclass has only a few members that really belong at a higher level in the tree. This is an alternative to dragging and dropping each class member individually.

Help Menu

This menu provides access to the user manual, to version information, and to information on where to report bugs and get further assistance.

Visualization Buttons/Pop-Up Menu

These buttons are accessible on the top of the Visualization panel.

Navigator

When a visualization plot displays too many classes at once, turning the Navigator "on" will refresh the display focusing on just the current class and its near neighbors in space. In this mode, clicking on a centroid will cause the plot to shift perspective, making the selected class the current class and changing the visible classes to be the nearest neighbors of the selected class.

Turning the Navigator "off" (by clicking on it again) will cause all the classes (of the current level of the class hierarchy) to be displayed.

Tour

Causes the dot plot to rotate continuously from one plane to another. The selection of plane is based on a random choice of three primary centroids. The Tour Location indicator shows how many of the possible ways to choose three positions you have seen so far. When the end of the tour is reached, the tour begins again at the beginning (see Figure A-21).

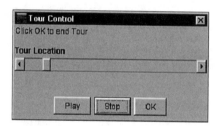

Figure A-21 Visualization tour control

The motion can be stopped at any time by clicking on the Stop button in the Tour Control dialog. The tour will then halt at the next primary centroid plane. To start the motion again from this point, select Play. You can also manually select the tour position by dragging the Tour Location control. Click on OK to end Touring.

Select Classes to View

Lets the user select which classes should be displayed in the visualization plot. The user should select at least three classes to view at a time. More than eight classes is not recommended to view at once.

Move Examples

Creates a blow-up window within the visualization that can be used to select examples and move them to a different class. You can drag the white square around the dot graph to see a magnified view in the side-car window.

Once you have the examples you want to move selected in the box, select Move Examples to move them all to a particular class. Select "Create Class" to create a new class containing these examples. Close the side-car box to remove the blow-up.

Class Tree Pop-Up Menu

This menu is accessible by right clicking on the Class Tree View.

Refresh

Repaints the graphics in case they have been messed up.

Rename

Give the selected class a new name. The user will be prompted for the new class name.

Subclass

Subclasses the selected class. Creates five subclasses using the k-means clustering algorithm.

Merge

Merges the selected classes into a new class. The merged classes are deleted, and all of their examples go into a new class, which is given a user-supplied name.

Merge as Subclass

Same as Merge, except the old classes are retained as subclasses of the new class.

View/Select

If the selected node is a leaf, then it goes to the Class View, displaying the selected node. If the selected node is not a leaf, then it goes to the Class Table with the selected classification displayed.

Class Tree Buttons

These buttons appear at the bottom of the Class Tree View.

View Selected Examples

Displays the full text of the selected example rows.

Nearest Neighbor

Changes the "Fit" value to be the distance between every example and the selected example. Sorting by "Fit" will now display the examples that are the nearest neighbors to the selected example(s). A "1.0" fit value indicates a perfect match. A "0.0" value indicates the examples share no words in common.

Visualize Examples

Displays a scatter plot with the selected examples circled.

Class View Buttons and Menus

These buttons occur in the Class View.

Move Examples

Allows the user to select one or more examples to remove from the current class. The selected examples may be deleted completely, or moved to a brand-new class, or moved to an existing class. Selected examples may also be copied to another class. They will then reside in two places at once. In general, this is not recommended because it reduces inter-class distinctness, thus making it harder to accurately classify new examples.

View Secondary Classes

Displays a pie chart indicating where the examples of the class would go if this class were deleted. The slices of the pie can be clicked on to display the actual examples that make up the slice.

Sort Menu

The following sort methods may be employed against the list of examples in the example display box:

1. **No Sort**—Show the examples in the original order in which they appear in the file.
2. **Most Typical**—Show the examples in increasing order of distance from the class centroid.
3. **Least Typical**—Show the examples in decreasing order of distance from the class centroid.
4. **Keyword**—Show first the examples that contain the last keyword search expression.
5. **Solution Authoring Usefulness**—Show first those examples that provide useful diagnostic or corrective actions. These are identified by counting typical diagnostic or corrective phrases such as "tried to" or "told customer."

Index

C

S

T

W–Z